MW00831467

Eleanor's Crusades

Being the True Account of the Noble and Historic
Adventures of the Great
Queen Eleanor of Aquitaine

In Her Glorious, Valiant, and Remarkable Efforts to Bring
Civilization to Christendom, and to Defend Civilization
from Assailants Both Within and Without.

Told by Her Friend, Comrade, and Companion
Marie De France

For Hope

Eleanor's Crusades

Polaris Books
11111 W. 8th Ave
Lakewood, CO 80215
www.polarisbooks.net

ISBN 978-0-9741443-7-5

Manufactured in the United States of America

First Polaris Books Edition 2017

Cover image of depiction of Eleanor of Aquitaine, painting by Edmund Blair
Leighton, *The Accolade*. 1901

Layout Design by Robert Zubrin
Cover Design by Hannah Criswell

Roster of Chapters

In the titles thus set forth ensemble, the astute reader may discern the many famous personages and splendid, horrid, or otherwise extraordinary events whose true report will be encountered within this chronicle.

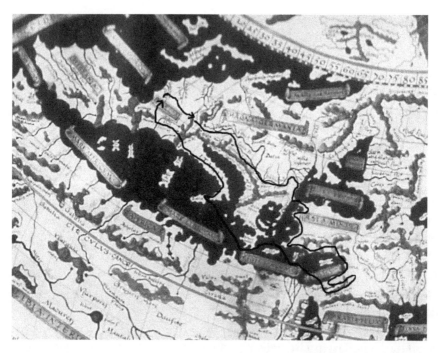

Map of the Known World, showing the path taken by Eleanor and I on the Great Crusade

The Bard's Prologue

I tell of a time when the world was in its spring. The nightmare age was over, and long sleeping Christendom was waking up. It was a time of new things, new thoughts, great deeds and great wonders, when Eleanor and I were young.

Men have said many things of the glorious Queen Eleanor, as slanderous men will, but of all who remain, I knew her best. The perfidious sycophants of King Louis have presented accounts that differ from mine, but that is because they are liars. As the holy Virgin who rules heaven is my witness, this is Eleanor's true story. That Eleanor was beautiful beyond measure, and possessed of a charm and wit exceeding all other women, even her enemies concede. But, faithless as they are, they call these gifts given her by God tools of the Devil, and naught but her deceitful weapons to bend men from virtue. Greater falsehood was never said. Yes, of course she was surpassingly fair, but the magic that enwrapped her came not from mere externals, fine though they were, but from the greatness of soul that radiated forth from within to fill her eyes, face, and voice with a light that inspired all with a heart capable of receiving it to join her cause. They say that the great Alexander, conqueror of the world, had a similar power. If so, then Eleanor was a female Alexander; equally gifted, equally possessed of fortitude and courage, equally chosen by Heaven to lead.

They say that she had no respect for tradition or custom, that in her pursuit of novelty she fomented heresy, that in short, she was not a true Christian, and failed utterly in her duty as a monarch to protect our holy faith.

To those who say this, I have only contempt. Yes, of course, Eleanor had many revolutionary ideas, but were these ideas less Christian than those they usurped? What was un-Christian about her insistence that all knights within her realm adopt the code of Arthur, pledging themselves to defend the weak? What was un-Christian about her demand they respect the dignity and persons of women?

Who but a true Christian would pledge a good part of her fortune to build the glorious cathedral of St. Denis, a building novel with wonder, its magnificent windows filling all within with the light of heaven   and heralding the dawn of a new age? Who but a true Christian would conceive a project like the Universitas of Paris, a place where the greatest scholars of Europe could join their efforts to use the tools of Reason to discover the truths of creation and prove the validity of our faith?

Yes, it is true that she refused to persecute the Jews, Cathars, Petrobrussians, and other heretics of Aquitaine, and even made some of them her friends. But where is it written in the Gospel that we are instructed to hate anyone, however erroneous their beliefs might be? Certainly her kindness towards these unfortunates cannot be confused with any lack of steel in her character when the need came to defend Christendom from its deadly enemies to the east. Let those who claim so explain the facts that the reader of this narrative shall soon encounter.

Let them explain how she, though a frail young woman, responded to the alarm of the Turkish threat to the Holy Land by donning armor and marching across half the world to meet the dreaded Nurradin in deadly combat. Let them explain how this "sinful strumpet" as they call her, faced battle with the evil Mohammedans amidst the plains of the Meaender, the mountains of Paphlogonia, and the hell that was Damascus. Let them explain how she had the fortitude to endure deadly floods, freezing snows, blazing deserts, sickness, famine, ambush, betrayal, ocean storms, shipwreck, and every other kind of hardship and misfortune, and defying all despair, push on.

These are just a few of things they cannot explain, and with this account, I will expose the slanderers of Eleanor as the foul lying knaves they truly are.

*** *** ***

Who then am I, to tell Eleanor's story?

My name is Marie. I was born in Brittany, but have lived in many places. I am a bard, and as I first gained fame while residing in the Kingdom of the Franks, I have chosen to style myself Marie of France. It sounds like a noble name, does it not? Yet I was not born to noble estate, but to that of a burgher. I am not ashamed of that, though, because my father was no ordinary burgher, but a builder, a master builder in fact, and not to put too fine a point on the matter, a genius.

The builders' trades include diverse crafts. There are the masons and stonecutters and glaziers, and many others, but the greatest of all are the enginators, those skilled in the secret and divine art of creating engines, or machines, as they are also known. For of what use would all the fine cut stone in the world be without the machines to lift them to their proper place? It is engines that allow weak men to move and lift all things, no matter how heavy, and by so doing transform mere rocks into mighty castles, noble palaces, and glorious cathedrals. The very word "engine" bespeaks a holy quality to this profession, as it shares its root with "genius" and "genesis," terms that name the quality necessary for, and the very act, of creation. Indeed, those who truly know their scripture will realize that Our Savior himself was also an enginator. Notwithstanding that he is frequently described as a "carpenter," at that time the word "carpenter" referred to those whose profession it was to create and fix carpentia, or carts, which were the first species of machine. Thus the work of the enginator can truly be said to be a continuation of Our Lord's own.

So I am in no way ashamed to say that my father was an enginator. Nay, I am proud of him, and doubly and triply so, as not only was his profession grand, but his accomplishments within that trade remarkable, as this narrative will surely show.

Suffice however, at this point to say, that as a result of my father's profession, my youth was spent in far travels, for builders are free people, and in those days walked the roads far and wide to go wherever work was to be had. Thus before my twelfth Christmas, I had seen Brittany, Normandy, Flanders, France, and Aquitaine, and finally holy Toledo itself, so recently liberated from the clutches of the unbelieving Moors.

Toledo was filled with scholars, young and ambitious, each desiring to make his mark by being the first to translate into Latin one of the many ancient texts newly discovered in the vaults of the great city returned to Christendom just fifty years prior. But these scholars were poor, for the most part, and before they could reap the rewards of fame and fortune due them from their great work of translation, they needed the wherewithal to eat. My father being, by comparison, rich, and I a curious girl desirous of both knowledge and better acquaintance with the handsome young scholars, I prevailed upon him to purchase me lessons, and so I became lettered.

Spain, however, was not a land in which good people could live in safety, for the wicked Mohammedans, haters of Christians, and women, and Christian women most of all, still lurked about the country, seeking to seize those they might sell as slaves in their unholy markets of human flesh to the south. It was thus that my own dear mother was surprised and taken, while out with the other townswomen to wash clothes by the river, and I myself would also have been took, had I, then a lass of some eleven years, not been so fleet of foot.

We had hardly begun our mourning for this loss when the news came that the brave knights of Aragon had been horribly slaughtered by the Moors at Fraga, and the alarm spread that the fiends might soon march on Castile in dreadful force to make slaves of us all. Wishing to protect our family from such a fate, my father decided that the time was ripe for us to return to the north.

So, fleeing warlike Spain, we crossed the mountains to happy Aquitaine, land of wine and music. There I encountered some troubadours, and convincing Papa again, (this was not difficult, as he loved me dearly) obtained further lessons in music and poetry, and thus educated and equipped with a serviceable lute, became a troubaritz myself, thereby adding to my ancestry the spirits of the bards of all the ages.

Papa though, would not have me cast my lot among the merry troubadours, for many were Cathar heretics or otherwise unfit companions for a young girl. So we traveled on, to France, where the customs were less novel and where, moreover, a freehold was found, which he bought, and upon which he erected his most marvelous engine. It was there that I first met Eleanor

*** *** ***

Every history contains two stories, the history itself and the tale of how it came to be written. In this case, the incident that made me realize that I might have an account to tell the world occurred within a moment as brief as the drawing of a breath, although at the time that breath seemed like an eternity.

It occurred ten years after our meeting, on the day before Christmas, in the Year of Our Lord, One Thousand, One Hundred and Forty Seven, on the banks of the Maeander River in Anatolia, the very morning when our valiant crusade first met the enemy.

The day was overcast, cold and windy, with intermittent showers of rain threatening bad weather to come.

On our side of the river, the knights massed in a long front of cavalry on a plain, slightly raised up a gentle sloping meadow leading down towards the stream. Behind our cavalry were the infantry.

Eleanor had gathered her company of armed female companions, her "Amazons," as she called them, in the space between our horse and foot. Because of the rising ground, we could see over the knights to the far side of the river, where the Turks were assembled in the meadows. Mounted on ponies, they dashed back and forth in front of their wagons, barking like dogs. In their hands many held the heads of those they had butchered near Dorylaeum. They waved them about, mocking us with the offer of a similar fate.

We stood mounted in a line abreast upon our horses, all in full armor. Eleanor faced us, looking up and down the line without saying word. Unlike the rest of our company, she also had a lance. A cart drew up to us, driven by one of our camp followers. I could see that it was filled with lances.

Eleanor gestured at the cart. "The time has come," she said. "Take your lances."

The Amazons looked at each other in agitation. Then Mamille de Roucy, one of the proudest noblewomen of the group, spoke up.

"Take lances? Surely you don't mean for us to charge into the battle?"

"That is what Amazons do," Eleanor said.

Mamille de Roucy shook her head. "We are not Amazons," she said. "We are ladies."

Eleanor looked at the lady in anger for several seconds. "Then what are you doing here?" she finally asked.

"My Queen," Mamille pleaded. "You yourself ordained our code. It is not our role to fight, but to encourage valor in the knights who carry our colors before our eyes."

Mamille then pointed to the row of knights, many of whose lances indeed were adorned with colored favors from the ladies.

Eleanor frowned. "That is well enough for gay days at court. But this," she shook her lance, "is for days such as today."

"You really intend to ride into the fight?" the lady Torqueri of Bouillon asked, her amazement evident.

"I would not miss it for the world," Eleanor answered, and we could all hear the steel in her voice.

Then she called out. "Who will ride with me?"

Without hesitation, Erika of Jutland and Sybille of Flanders spurred their horses and rode up to pull lances from the cart and array themselves besides Eleanor. That these two dared the challenge did not surprise me. Erika was taller than most men, and tanned and wiry as a sailor, her long blonde braids recalling one of the fierce warrior maidens whose valor is still sung in the sagas of her people. There were deep nicks in her sword already. Sybille was shorter, but stout and gruff; her brave defense of her absent husband's castle was the stuff of legend.

A moment later the Lady Alicia of Bordeaux looked at me and smiled, then also rode forward. Alicia was no toughened fighter like the other two, but a tall and graceful beauty. Yet she had been Eleanor's companion since childhood, and was an equestrian beyond compare. If her sword arm was not particularly strong, it was skillful, and the elegance with which she could dance with a weapon might well make her deadly. Where Eleanor would go, she would follow. But the threescore other Amazon ladies, though all proud dames from warlike families of famous ancestry, backed their horses away.

I sat in my saddle, unmoving, stranded between the two groups. I didn't know what to do. The cold rain wetted the clothes beneath my armor, the wind blew, and I felt a chill.

Then I heard Eleanor's voice, harsh and imperative. "Marie? Your choice?"

My choice. What could I do? I was no veteran, nor a daughter of a knight or noble who might have bred me to arms. Eleanor and Alicia had taught me to ride a horse, but when it came to the gallop, I could barely keep in my saddle. The Queen had provided me with a good suit of chain mail, but given my small stature, the helmet was so oversized for my head that its bottom hung most of the way to my shoulders, making me look like a fairground comic imitating a German. I had never even touched a lance before.

And there, across the river were the merciless Turks, swarming in their multitudes, shouting their unholy vows to massacre and mutilate every one of us, just as they had already done to so many of our friends. Eleanor was asking me to join her on a charge right into their midst.

They say that women must avoid battle because we are weaker than men, and the consequences of defeat for us much more horrible. But our difficulty is greater than that.

Women can and will fight to save themselves, or those they love. Men will fight for these reasons too, but also for revenge, for their faith, or to prove their worth. Whether they or we are more rational in this respect, I will not say, but it is clear enough that when the time comes for battle, this difference of mind affords them their greatest advantage. They lust for combat. We don't.

Yet Eleanor did. Why? Was it truly to seek glory, as a man would, and perhaps gain more from the sensational audacity of her conduct? Was she willing to take such a risk simply to prove to one and all the true capacity of women? Or did she think that by charging home herself, she could set an example that no man would fail to match, and thus assure our victory? Or did she simply wish to experience the thrill of the charge, to know in that one supreme moment the great secret that only the brave know, a secret whose entrance she would not be denied? Who can say which reason moved her most? Perhaps it was all of them.

But charge she would, and the choice was now mine to join her, or abandon her as so many others much better suited to such an exploit already had. To say I was terrified would be to fail at words, for my fear in peering out across the river at that horde of savage demons screaming for our deaths defies description. Yet as I looked at Eleanor on that freezing morning, sitting armed and armored upon her steed beneath the grim leaden skies, her tunic soaked and long red hair turned into a crazed mass of damp spirals by the rain, her green eyes flashing fire as she waved her lance about, I knew I was looking upon a spirit from a world beyond our own. Our Savior said: "I come among you not to make peace, but with a sword." So Eleanor had come among us, like a whirlwind, to separate the wheat from the chaff, challenging us all to rise to our higher natures. There was no choice. Come what may, I could not fail her.

I took a deep breath. They say that in a man's last moment his entire life appears before him in a second. I think this is true, because in that passing moment as I inhaled the air that would come out with my fateful reply, memories raced through my mind, all seeking to answer my soul's desperate inquiry: "How did I ever come to this?"

So I remembered, and in that moment of recollection realized what an extraordinary life I had had since this incredible new Demiurge had swept me up from my humble existence into her wild career. It was in that instant that I saw that her adventure – our adventure together – had been epic, and vowed, should I survive the day, to record it for posterity. Little did I know then the still more stupendous and horrifying exploits that were shortly to follow. These also have been writ herein so that all may learn the truth of these famous events, and glory and infamy assigned to all in accord with their just desserts.

Hear then, my lords and ladies, the words of Marie, who does not waste her talents with chatter or slander, but who speaks the truth of that which she truly knows. Hear then, the true tale of my friend, the great Queen

Eleanor of Aquitaine, the most remarkable person of our remarkable time.

Book the First

Young Eleanor

Chapter 1

In Which I First Encounter the Great Queen Eleanor

It was a midsummer in the year of Our Lord One Thousand Eleven Hundred and Thirty Seven, and the bright sunny morning would have been most excellent except for the circumstance that the magistrate and his men had us at the point.

My father was a strong man, as were my two brothers, both nearly grown, but what could they do when faced by a half dozen brutes with swords and chain mail, and one who claimed to speak for the law? Papa tried to reason with the magistrate, to no avail, while Patrick and Michael stood frozen, facing off against two huge men at arms, who dared them, with hands on hilts, to come on with their bare fists. Another guard held a villager bound and noosed, ignoring the desperate pleas of his wife, while the last two, assisted by a rotten-toothed village elder, tried to cast a rope around the swiftly moving arms of my father's engine.

It was to these that I directed my attention. All the ragged peasant girls were on our side, and making avail of the cattle droppings with which the Lord in his wisdom had chosen to adorn the hillside, we pelted the miscreants who were endeavoring to stop the machine with such a furious barrage of splendid projectiles and choice insults as might have saved Troy, had only we been there to defend the city. One of the guards tried to drive us off, but a man in armor makes a poor foot racer, and the barefoot village maidens dashed about flinging so much filth at him from every side that he soon thought better of his enterprise and beat a hasty retreat to his fellow. Cheering our triumph and jeering at the oaf, we redoubled our efforts. Yet despite everything we could throw at him, and all the abuse we could scream at him, the man casting the rope kept improving his attempts, and it was apparent that all would soon be lost.

Suddenly I became aware of a great sound behind me. I turned and was astonished to see an army of mounted knights and two fine ladies on horseback galloping straight at us.

I say it was an army, because that is what it seemed to me at that time. Since then I have been to war, and seen real armies in their thousands and

tens of thousands swarming across plains like ravaging locusts, and this was not a force to compare with such. Still, there were more than two-score of them, and the galloping hooves of their steeds pounded the meadow like thunder.

At the last moment before running us all down, they reined in their horses and stopped, not three fathoms away. I looked up at them in amazement. The knights were all handsome men, with well-trimmed beards, colorful clothes and horse trappings, and their armor and weapons shone like silver. But the two young ladies were more magnificent still. Perhaps a year or two older than me, both were as tall as the men, and they rode like them, astride, except that they were far more graceful, and their mounts were wonderful horses of the Andalusian type. Each had long hair, one fiery red, the other golden blonde, which they wore loose and uncovered to frolic in the wind. Their clothing was fine, such as only the richest ladies wear when out riding, and the red-haired one also had a jeweled necklace, fur lining her clothes, and golden buckles on her boots, all of which marked her as a person of great importance. The golden maid could fairly be called beautiful, but the red-haired one was simply beyond compare. For a moment she looked at me, and I saw keen intelligence in her green eyes, and a spirit high, proud, and unconquerable.

The fire-haired noblewoman turned and spoke to her chief knight. "Sir Robert, would you be good enough to quiet this rabble. I would like some answers."

Sir Robert nodded, drew his sword and yelled. "Silence, knaves! Be silent and hold fast."

That was enough. Magistrates and builders, peasants and guards, everyone stopped and froze in utter silence.

The noblewoman surveyed the crowd for a moment then gazed curiously at the engine. Finally she turned to the constable. "Master Magistrate, what is the meaning of this?"

The magistrate gulped nervously. "Great lady, I am here to stop this, this... thing."

Lady fire-hair nodded, then gestured again at the engine, whose canvas sails were causing it to spin rapidly in the freshening breeze. "Yes, I can see that. But what is this thing?" The rotten-toothed village elder rushed forward, his clothes well spattered with the effects of our barrage.

4

"It is the work of the devil!" he cried.

Reacting to his smell, the lady twitched her nose. But then the wind shifted, causing the engine to turn about its center post. The two men at arms who had been trying to grapple it scrambled away in terror.

The elder shouted. "There, you see!"

Papa interjected. "No, no. It is but a machine for milling grain."

The elder pointed at Papa. "Don't listen to him. He is a stranger. He does not belong here. He is corrupting our daughters."

The fire-haired lady looked bewildered. "With this engine?"

"Yes," the elder nodded emphatically. "God has given that girls should grind wheat. But now, they just bring their grain to his infernal machine, and do nothing, while he keeps one part in twenty-four."

Papa folded his arms and looked up at the lady. "It is a just portion. The river mills keep one part in twelve."

"And thus are too costly to tempt our poor folk," the elder cried. "But now, he takes our grain!"

The lady looked down on Papa from her saddle. "Is this so?"

Again my father responded, respectfully, but without cowering. "The trade avails them. For now, instead of slaving their mornings at hand mills, these girls can sew clothes, attend to other chores, or help their mothers care for smaller babes."

The lady tilted her head and nodded slowly, considering Papa's words. This clearly did not please the elder, for he broke in again. "Listen to him! They can sew, do chores, and help their mothers! Hah! If only that was so. Instead they play, and laugh, and sing, and dance, from dawn till breakfast. It is sinful. I say it is sinful."

That made me furious. Who was he to call my father's noble creation sinful? I could not hold my tongue any longer. Ignoring my proper place, I spoke up.

"No. It is right."

The great lady turned and looked at me, up and down. Suddenly I became acutely conscious of my appearance. How must I appear to so high and mighty a person? She, so tall, with her magnificent red hair hanging down to her waist, and dressed in silk and fur and leather with a necklace of jewels, while I was of but ordinary stature for a girl approaching fourteen, with ordinary brown hair cut at the length of the shoulder. I was no barefoot peasant in linen rags, it is true. My clothes were of good dark dyed wool, with only a few holes here and there, and I wore stout, if unfashionable, shoes. But my only marks of distinction were the builder's guild medallion I wore about my neck, my fantastical green troubadour hat with its long yellow feather that I wore on my head in the style of a lad, and my lute carried by its strap upon my back. But there was nothing for it. I was who I was. I advanced several steps, bowed low, and looked up boldly at the noblewoman.

I took a deep breath, whispered a silent prayer to the Virgin for eloquence, and spoke. "Great lady, I beseech you. For what end did the good God make young girls, but to play and laugh and dance and sing? If not for this end, why did he give them such sweet voices, made for song and laughter, and graceful forms, made for dance and play? Does not the Bible tell us that it was Satan who effected the fall of man, thereby condemning us to toil, in defiance of God's true plan, which clearly designed girls for happiness?"

The high noblewoman raised her eyebrows, laughed, then turned to her fair companion. "Well, Alicia, what do you think? I must say, I like her philosophy."

Alicia nodded and smiled, apparently agreeing as well. Then the great lady turned back to me. "So Miss, you seem well-spoke, although of foreign stock. From the sound of your voice, I would say you hail from Brittany."

"Yes, great lady," I responded modestly. "The glorious land of the Bretons, famed throughout creation for the bravery of its men, the beauty of its women, the brilliance of its poetry, the sweetness of its fruits, and the savor of its wines, that land indeed was our first home."

"Then, how came you here?" she inquired further.

I clearly had her interest, so I took advantage of the moment to explain our entire case. "We are free people," I said, "of the guild of builders, and have traveled to many far off countries, from Flanders to Normandy and even to Spain. And in living thus, through many projects we gained some wealth, and so resolved to buy ourselves a freehold safe in the bosom of the great kingdom of the Franks.

"But my father is more than an ordinary builder, he is an enginator, a constructor of rare engines unknown to even the wisest of the ancients, and here upon our own land, has built this, the noblest machine ever conceived by the mind of man. For through this wondrous engine the breath of God sets every humble village maiden free from the grinding slavery that the Tempter, in his evil, had doomed them to since our first parents fled Eden.

For unlike the rivers, the wind is everywhere, and never freezes, shedding its blessings on all willing to accept the grace that God-given wisdom offers to lighten our burdens in this vale of tears."

The great lady laughed again. "Such eloquence. I must admit, I never heard a mill so highly praised. Have you Alicia?"

Alicia shook her head. "No, I can't say that I have."

Lady fire-hair turned back to me. Gesturing at the lute on my back she said, "So Miss, are you then a Troubaritz of some renown in these parts?"

I nodded. "Indeed, great lady, if I may say so, my name is famous, and acclaimed throughout all the world."

Obviously impressed, she raised her eyebrows and leaned back in her saddle. "Really! Then what is your famous name. Perhaps I have heard it."

I faced her with confidence. "I'm sure you have. For I am called," and here I bowed grandly, "Marie."

She looked at me curiously. "Marie. That is your famous name?"

"Indeed it is," said I, quite truthfully.

The golden-haired one called Alicia now snorted. "A common name for a common maid."

How could she say that? "It is the name of the mother of God," I cried.

Alicia snorted again. "And commonly used by the common sort."

That raised my ire. "Common! You shall not call me common when I am done. For I am lettered, and someday I will write my tales into a book which will make me remembered when you are long forgot."

There, I thought. That should set her back. Who today would know of Helen or Menelaus if not for Homer? How many other kings and queens have lived, died, and turned to dust during the ages since, without leaving a trace in human memory? The highborn may wear the finest clothes and eat the rarest spiced meats while yet they eat and breathe, but without bards to commemorate their deeds, they have no hope of living on in this world. And in the other, we are all equal.

However this may be, the knight called Sir Robert now mocked. "Hah, there's a claim we can make merry with. A woman, write a book. What nonsense."

At this, several of the other knights laughed, but the great lady of the fire-hair shot them a dark look, and they silenced themselves with haste. Then she turned to me thoughtfully. "It is an uncommon thought. I don't think it has ever been."

I returned her gaze, and nodded. "Just so." Then I turned to her light-haired and apparently equally light-minded companion. "Now tell me, haughty one who rides in company with this great lady, what uncommon thoughts have you ever had?"

"I don't need uncommon thoughts," she replied. "I have uncommon blood."

"I can see that," I said. "But is not the spirit greater than the flesh?"

"Yes," she admitted.

I seized my chance to strike home. "Then I am as great as any who claim the finest blood. For I am a bard, and in my spirit flows the spirit of the great poets of all the ages, and thus I am the granddaughter of Homer, and Virgil, and Ovid, and even he who truly brought the Muses to Christendom, that glorious hero, the first of troubadours, William of Aquitaine!"

Something I said appeared to arouse the mirth of the red-haired noblewoman. "You claim to be a granddaughter of Duke William of Aquitaine?" she inquired.

There was a mischievous look upon her face, and I sensed some kind of trap, but I was not about to back down. "Yes, in truth I am," I asserted.

She looked at me like a cat that had just placed her paw upon a mouse. "That's odd, so am I," she said pleasantly.

My thoughts raced. "Oh. Then you must be…," I stammered. Then my blood froze as I finally realized who I was talking with.

"Eleanor," she said with deadly softness. "Perhaps you have heard my name?"

Eleanor! Eleanor of Aquitaine! I stood transfixed with my mouth agog. Eleanor was Duchess and sole heir of Aquitaine, a vast realm twice the size of the Kingdom of the Franks. The word was everywhere that she had just arrived in France and married King Louis, and by so doing, joined the two kingdoms to form the greatest empire in Christendom. She was my Queen, and I, a mere burgher, had just boasted to her person that her grandfather was my own! I felt faint, and every bit of wit I had fled me, leaving me speechless in terror.

The lady Alicia smiled at my discomfort. "The bard has lost her tongue. Perhaps it is the shock of having met her long lost sister."

"No," Eleanor said, still looking calmly at me. "We are only cousins."

Papa rushed to my side, and pushed me to my knees, and then fell to his knees beside me. "Your Majesty, please," he implored desperately. "You must forgive my daughter. It is my fault, thinking I could raise her without a mother. She has a saucy way, but she meant no disrespect."

I quaked with fear. But Eleanor smiled, and it was not the smile of a captor to a captive, but of a friend to a beguiled friend. "Fear not, Enginator," she said. "I can appreciate a saucy girl."

Then, as sunlight reentered my world, she turned to her companion. "What say you, Alicia. Do you think this famous bard might lighten our dreary hours in Paris?"

Paris! Was I was hearing correctly? A moment before I had been expecting an invitation to a gallows. But now, Paris!

The Lady Alicia looked at me keenly, then nodded. "She might."

The Queen returned her gaze to me. "So bard, what say you? Would you like to join me as one of my ladies?"

My heart leapt. To be one of the great Queen's company! But then I saw behind her and Alicia two girls sitting silently on horseback. They wore better clothes than I could ever expect to own, yet by their countenance and patient silence I could see they were nothing but servants. Such a role was not for me.

Though it cost me my opportunity, I had to tell the truth. "Your Majesty is very kind," I said. "But I am a free woman. And though they wear clothes of silk, I would not be a maidservant, even to a Queen."

Eleanor raised an eyebrow. "Nor would I, were I in your place. But I am asking you not to be my servant, but my bard and my companion."

That put a different face on the matter, but I was now unsure. The sight of the servant girls had made me reconsider. She said I would not be her maid, but what would I be? For certes I would be leaving behind all my family and friends to place myself utterly in the power of one whose will knew no limits. Could I trust her? "In that case…let me think," I stammered.

But Papa had heard enough. "Marie! This is a chance that comes but once in a lifetime!"

Then I had an idea. "Father, I need some moments to decide." I gestured to the peasant bound and noosed by the magistrates. "Perhaps if the Queen would dispense justice," I said.

Eleanor frowned, irritated with my insolence. Clearly she was not used to such treatment from a commoner. Yet I met her eyes with mine and stood my ground. "A saucy girl indeed," she snorted. "Very well. Magistrate, what is this about?"

The magistrate pointed at his captive. "This man was caught poaching. He already had shot one of the King's deer. We are taking him to be hung."

Eleanor seemed surprised. "What, hang a man for shooting a deer?"

The magistrate nodded gravely. "That is the law."

Eleanor shook her head. "Then the law is too stiff. Give him twelve sound lashes on his back and then release him."

At this, the poacher's wife fell to her knees before the Queen. "Oh, thank you, Your Majesty," she cried. "Bless you. Bless you!"

Eleanor let the poor woman kiss her hand and then turned back to me. "So famous Marie, does my verdict meet your approval?"

Indeed it had. For mercy is the finest of virtues, and while without it, the high and mighty can be great, they cannot be good, and afore I pledged myself to follow this Queen, I first needed to know that she were both. But yet one matter remained.

"And the mill?" I asked.

"You need not worry," she said. "Magistrate: The mill stands." Then she reached into her saddlebag and pulled out a little leather pouch that clanked with the sound of heavy coins.

"Enginator," she said, tossing the bag to Papa. "Build more of your blessed engines."

Papa caught the gift with both hands. From its heft, we could all see that it contained a small fortune. "Thank you, Your Majesty," he said bowing.

Again she turned to me. "So bard, will you accompany us to Paris?"

What could I say? I bowed like a troubadour. "My lady, I will follow you to the ends of the Earth." And while I meant my words without reservation, I had no idea how true they would turn out to be.

Alicia gestured to one of the knights, who led a lively steed by its halter. Then she turned back to me. "So, uncommon Marie," she asked, "Can you ride a horse?"

This was an interesting question. Our family was rich enough to own a horse, but we bought her after her middle years, and only used her to pull our cart. Horse riding was a sport for nobles. So I answered honestly. "I don't know. I've never tried."

Eleanor grinned. "Don't worry, you'll learn."

The knight walked the horse up to me. It was a beautiful young mare, with a soft brown coat. I patted her mane. Then the knight showed me how to put my foot in the stirrup, and I pushed it down to mount the horse astride, just like the knights, Eleanor, and Alicia. Sitting on such a fine horse, I felt so proud. Then I looked down, and saw my father regarding me with tears in his eyes, and tears grew in my own.

"Farewell, Marie," Papa cried. "Take good care of yourself, and be faithful to God."

"Farewell, Papa," was all I could say.

Then Eleanor said, "very well, let's go," and led the company all away at the trot, with my horse following the rest. At first I was frightened, being bumped up and down on a horse like that, but after a minute I felt secure enough to look back.

The magistrates had departed. Papa, Patrick and Michael were standing, looking at me, the bag of silver still unopened in Papa's hands. Near them, the village girls had joined their hands to form a large cross imitating the form of the engine's masts and, holding the ends of their dresses in the air to represent the sails, were skip dancing in a circle, mimicking the mill's rotation.

As one, they began to sing. "Spin wheel, wind mill. The breath of God, sets us free."

Then Eleanor cried "Yah!" and the horses started to gallop. I clutched the mane of my little mare and hung on for dear life.

***   ***   ***

And so it was that I, the daughter of a builder, was adopted as a companion of the great Queen Eleanor. Why did she do this, when I, some might say falsely, had demeaned her by claiming a common lineage with her illustrious self?

It was because I was a troubaritz, which is to say a female troubadour, and Eleanor loved all troubadours. For we had introduced a new and grand idea into the world, and that was this; that when Our Savior had commanded us to love one another, he also meant that to hold between man and woman, so that when a man should seek a woman to wed, he should not do so by snatching her through his mighty prowess, or even by impressing her father with his wealth and worldly success so that she should be given to him, but that rather, he should through valor on her behalf, and kindness to her, and courtliness, and handsomeness, and merriness, and wittiness, and other such fine things besides, so win her heart that she should freely choose to love him even as he loved her. And of this idea, Queen Eleanor, though her station in life denied her its custom, greatly approved, and thought to spread everywhere, even, or should I say most especially, to the court of the King of France.

Chapter 2

Of Eleanor and Louis

The Queen and her party, I soon discovered, had been out and about in the country for the purpose of engaging in hawking. In this noble occupation we spent some several hours, riding this way and that as Eleanor, Alicia, and Sir Robert released falcons into the air to kill birds of various sorts. In this sport, Eleanor again displayed her merciful and virtuous character, for as I observed, she never allowed her sharp-clawed hawk to be set upon the helpless little songbirds of the meadow, but always waited for a more worthy opponent, such as a big fat duck or goose to fly out from the bushes to test the warlike mettle of her bird. And she was rewarded for her kindness in this matter, for as a result of her insistence that her hawk only be employed in such chivalrous style, several fine capons were obtained, suitable for gracing any table.

Everyone in the Queen's retinue enjoyed this sport immensely, excepting only me, since as a result of my lack of tutoring in the equestrian art, I found myself flying nearly as often as the falcons. However since, unlike them, I lacked wings, my aerial exploits were shorter, and far less bountiful of positive results, although it must be said that among the other members of our party, they produced nearly as much mirth.

Yet, not being one to surrender easily, after each instance I was thrown off my horse, I climbed back on, until finally, in grudging admiration for my persistence, the Lady Alicia took pity on me, and leading me aside, schooled me in some of the secrets which allow riders to remain seated upon their steeds. This lady, was in fact, a noble daughter of the house of Bordeaux, and had been instructed by her father, a fine chevalier, so well in the art of horsemanship that it can fairly be said that, in the saddle, neither man nor woman was her peer. I have since seen her upon her horse win races, leap fences, ride standing up and backwards, and do so many other diverse and amusing tricks that I truly believe that had she not been born rich, she could have made herself so by displaying her skill at the fair.

She was a demanding teacher. Her pedagogy consisted in riding by my side and shouting instructions: "up! down! lean forward! lean back! up straight! I said straight!" Then, when I did not respond instantly, she would strike me with her stick, so that between her blows and the bumping up and down in the saddle that she commanded, I soon wished that she had left me to my earlier, less arduous method of learning through experience.

Thankfully, however, the noontime arrived, and we all sat down to eat our dinner. Eleanor's maidservants stretched out a blanket upon the meadow, and accepting the Queen's invitation, I gratefully took the opportunity to seat my aching body down upon it. Alicia joined us, as did Sir Robert, and then the maids opened up before us sheets of leather containing delicate foods of every type. There were pieces of meat and fish spiced with the rarest of herbs, and little cakes and many kinds of fruit, including one that I had never seen before. This novelty had a thick skin the color of flame, with a wet inside that stung the tongue, yet was so sweet that its taste can hardly be described. So taken was I with this wonderful fruit that I ate far more than my share, and would have eaten it all had not the Lady Alicia sounded the alarm in the nick of time. For a moment I feared punishment, but the others just laughed and redirected my attention to the other foods, and the flagons of fine wine being offered by the maids. All this occupied me for some time, so that when I finally looked up from my repast, I saw that the others had long since finished their eating, and Eleanor and Sir Robert were facing each other over a game of chess.

I had seen chess before, of course, and even played it some, because in Toledo the game was all the rage, and enterprised not only by nobles, but scholars and burghers as well. But the chessmen I had played with were but crude things carved of wood. Eleanor's pieces were made of ivory, which is an elegant substance made from the bones of giant beasts that dwell in Africa, and each one was a work of art, a perfect statue of the personage it was intended to represent. The board was of fragrant wood, with inlaid squares made of native marble of each color, and as the brave knights, loyal pawns, holy bishops, formidable castles, beauteous queens, and grave kings moved about it, they seemed like living beings doing battle in the palace courtyard of a magical kingdom.

Sir Robert looked thoughtfully at the board. "I see, my Queen, that you are well versed in this new game."

"Yes," Eleanor said. "I like it a great deal, for the most part, because it prizes brains over brawn."

This, I thought was a most excellent judgment. But I would go farther in my praise of chess, because unlike the dice, whose use convinces players that fate is a matter of chance, in chess it can clearly be seen that salvation

13

is won throgh the wise and virtuous exercise of the free will that the good God has given to each of us.

Sir Robert, apparently also found Eleanor's limited approval of the noble game curious. "For the most part?" he inquired.

Eleanor sighed. "Yes. I question that the Queen, a noblewoman of such importance, should be limited to moving but one square a time."

Saying this, she moved her Queen one square diagonally in the direction of the far left corner.

Sir Robert surveyed the results of her move critically. "Your game appears to be

off, my Queen."

Eleanor frowned. "I don't think so."

Now it was Lady Alicia's turn to speak. "Your mood certainly seems off," she said. "What's wrong, Eleanor?"

In response, the Queen just looked sour. There clearly was something bothering her, but she wouldn't say what. I thought that, as her new companion, it was my duty to help her unburden herself of her troubles, so with the innocent boldness of youth, I inquired softly.

"Is something amiss between you and the King?"

I thought this might be the case because it seemed to me strange that one so recently wed should be out and about hawking without her husband. Little did I expect how pointedly my arrow would hit its target.

The Queen glared at me. "The King?" she said. "What King?"

"The one you married," I responded, amazed at her question.

Eleanor shook her head. "Marie, my little friend, you are mistaken. I have married a monk, not a King."

I looked at her, then at Alicia, in shock. Alicia smiled at me in a knowing way, while Sir Robert whistled softly and stared at the chessboard as if it were it were the sole item in all creation that he wished to ever look upon.

"I don't think that I just heard anything," he said.

Eleanor left no room for misunderstanding. "You certainly did not. Nor will you hear what I am about to say."

Then she turned again to me. "I see you are confused," she said. "But if you are to be my friend, then you must understand my predicament. So allow me to explain."

She leaned back on her cushion and paused for a moment thinking. "Imagine yourself in my boots. A young princess from a civilized land, you are forced by reasons of state to marry the King of another country. Of this you cannot rightly complain: After all, if you are to enjoy the pleasures that rulers enjoy, you must expect to endure the travails that rulers endure.

"Very well. Yet must you also accept the fact that everything you were told about this so-called King and his sainted kingdom were nothing but perfidious lies?

"You were told he lives in the magnificent city of Paris. So when you arrive at this renowned capital, what do you discover? That the town is big, yes, in fact beyond all reckoning, at least eighty-thousand souls, which you can hardly believe. But for the rest, it is a dung heap, with pigs running amuck amidst the never-removed night soil that fills its muddy streets.

"Bordeaux, Poitiers – these are cities of your own country. Smaller than Paris, for certes, but with good Roman streets made of stone, cleaned every week by the hired men of the Lord Mayor.

I nodded. I had been to Bordeaux. It not only had Roman streets, but fountains, which flowed with the clear water that the grand aqueducts built by the Roman enginators in ancient times still brought to the city.

She continued. "Then you reach the palace, if a heathen lodge recast from logs to stone can be dignified with such a name. In front of it are the King's knights. That is, we'll call them knights to be polite, but really little more than greasy bearded brutes with sufficient land to their names to purchase some serviceable armor. These and some men at arms greet you with a trumpet fanfare so loud and utterly lacking in harmony as to penetrate the very bowels of the Earth and torment the damned beyond the limits of their sentences.

"Surviving this, you go inside, and find the palace interior differs from the rest of Paris primarily in the particular that it is dogs that play havoc amidst the offal on the floor, rather than pigs. It is dark, for they still use torches for light, rather than candles as modern people do, yet it must be said that the smoke that fills the air is not completely unwelcome, as it shields your nose somewhat from the fatal offense that must otherwise be delivered by the foul stench of the place.

"Finally, you meet the King. Only he does not look like a King. His face is the color of paste, his shoulders stoop, and he wears the habit of a monk. When you approach him, he does not greet you like a man, but rather, casts his eyes down on the ground and starts jabbering prayers, as if fearing for his soul should he imperil it with the carnal experience of gazing upon the face of a woman."

Here Alicia broke in. "In truth, when we met him, we thought he <u>was</u> a monk, and requested of him that he lead us to the King!"

Eleanor nodded. "Quite so. Then imagine your consternation when this person, finally collecting himself from his holy terror, finally risks addressing you, and speaking in his eunuch's voice, informs you that he is the royal lord to whom you have been espoused.

"Now, you, being an educated girl, had always known that the Franks were a rough sort of people, and that in casting your lot among them, you could not expect to encounter gallant gentlemen of the quality found in Aquitaine."

Here she gestured at Sir Robert and then at the other knights of her party seated more distant. Then she continued. "However, inasmuch as they are rough men, you might have thought, you might have believed, as indeed you were led to believe by the King's ambassadors, that the King of such a nation might at least exhibit some of the manly virtues that rough men are generally reported to have." She shook her head angrily. "But no."

"It being far too late to cancel the union, you proceed into the church, which is but a little cleaner and even darker than the palace. There you stand, before all your vassals and those of the king, dressed in your finest silks and jewels, appearing as you always dreamed you might on your wedding day, while besides you stands this monk!

"The ceremony concluding, you retire to supper in the great hall of the palace. On your side of the table, sit your friends and vassals, dining like civilized people. On the other, the King and his men, all in a row, tear at their meat like animals.

"You are aghast. You try to lighten the mood by telling a joke. But the King does not like jokes, and will neither laugh at yours nor tell one in return. You ask for a story, but the King has no bard."

"He does now," I broke in.

Eleanor acknowledged my comment with a tilt of her head, but then continued. "So you ask for music. It is a wedding feast, after all. Let us make merry, let us dance! And what does the King say? He says, 'Oh no, what? Dance here? In the palace? No, no, we can't do that! It would not be proper!'"

"Apparently, they don't dance in France," Alicia interjected, then rolled her eyes.

Eleanor went on. "So you endure more of this disgusting banquet without benefit of any kind of entertainment, and that being the case, you are positively relieved when, at barely the eighth hour, the King announces that it is time for the two of you to retire for the night."

Alicia said. "It was so early for a summons to bed, that I thought for a moment that we might have been mistook, and that perhaps the monk-King could be hiding some liveliness beneath his habit that had not been apparent upon our first acquaintance."

Eleanor said, "Yes. In that instant, you think, perhaps, that your husband was only playing the penitent during the day, but now that night has come, the true man will emerge. So off you go hopefully to the bedchamber. There is a good mirror there, and by the light of fragrant candles that you had thoughtfully ordered your maids to bring thither, you prepare yourself. You stand before the glass in your elegant silken nightgown, and brush your hair to make yourself as perfection for your lord on your wedding night. When all is done, you go, and recline on the bed, content in the knowledge that you have achieved all that nature and art can aspire to achieve, and that now, at this highest moment of your life, you have become, as you always dreamed you would become, a true vision of feminine beauty.

"So, you call out to him. 'My lord husband. I am ready.' And a minute later, he enters, still wearing his monkish garb. He looks at you for but an instant, then quickly averts his eyes towards the floor. He commences an advance at the pace of a snail towards you from across the room, but having managed about half the distance, suddenly falls to his knees before a large cross affixed to the wall. He begins to pray. At the start of his prayer, your candles are new and tall. But as he continues, they shrink, and shrink, and still he prays. When they are nearly gone, he is still praying, until finally, he stands up, crosses himself, and turns to you.

"'I needed to speak with God,' says he. You reply to reassure him. 'Well, I'm sure he heard you.' Then you pat the bed to coax him in. 'Come on, it is time,' you say. 'The candles are nearly gone.'

"He seems to agree, but then completing his approach, climbs into bed and goes under the covers without removing any of his flea-ridden clothes. So you go under the blanket as well, and reach over to try to touch him under his robe. And what does he do then? He rolls away and turns his back towards you, tightening his habit about himself to protect his precious body from your sinful touch.

"So you cross your arms and look up at the ceiling and ask God what did you ever do to deserve this. Then, since not even an omniscient being could possibly provide an adequate answer to such an inquiry, you lean over and blow out the candles in disgust, and spend the rest of your wedding night sitting up awake in bed, furious in the dark.

"And so, my dear bard, you may now understand why, even if he did hawk, which, needless to say, he does not, I would not care to take the King hawking with me."

Indeed I did. For the pleasures of the Earth have been set here for our enjoyment by the good Lord, and to refuse them is to defy His plan. For one so pious as the great Queen Eleanor to then have found herself with so ungrateful a husband must surely have caused her dismay nearly beyond all endurance.

Sir Robert exhaled deeply. "Is the narrative that I could not hear now concluded?"

"Yes," Eleanor said, still looking at me.

"Well, then, begging her majesty's pardon…" Sir Robert moved his castle several squares. "Check."

Eleanor now turned her attention back to the game, and spent a full minute staring at the board in anger. Then deliberately, she picked up her Queen and moved it slowly diagonally five squares across the board to remove the offending castle. She then faced up and looked defiantly at Sir Robert.

The nobleman was taken aback. "But Your Majesty," he said. "Your move is not within the rules."

Eleanor smiled. "I'm changing the rules. From now on, the Queen will go as far as she wants."

Chapter 3

In Which I Tell the Franks of the Great King Arthur

It was late that afternoon that we reached Paris, riding into the city at a walk. Sir Robert and a standard-bearer led our column, then came Eleanor and Alicia riding side by side, then I behind these two, followed by the maidservants, with the remaining knights traveling in a column of twos bringing up the rear. As we rode in, I could see that the town was a messy place, as Eleanor had described, but it also was a lively one. Everywhere I looked there were merchants hawking trade goods from their stalls, and in several little plazas, jugglers and other street entertainers played to small crowds. There were many pigs in the street, of course, but they were good fat ones, and gave promise of excellent fare in the town's numerous taverns. I saw many little churches, as well as a big one, and observed a working ground near a church of middle size where stone was being cut, apparently in preparation for a major enlargement.

There was also a synagogue, which is a kind of church used by Jews. It was only a small one, however, much less impressive than the one in Toledo, or even those of the Aquitainian cities of Poitiers, Toulouse, or Bordeaux. Clearly, while there were some Jews in Paris, there were not many. I felt this to be unfortunate, because the Jews are venturesome merchants, and their stalls sell many amusing things from faraway lands that you cannot get from anyone else. They are also very skilled in the healing arts. It is said that they are all cursed because some of them killed Our Savior, but I do not believe this can be true, since the holy Virgin herself is also of this race. They are heretics though, and will never listen to anyone who tries to convince them of the true faith. I know this because I have tried many times myself.

At the time we passed the big church, we encountered a group of scholars, perhaps just returning from a lecture. Dressed one and all in the distinctive square-topped caps and gowns that mark their profession, and carrying books, quills, and writing tablets, most of the scholars were clean-shaven, young, and handsome, a circumstance which greatly added to my pleasure in observing them.

The scholars bowed low when Eleanor and Alicia passed them by, but looked up curiously at me, no doubt puzzled to see one of my station riding a fine horse in a royal train. Hoping, peradventure, to make further acquaintance with them at a more propitious time, I favored them with a smile and a wink, but then, lest they become too confident of me, quickly looked away to point my head forward in same style of aristocratic bearing as Eleanor and Alicia. This confused the lads even more, which made me happy.

It was well that this encounter occurred some distance from the palace, because when it was time to dismount, I found that my legs were stiff, and wanted to spread outward, so that in climbing the stairs towards the door, I struggled to walk in the most awkward manner imaginable.

We then entered the great hall of the palace, which, Eleanor to the contrary, was truly a grand place. There were sleeping spots on the floor for hundreds of people, long tables with space for an equal number of diners, and while it did lack candles, a thousand torches made the place nearly as light as day. The dogs that cleaned the scraps were fine, strong hounds, of the best breeds, and more to the point, it was clear that they were all well fed, which augured well for what the tables might offer.

Eleanor and Alicia led me to a bowl of water and rubbed their hands together in it, ordering me to do the same. Then, after observing this curious custom, we sat down for supper.

Our table was of the long kind. The order of seating was as follows. At the head sat Eleanor, and a young man dressed as a monk, who I soon surmised was King Louis. Then, along Eleanor's side of the table sat first Alicia, then me, then Sir Robert, followed by the rest of the Aquitainian knights who had accompanied the Queen on her hawking expedition. Along Louis's side of the table sat first two other men dressed as monks. The first was Odo de Deuil, whose devilish name would prove to be well-chosen. He was of the same age as the King, his garb was equally sparse, and a sour expression never left his face. Both the King and Odo wore unadorned crosses made of silver on their cassocks, with the only difference in their costume being that the King was not tonsured.

The other monkish man, however, was a more comfortable man of the church. This was the Abbot Suger. Suger was older than Louis by at least a generation, and served as his chief secular minister, as he had for the King's late father, Louis the Fat. His cross was of gold, with several inlaid jewels, and some ermine lined his robe. These vanities suggested worldly interests unfortunate in a priest, but his eyes were merry, which made him more likable than Odo.

After these sat the Frankish knights all in a row. Big hulking men, with, as Eleanor had said, bushy grease-covered beards, and dark, dirty clothes, they made a poor contrast with Sir Robert and the other well-trimmed, well-dressed, knights of Aquitaine.

When all were seated, serving wenches came and placed a big slab of meat on each trencher, including mine. Then the King said the Lord's Prayer. This being done, I reached for my meat, but stopped when I saw that no one else was moving and heard the King begin the prayer again. This went on four more times, and as my stomach began to growl about the wonderful piece of beef that was lying before me untouched, I looked to my side and saw Eleanor strumming her fingers impatiently on the table.

The King continued. "And so for the Seventh time, I pronounce, as we are more than seven times thrice blessed. 'Our Father that art in heaven, Hallowed be thy name. Thy kingdom come, Thy will be done, On Earth as it is in Heaven. Give us this day our daily bread…'"

"Amen," Eleanor broke in.

Louis looked offended. "I have not yet concluded," he said.

Eleanor was firm. "No. You have. Seven times."

"But not seven times thrice," Louis objected.

Abbot Suger spoke in a soothing voice. "Seven times is sufficient, my son."

Louis seemed disappointed, but he acquiesced. "Very well. All may dine."

At last! I picked up my meat and bit into it. It was delicious, and I had never had so much meat on my plate in my life. As I chewed my piece, I looked across the table at the Frankish knights, who were all enjoying themselves in the same way, in the process layering another coating of grease upon their beards. It was somewhat grotesque, but I did not worry, since I did not have a beard. So I merrily bit off another piece.

But then, next to me, I heard a coughing sound. I looked to my side and saw the Lady Alicia glaring at me. What's more, she did not have any meat in her hands. Instead she held a knife in her right hand and a spoon in her left. Then, confident she had my attention, she deliberately put her spoon down on the meat to hold it in place, and cut several small pieces off the slab with her knife. Only after having done so did she put the knife down, and then, with her right hand, pick up one of the small pieces of meat she had severed from the main slab, and held it to her mouth to nibble on until it was all gone.

Amazed at this strange method of eating, I looked over at Eleanor, and observed that she was dining in the same style. Turning to my right, I saw that Sir Robert and the Aquitainian knights were doing it as well. In fact, I was the only person on Eleanor's side of the table who was eating in the manner of the Franks. The thought struck me. Is this what Eleanor had meant when she said that the Franks "tear their meat like animals?"

Greatly embarrassed, I put down the slab, and picking up my spoon and knife, tried to eat in the polite manner of the Aquitainians. My method, though, was not quite correct, because even as I hacked away with the knife at the slab, Alicia saw fit to gently reach over, grab my hand, and switch the position of the knife so that the blade emerged from the upper part of my grip instead of the lower. Apparently, in Aquitaine, polite diners must not only cut their meat with a knife, but hold the knife in an underhand grip like a sword, instead of an overhand dagger grip, which really would make more sense seeing as a table knife is just a dagger anyway.

But since I wanted to be Eleanor and Alicia's companion, I put reason aside on this matter and copied their eating style as best I could. I know I didn't get it completely right, because I saw them watching me and exchanging amused glances throughout the meal, but under their mirth they seemed pleased with my effort, which made me happy enough.

We had a pie of many fruits for dessert, and as this was served, I heard Odo speak to the King. "Your Highness," he said. "We received more bad news from the Holy Land this day. Several outlying castles of the Christian kingdom of Edessa have fallen to the Turkish warrior Zengi. The King of Edessa begs for knights, or if not knights, then gold, so he can hire men at arms to defend his realm."

Eleanor waved her pie spoon and grinned. "The gold is what he wants. There can be no real threat to Edessa. If there were, my uncle Raymond, who rules in Antioch, would send us due warning."

Louis looked mournful. "Still, perhaps we can help the King of Edessa with our prayers."

"That's a good idea," Eleanor said sweetly.

At this point, Abbot Suger, who was sitting directly across the table, addressed me. Looking at the square and caliper medallion that hung around my neck, he said, "I see your family is of the builders."

22

"Yes," I said quietly, a little embarrassed to be called out as a burgher when seated amongst such a noble company.

The Abbot consoled me. "There's no need to be ashamed of your birth, my child. I was born a peasant."

He said this loud enough that others could hear, as if he were proud to have risen from such a low estate, and wished to push it in the face of those about him. I found this admirable.

But then Odo interjected. "However you should be concerned for your soul." He pointed at my medallion. "I have heard rumors that the builders have a secret ritual not sanctioned by the Church. Is that true?"

I felt a chill. The free builders did have a secret rite, and no one was supposed to know about it, least of all a man of the cloth. This was not because it was un-Christian. To the contrary, our secret oath pledged all of the brotherhood to be friends to all who would be friends with us, which seems to me to be fully in accord with the preaching of Our Savior. But this code, so necessary for traveling people who need shelter when arriving in strange places, could never be approved by the shepherds of the holy mother Church, or those who fancy themselves her sheep dogs, who seek to keep her flock separate from those others who might lead it astray.

"We have our own peculiar hand grips, for mutual recognition, as all guilds do," I replied, truthfully enough.

"Yes, I'm sure you do," Odo looked at me as if trying to peer into my soul.

Uncomfortable with his gaze, I picked up my flagon and took a sip for as long as I could, thereby blocking his view. Then putting it down, I turned quickly to the King.

"Your Majesty, this is excellent wine," I said like a true connoisseur.

Eleanor and Alicia looked at each other and grimaced, as if they found my statement past laughter. Then Eleanor shrugged and stood up and addressed everyone at the table.

"Your Majesty, wise Abbot, noble knights of France and Aquitaine," she began. "Tonight we shall have the pleasure of music with our repast. For on my travels, I encountered this fine young woman, who is a troubaritz of great renown, and telling her of your glory, prevailed upon her to join our court. So Gentlemen, I introduce you to the famous Marie, poetess, singer, and teller of tales beyond compare."

Eleanor then gestured to me, and taking my cue, I took my lute and, rising from my chair, walked over to an area that seemed to me best for giving a performance.

I strummed a few strings to make sure it was in tune. Then I faced the crowd at the table and began. "I sing of Troilus and Cressida, Unlucky lovers who…"

This far I got and no farther, when a huge hairy Frankish knight named Sir Bertrand stood up. "Let's have no tales of whining lovers," he shouted. "Sing a story of swords and war."

At this, the rest of the Frankish knights started to bang the table in agreement. "Swords and war! Swords and war!" they yelled. "Tell us tales of swords and war."

"Very well," I said, changing my plan. Then I began again.

"I sing of Arthur, Breton King of might
Who in Rome's dread hour of greatest fright
Fought Goth, and Vandal, and Huns accurst
And with bloody sword gave them the worst.
He saved the faith. He saved the cross.
He saved the world, when all seemed lost.
He met Alaric, and him he slew.
With battleaxe he cut him through."

This seemed to go over much better, for Sir Bertrand soon resumed his seat, and he and other French knights started to nod to each other in approval.

"She's good. She's good," I heard Sir Bertrand say to another Frank.

And so I sang on. I said the hall was lit by torches, but in fact the table itself did have candles, no doubt the doing of Eleanor. Watching these, I could gage the passing of time, and it was amazing to see so many rough men of the sword listen with the rapt attention of little boys as I related the heroic deeds of the noblest and most valiant King ever to grace the annals of history. Eleanor and Alicia were not so captivated, and in fact seemed a bit bored with the war story, but this did not concern me too deeply, as my assigned target for the evening was not them, but the knights.

With the candles almost gone, I reached the climactic conclusion of my history.

"So Rome's last hope was but to pray
As Attila's host had won the day.
Mothers blocked whelps' ears and eyes
To hide gore's sight and dying cries

The Emperor hid beneath his bed
Whilst Pope and Bishops wept and pled.
The Huns' ram crashed at the gate
In seconds it would be too late!
Then Arthur and his knights appeared
And the Huns saw what they most feared.
Three times round the walls they ran
Arthur slaying horse and man.
Till at last Attila turned and stood
The giant chief of the unholy brood.
He drew his sword, but was not so brave
For twelve tall Huns were with the knave.
'Repent!' cried Arthur. 'Your lives are spent!'
And with one great blow twelve Huns he rent
But in the heathen last Arthur's sword was stuck
And Attila sneered at the King's bad luck.
'Die you now, bold Christian knight!'
Then swung his blade with hideous might.
But unseen by Hun, the holy Virgin maid
Had to Breton's King his sword repaid.
And bravely on that bloody plain
Arthur cleft the Hun in twain.

Christendom's victory thus secured, I strummed my lute a last time, then bowed. The French knights all applauded me vigorously.

"Well done, bard! Well done!" Sir Bertrand shouted.

Eleanor and Alicia looked at each other and shrugged, then they applauded politely. As much as I wanted to please these two new companions, taming a hallful of boisterous knights remained quite a feat.

Oh well, I thought, oh well, you can't please everyone.

Louis spoke. "An admirable history, for it clearly shows that God will give victory not to the strong, but to the pious."

"Yes, clearly," Eleanor said.

Sir Bertrand was much more enthusiastic. "I liked the finish where he cut his enemies in half," the knight said. "He must have been a very great King."

He was right about that. "Arthur was the greatest King who ever reigned in Christendom," I replied.

25

"Do you know more histories of his life and feats of valor?" Bertrand asked.

"Yes, many," I said, pleased with his interest.

Sir Bertrand wanted more. "You must sing them to us."

Eleanor interrupted. "On other nights, perhaps. It grows late. Come Marie, Alicia will show you to your quarters."

I bowed again, and all the knights gave me another round of applause. I was in heaven. Troubadours live for such moments.

***   ***   ***

And so, my talents being recognized, I was given a place in the Great Hall of the Palace, right next to that of the highborn lady, Alicia of Bordeaux It was Alicia herself who showed me to my sleeping place, leading our way through the great hall by torchlight. Around us, on the floor there were many pallets, as befitted the palace of a mighty monarch with many retainers, and each place had its own pot, so no one would have to share. Dogs ran around among the beds carrying bones they had taken from the dining area, and offering themselves as fine bed-warming companions to sleepers unsatisfied with their blankets. Many people were already sleeping, and in some of the beds, knights and maidservants were making good use of the night to become better acquainted.

We picked our way past several such couples, then Alicia turned to me. "A rather crude and bloody tale for a royal dinner, don't you think?"

"Mayhaps," I said. "But an artist is like a fisherman, and must account for the tastes of her audience if she is to draw them to the hook. Once they come to admire Arthur for his prowess, they can be taught his courtly virtues as well."

Alicia nodded in grudging acknowledgment, and we continued on our way. Finally we reached an area of the hall where only women were sleeping. There were two vacant beds on the floor, each with a pillow. A cross was mounted on a column which stood near the heads of the beds, and below that there was a small mirror, and also a little wooden clothes box upon on which there sat a candle holder with three tapers. Alicia used her torch to light the candles, then put it out and turned to me.

"Well, these are our quarters," she said. Then she sat down on her bed and pulled off her fashionable pointed shoes, revealing silk stockings which she also removed. I glanced playfully at my image in the looking glass, then quickly sat down on my own bed to pull off my stout rounded shoes and woolen socks. As I did this, Alicia watched me curiously, with a trace of a smile on her face. But I was not ashamed. I was a burgher, and never pretended to be otherwise. Why should I be ashamed? Abbot Suger wasn't, and his birth was even lower than mine. In point of fact, when it comes to walking down a cold long winter road, woolen socks are better than silk, and blunt shoes better than pointed ones. The more elegant attire simply costs more, but it is not better. And is it not the soul of wisdom in practical affairs to buy the best things for the least silver, rather than the worst things for the most?

So you see, burghers choose their clothes more wisely than do nobles - as Lady Alicia would discover for herself when we went to war.

Be that as it may, our shoes and stockings removed, both of us retired under our covers.

Alicia turned to me. "You did well today."

"Yes," I said. "Arthur is always a good choice for a performance to knights."

"No," said Alicia. "I meant on the horse. You are a brave lass. Perhaps we shall get along."

"I hope so," I said, happy to have earned her approval.

"Sleep well," said Alicia.

"Good night, my noble friend," I replied.

Alicia smiled and then turned away to snuggle herself to sleep. But I lay back upon my pillow thinking. A good dog came and nuzzled me, and I patted her so that she lay upon my blanket to keep me safe and warm. I looked up at the ceiling, and by the flickering light of the candles, I was delighted to discover an image of the Blessed Virgin Mary, my dearest friend, gazing down on me from above.

I spoke to her. "Thank you, holy Virgin," I said. "Thank you for all your gifts. This is magnificent."

Chapter 4

The Hero of Reason

The next morning, we met Eleanor on her terrace for breakfast. We dined on fine breads, honey cakes, fruits, and choice pieces of salmon caught that very dawn in the river. Afterwards, I sang for the entertainment of the ladies and their maids. With such an audience, I was able to choose a softer theme than that I had used the previous evening at supper. Everyone listened to me with pleasure and attention, except for Eleanor, who seemed distracted.

I concluded:
"And so they did love
And so they did kiss
And live ever after
In heavenly bliss."

Finishing by plucking three delicate notes on the lute, I looked up. Alicia sighed, as did the maids, then all applauded, obviously delighted by my performance. Eleanor, however, had a sad expression on her face.

Alicia turned to her. "Your Majesty, what is wrong?"

Eleanor shook her head. "I'm afraid that such bliss as we have managed to find here in Paris has now come to an end," she said.

Alicia seemed puzzled. "How so?"

"The King has ordered my knights to return to Aquitaine," Eleanor said gravely.

"The King?" Alicia asked. "How is that possible?"

Eleanor picked up a bread roll and started tearing off pieces which she tossed absently to the terrace birds. "It is the work of his spiteful advisor, Odo de Deuil," she said. "It matters little, however. With summer ending they would have left soon anyway."

"When do they leave?" Alicia said.

Her roll now completely ripped, Eleanor scattered the last remaining pieces with a single toss, then slapped the crumbs off her hands. "They are already gone," she said. "And now we here are alone in the palace among all these barbarous Franks."

"Mother of God!" Alicia cried. "Whatever shall we do?"

There were several moments of silence. Then I had an idea.

"We could go into the town," I said.

Alicia looked at me as if I had just praised the King's wine. "The town? Why ever should we go there?"

But I was not to be put off. "There are many amusements in the town," I explained. "There is the fair, and the market, and the school of Notre Dame." Notre Dame, I had learned from one of the maids, was the name of the big church where we had seen the scholars.

Eleanor laughed. "Now there is a new thought. The Cathedral school as entertainment. How many delightful hours we shall be able to spend there, watching instruction in the dialectic."

I, however, was in earnest. "Indeed my lady," I said. "So, shall we go today?"

Eleanor now became cross. "Are you mad?"

I would not back down. "Have you ever done it?" I challenged her.

"Of course not!" Eleanor said, clearly frustrated with my apparent obtuseness.

"Then try it," I said, with the self-assurance that comes from experience. "It is more amusing than you can imagine."

Eleanor found my statement incredible. "Tush!" She waved her arm at me as if shooing away an annoying peddler. "There is nothing amusing in Aristotle."

This last statement was true enough, but missed the essential point. I realized I had to spell it out.

"But there is in those who study him," I explained, with the patience of a saint. "The scholars, my lady. The young, handsome, witty, scholars, my lady."

Eleanor appeared struck. "Oh," she said, looking at me with much improved appreciation. "That does put a different face upon the idea."

Alicia remained unconvinced. "But they are commoners, Eleanor," she said.

Eleanor smiled. "Young, handsome, witty, commoners, Alicia."

"And better company by far than these loutish Frankish knights," I added, happy that I now had the Queen on my side. "But she has a point. They also know their birth to be too low to spend time with you. If you wish to be in their company, you cannot go in your own persons." Eleanor's eyes sparkled, her face now full of mischief. "Go in disguise?"

she said, the delight apparent in her voice. "It sounds like an adventure! What say you Alicia? This could be sport."

Alicia shrugged as she smiled, then sighed as if she had been on adventures with Eleanor before, and not all had gone well. But she went along.

"Thy will be done," she said resigned to the proposed course. "I'll have suitable garb fetched."

***   ***   ***

So into the town we went, all dressed as respectable unmarried burgher girls. In my case, this had simply required replacing my troubadour hat with a wimple, but Alicia and Eleanor had needed the entire outfit, and I had greatly enjoyed watching the initial efforts of the two noblewomen to discover the proper manner of wearing, what were for them, strange and unfamiliar clothes. The noise and bustle of the town were also wonders for them, and more than once I had to drag them away from some puppet show or street side magic act in order to get them to the school before the commencement of instruction.

We reached the church just as the last of the scholars were filing into the hall, and so we followed them inside, quietly taking seats in the backmost row. We had apparently chosen a popular lecture, for the entire place was filled with clean-shaven young men, more than a hundred I would hazard, all very sweetly dressed in their academic hats and gowns. A few of those sitting closest to us noticed us, and whispered to each other, but then quickly quieted down when the lecturer, a priest named Father Stephen, began to speak.

The first part of his talk was quite boring. But then things began to heat up.

Father Stephen said, "And thus we see the fallacy of trusting too much to the pagan Aristotle, who for all his wisdom, did not have the revelation of Our Savior. For it is better to be saved by divinely inspired Faith, then led astray by man's flawed Reason."

That's when a man rose up from the front row. Unlike the other scholars, who were of our age, he was an older man, perhaps of fifty years or even more.

He spoke with the accent of the land of my birth. "You sir," he said pointedly, "do not know what you are talking about."

A tense hush fell over all the scholars, and we heard them whisper "Abelard" to each other. I craned my neck to see the man. Sure enough, it was he. One of the scholars in Toledo had once shown me his miniature. No wonder the hall was packed.

I turned to Eleanor. "It is Peter Abelard!" I cried.

Eleanor was astonished, for Abelard was famous, and not just for his scholarship. "What, the teacher who paid with his manhood for his love of the fair Heloise?"

"Yes," I nodded. "The bravest philosopher in Christendom, and a Breton besides."

But Father Stephen was less impressed. "How dare you interrupt me?" he said indignantly. "I am a Doctor of Philosophy in this school."

Abelard laughed out loud. "Through some misunderstanding, I'll warrant."

Father Stephen reddened, then gathered himself. "So," he said. "I suppose you believe that Aristotle's doctrine of God as the Prime Mover, who creates Nature, but leaves all things that follow to Nature, can be reconciled with our holy faith, which instructs us that it is God who makes all things happen? Perhaps you would care to defend such views before our school?"

"Yes, I would," Abelard answered. Then he walked right onto the lecture dais and faced the assembled scholars. He held up a book, which from its beaten appearance and cheap wooden covers I ascertained was not an illustrated work or a bible, because no one would treat a volume of true value thus.

Abelard said, "I have here a book, whose famous author says that it is God who makes the birds fly, and it is futile to inquire how they fly, for it is the inscrutable will of God alone that keeps them aloft. Would you say that this exemplifies your view?"

Father Stephen seemed happy to have his argument so nicely summarized by his opponent, for he nodded without hesitation. "Yes, precisely. Tell us the name of this wise authority, so that the scholars may take note of him and seek further instruction from his pious book."

A smile like that of a chess player whose adversary had just blundered crossed the face of Abelard. He shouted, "It is none other than the damnable heretic Mohammed! And his book is the cursed Koran."

All the scholars hissed. Then Abelard dropped the evil book on the floor and kicked it towards Father Stephen. The priest recoiled in horror, as well

31

he might, since the teachings of Mohammed are very bad. They say that heaven is a brothel, forbid the drinking of wine or beer, and command his followers to try to destroy Christendom.

Having thus linked his opponent to the worst of all heresies, Abelard continued his polemical onslaught. "There," he said, pointing at the foul volume. "That is the faith that you would set against Aristotle! What madness is this, saying that is God's inscrutable will that keeps the birds aloft? No, God made the birds, and God made the air, but it is the beating of the birds' wings against the air that keeps them aloft. This any man of reason can see."

But Father Stephen had dialectical training too, and was not one to surrender easily, especially on so important a matter as the role of God in governing nature. Counter attacking, he said, "Then why cannot men fly by beating their arms against the air? Angels can. What is the difference? Clearly, it is simply the will of God that allows one to fly and denies that ability to the other."

Abelard, however, denied any contradiction within his argument. "Why can one man swim and another man drowns?" he asked rhetorically. "It is because the swimmer knows how to push against the water but the drowner does not."

Now Father Stephen eyes lit like that of a hound that has smelled blood.

"So you say then, that the only cause of man's inability to fly is our lack of proper knowledge of the method of pushing against the air? That through inquiry and reason we can gain such knowledge, and so informed, be able to take wing, just as birds and angels do?"

This seemed like such a strong argument, that my heart went out to Abelard, for my sympathies were entirely on his side. He was my countryman, and now he would be humiliated in front of the entire school. But like a saint proclaiming the true faith in the face of a thousand heathen swordsmen, the Breton sage stood firm. "Yes," he said, without hesitation. "If Nature allows it, then it is possible. If it is possible, reason can discover the means by which it is possible. Therefore it is apparent that someday, men will learn to fly."

Everyone in the hall gasped. I looked at Eleanor and Alicia, and saw that they, like me, and all of the scholars, were utterly astonished at the boldness of Abelard's thought. Father Stephen, though, was unimpressed. "Preposterous," he pronounced. "And dangerous. You undermine our faith and claim divine powers for man."

Abelard spoke calmly. "In no way. I only say that we should hearken to the words of Our Savior. For did he not tell us, in the Gospel of John: 'Seek the Truth, for the Truth shall set you free.' How do we seek truth, but through inquiry? What capacity did God give man to inquire, but human reason? Tell me Father, should we refuse a gift from God?"

Hah! I said to myself. The greatest philosopher in the world agrees with me. No one should refuse God's gifts.

Father Stephen said, "No. For that would make us like the stubborn Jews who rejected Jesus."

Abelard said, "Sir, we agree. Now answer this: Can any truth contradict our true faith?"

"No," the priest said without hesitation. "Truth cannot contradict truth. So all truth must support our faith."

"But can truth contradict heresy?" Abelard asked.

"Of course," Father Stephen said, apparently bored with the obvious nature of the question. "Heresy and false religion must always be in contradiction with truth."

"So then," Abelard continued. "It is heretics, such as Mohammed and his followers, who should fear the search for truth?"

Father Stephen did not see his peril. "Yes," he responded confidently.

"Then why do you?" Abelard shot back.

The entire hall full of scholars burst into laughter.

Father Stephen's face turned as red as a beet. "I'll have no more of this!" he cried, and stalked off the lecture dais and out of the hall.

All the scholars started to stamp their feet. "Abelard! Abelard! Abelard!" they chanted. Then a Master scholar somewhat older that the rest jumped on the stage, and held up Abelard's hand in the same manner as the judge does with the winning boxer at a fair. Everyone applauded, including us, because Eleanor and Alicia were equally delighted as I with the outcome.

Finally, the applause died down, and Abelard faced the scholars. "So, are there any queries?" he asked.

While I liked Abelard, there was something in his philosophy that gave me pause. So after seeing that no one else in the hall had a question of their own, I raised my hand.

Age and the work of scholarship had apparently weakened Abelard's eyes, for he squinted at me. Then his expression brightened and he said, "What's this? Three pretty ladies in the back row."

The attention of the entire hall thus being drawn to us at once, all the scholars started to whistle like a giant flock of birds. I was frightened, and blushing, started to hunch down and draw my wimple about myself. But then I saw that Eleanor and Alicia had chosen instead to sit up straighter, and raising their heads, nod and smile to each portion of the room, just like troubadours acknowledging an appreciative audience. Taking courage from their example, I decided to do the same.

When the whistling finally ceased, Abelard said, "Welcome, ladies. But would you not prefer private instruction?"

That, it is said, is how he had gotten Heloise with child. But Eleanor, apparently, was quite prepared to engage in merry sparring with such a suitor. For so young ladies are practiced in Aquitaine.

"I'm afraid we'd find something missing in such an encounter," she called out.

Alicia joined in as well. "Twere best you stick to Heloise!" she shouted.

The scholars all laughed uproariously, and now it was Abelard who reddened, as well he might, since the missing part was that which he had shared with Heloise, to whom though he was still an adequate partner in love, as she had since become a nun.

But the sage had apparently not lost the ability to laugh at himself. "Those were low blows," he grinned ruefully. "Oh, well, I know when I am bested. Young lady, what is your question?"

Gathering my thoughts, I posed my dilemma. "Master Abelard. You say that everything can be understood from natural causes. But what of miracles?"

Abelard nodded, clearly acknowledging the importance of my question. "God can still make miracles. But only a few does he make directly. Many he makes through Nature, and others through men."

Eleanor, though, was not satisfied. "And through women?" she inquired.

At this, the Master scholar standing next to Abelard seemed to startle, and he whispered something to the sage.

Abelard nodded, then looked at Eleanor, and though I know his vision must have been blurry, it was as though he could see her clearly. "Most definitely," he said in a voice soft, sad, and wise. "It is through women that the greatest miracles are done."

34

Chapter 5

The Joys of Scholarship

An hour later we found ourselves in a tavern, celebrating the end of the day's lectures with some score of youthful scholars who had invited us hence. The wine was better than the King's, which surprised me, since I have been to many taverns that cater to scholars, and this wine was not of that sort. And if it were not as good as Eleanor's, neither she nor Alicia made any complaint, but instead joined in and made merry with the rest.

Scholars love to sing while they drink and drink while they sing, so we quaffed from our cups and joined in the song.

"Eat to satiety,
Drink with propriety;
Tara, tantara, teino!"

Another drink, then another verse!

"Laugh till our sides we split,
Rags on our hides we fit;
Tara, tantara, teino!"

And yet another swig from the cup!
"Jesting eternally,
Quaffing infernally:
Tara, tantara, teino!"

Three handsome young scholars, who had earlier introduced themselves to us as Alan of Cherbourg, Thomas à Becket, and John of Salisbury, approached us, extending their arms in an invitation to dance. I took a quick final quaff from my goblet, then put it down to take Alan's hands. I knew the step, and as we began to dance some of the other scholars banged the table with their hands to drum out the beat. Eleanor and Alicia seemed to hang back for a moment, so I encouraged them by beckoning them on. Throwing away their doubts, on they came, Eleanor taking Becket for her partner, while Alicia took John. At first they were awkward, as they watched my feet to copy the steps, but it took them but a minute to learn the movement, to the evident approval of their dance partners. But they did not leave matters there, for shortly after they had the dance mastered, I saw Eleanor and Alicia smile mischief at each other and nod, and instantly the two started to elaborate the steps by adding in further rapid foot movements. Eleanor motioned to the lads at the table to quicken their beat, and as they clapped their hands ever faster, it became impossible for anyone else to keep up. So we stopped and watched and clapped with the rest as Eleanor and Alicia, with each other as partners, put on the most remarkable display of Spanish style dancing that I have ever seen. When finally they ceased, the cheers were loud enough to raise the dead. Then Eleanor reached for a goblet and held it high.

"To Terpsichore, Goddess of dance!" Eleanor proclaimed.

Alan raised his cup. "And to Ladies who can dance like Goddesses, and who are scholars besides!" he replied.

Alicia made her toast. "And to Peter Abelard, a gallant scholar to delight such ladies!"

Thomas à Becket waved his goblet. "Yes! To Abelard! Hero of Reason!" he shouted.

Eleanor and Alicia looked at each other and raised their cups together. "To Abelard, Hero of Love!" they hailed as one.

Now I took my turn. I held up my goblet and said, "To Abelard, who knows that it is women who make the greatest miracles, and will someday teach men to fly!"

The scholars laughed, and one shouted, "Then teach us now!" He was quickly joined in this call by several of his fellows.

I was up to the challenge. "Very well, I will," I said.

I took another drink and then jumped up onto the table. Stretching my arms wide, I flapped them like a bird, and then, without further ceremony, dove over a group of scholars. The boys caught me and then start passing me over their heads as I continued to flap my arms.

"She flies! She flies!" the scholars exclaimed, and several were kind enough to raise their cups so I could slake my thirst during my flight.

Eventually, they flew me back to a table, and alighting thence, I snatched up another goblet. "To good wine, and good friends!" I cried, "Which allow all to fly!"

Suddenly, I heard the sound of a door slamming open against the wall. I turned to look, and as I did so, saw several magistrates barge into the tavern, with the Abbot Suger following close behind

Alan yelled, "It's the Magistrates!"

The Chief Magistrate spoke loudly. "In the name of Abbot Suger, you are all under arrest."

There was a dead silence in the room. Then Becket faced the man. "For what, may I ask?" he challenged.

Abbot Suger stepped forward. "For stealing my wine," he said. "A barrel of the best claret has been took from my cellar, and I know it was one of you that did it."

So that explains why it was so good, I thought to myself.

Thomas à Becket, though, manifested innocence from his every aspect. "One of us, steal wine?" he intoned. "Impossible."

The Chief Magistrate was unconvinced. "Then what is that you are drinking?" he said, pointing at Becket's cup.

Becket smiled. "Why, water, of course," he said.

"Give me that!" the Chief Magistrate said, grabbing the goblet from John, who was the lad standing closest by. The he took a sip and handed the goblet to Abbot Suger.

"It tastes like claret to me," the Chief Magistrate said.

Thomas à Becket seemed amazed. "Water to wine!" he cried. "Praise God! It's a miracle!"

The scholars all stood, faced the magistrates, and raised their goblets in salutation.

"Hosanna in Excelsis!" the scholars proclaimed, all together.

"Arrest them!" Abbot Suger commanded.

The magistrates charged forward. So we all took a final quaff and hurled our goblets at them in a volley. The violence of our barrage and the spray of the wine caused the constables to stumble, and making good use of the bit of time thus afforded, we armed ourselves with such pottery and furniture as was ready at hand to meet their renewed onslaught.

The combat that followed was of an epic nature, and would have added luster to the renown of Arthur and the knights of the table round, had only they been there. Although I dare say that the table itself might not have fared as well, since the casualty rate among the tavern's furnishings was nearly as great as that endured by the companions of Roland. There were no cowards in the tavern that afternoon. Everyone fought, with neither constable, scholar, monk, bard, nor highborn lady hanging back from the fray.

I had just hurled a well-aimed clay pitcher at the Chief Magistrate, when

37

a burly constable grabbed me from behind. As I struggled to break free, the brute slipped his hand to squeeze me in a place that was not polite at all.

Barely had I bent down to deliver the discourteous hand an instructive bite, when Alan of Cherbourg, who had been nearby wielding a bench top against the enemy like a mighty battle axe, swung it at my assailant in a way that would have brought pride to any school of disputation. Indeed, the smack of the valiant scholar's board upon the constable's ear was so convincing an argument as to immediately induce complete repentance. The sinner flung me aside and stumbled away, his character no doubt much improved.

I scrambled out from the havoc, then turning, saw Becket interpose himself between a constable and Eleanor. Unfortunately the slim young man apparently had no skill at fisticuffs, and grappling with the constable, soon found himself forced back several paces. But the great Queen was not one to leave her defender to his fate. She seized a wooden chair and brought it down on the Magistrate's head from behind, causing him to depart from the ranks of the conscious.

Becket seemed astounded with his rescue. "Well done," he said, eyeing his assailant sprawled across the floor.

Eleanor smiled. "For what other end was such a chair made?" she responded like a true student of Aristotle.

I stepped over quickly to join them. We looked around. Scholars were streaming out of every unguarded portal. It was apparent that if we stayed in the tavern much longer, we would be fatally outnumbered. Becket spied an exit and pointed to it.

"Quick," he said. "The door's unguarded!"

Eleanor nodded, and we all ran for the door, with Becket in the lead. The scholar made it through, but before Eleanor could follow, a hand reached out and snatched her. It was Abbot Suger.

"Not so fast, Miss!" the Abbot said harshly. Then he swung her about, and as he did so, her wimple fell off, allowing her magnificent long red hair to become visible and fall behind her neck.

Suger recognized her with a shock, and released his grip with the alacrity of a man who had unknowingly picked up a hot kettle.

"Your Majesty!" he cried, his voice distraught.

Eleanor was ready for the occasion. "Why Abbot Suger!" she said, as if she had just caught him out in a demeaning act. "Father, what on Earth are you doing here?"

As he stood speechless, Alicia and I removed our wimples and let down our hair, and imitating Eleanor, adopted aristocratic poses, silently reinforcing the Queen's demand that the good Abbot explain himself.

Suger looked around. All the scholars had escaped, leaving him alone in the tavern with the magistrates and the three of us. He gulped, then spoke to Eleanor. "Well I'm delighted to have encountered you. There is a project I am working on nearby. Would you like to come and see it?"

Eleanor exchanged glances with Alicia and me, smiled, and shrugged. Then she turned back to the Abbot. "Why certainly, Father," she said. "Lead on."

Chapter 6

The Cathedral of Light

Suger was the Abbot of St. Denis, but he also maintained an office chamber at the Cathedral of Notre Dame, and it was to this closer place that he escorted us from the tavern.

Wonderful paintings illustrating Holy Scripture adorned three walls of the Abbot's chamber, while the fourth featured a large silver crucifix. Upon one small table sat a fine marble bust of Plato, while another featured that of Aristotle. But what was most magnificent was his library. He had – I swear this upon my soul – no less than thirty books upon his shelves. His windows were large, and through their ample transparency the light of the late afternoon Sun flowed to illuminate the room.

In the center of the room stood a spacious table of excellent dark wood, and upon this surface the Abbot unrolled a large sheet of parchment etched with ink. We gathered round to look at it, and stood amazed as he showed us the marvel he had illustrated therein.

"So you see," the Abbot said. "This is my plan for a cathedral of an entirely new type."

The Queen regarded the design in silence for a while. "Remarkable," she finally said.

But I, who had seen many building drawings before, was confused. The plan did not make sense. "I do not understand," I said. "The windows are so vast, and the walls are so tall. How can it stand?"

"The large windows do make thin the walls," the Abbot explained. "But I strengthen them with these buttresses that protrude sideways, which steady the arches, whose bases will push out in their direction."

I studied the parchment anew, and imagined the building stones pushing against each other, each in their own way, just as my father had taught me to do. Suddenly, all became clear. "Oh, I see!" I cried.

Alicia perceived another difficulty. "But how do you propose to build it?" she asked. "Surely there is no way to lift so much stone so high."

"I have faith that our ingenious craftsmen can do the feat," the Abbot said.

I looked at the Abbot, and fingered my medallion. Suger understood my inquiry, and answered it with a reassuring shrug, signifying he did not share Odo's prying zeal. That was good enough for me.

"My father could devise engines to lift such stones," I said. Abbot Suger smiled. "There, you see," he said.

Eleanor shook her head in admiration. "I have never seen anything like it," she said.

"That is because there has never been anything like it," the Abbot replied. "Not even the greatest of the ancients ever built such a structure."

"You propose to outbuild the ancients?" Eleanor asked, incredulous at the Abbot's bold claim.

"Yes," Suger said. "And why not? They were pagans, we are Christians. Are we less than they? For six hundred years, we have wandered amongst their works, living in their decay, like orphans hiding in a ruined house. But this should not be. Theirs was not the Golden Age. That age is yet to come. It is the age of the City of God, and it is for we moderns to build. The sight of this cathedral will tell all that we have started to do so. I will name it for Saint Denis, the patron saint of France."

Alicia marveled at the building's most prominent feature. "With such windows," she said, "it will be as daytime inside."

"Yes, I wish it so, because..." Abbot Suger said, then stopped in mid-sentence. We three regarded him intently, waiting for him to complete his thought. Then he did.

"God is light," Suger said.

We gasped, and exchanged astounded looks, one to another. God is light! The thought soared, and we soared with it.

I turned to Eleanor. "It is a concept of extraordinary genius, Your Majesty," I said, now totally devoted to the project.

Eleanor nodded. "Yes," she said, then turned to Suger. "So, Father, why are you showing these plans to me?"

Abbot Suger seemed embarrassed. "In a word," he began, looking at the ceiling. "A project of this type involves many elements, which..."

"You need money." Eleanor instantly put her finger on the matter.

"Precisely," the Abbot said, glad to be relieved of the necessity of making his explanation.

Eleanor, though, was slightly puzzled. "Why not ask the King for funds?" she asked. "He is a pious man."

"Pious, certainly," the Abbot agreed. "However he lacks a taste for novelty. But you, on the other hand…"Eleanor nodded. "I see," she said, appearing to deliberate silently for a few moments. She then asked, "So, would this cathedral provide a place for a community of scholars?"

"It might," Abbot Suger answered cautiously.

"The largest in France?" Eleanor persisted.

"If Your Majesty would have it so," the Abbot said.

Here I interjected. "I'm sure she would. She likes scholars."

Suddenly I felt the pain of someone stamping on my foot. I turned to my right, and Alicia met my gaze with a stern look.

"I mean she values their dedication to the search for truth," I quickly corrected.

Eleanor said, "Well Father, I admit your project appears to have merit, yet I must think on it for a while."

I was alarmed. The marvelous project could not be allowed to fail. I turned to Eleanor.

"Oh, Your Majesty, please!" I cried. "It is so grand. Were you to sponsor such a magnificent work, your fame would be immortal, and God would surely bless you forever. Besides, think of all the scholars! The young, handsome, witty…"

"Marie, be quiet," Alicia said. Her tone left no room for argument.

"Right," Eleanor said. "Tell me, Father, while I am considering. Is it not true that you have been made the guardian of a number of noble young heiresses who have been orphaned by their parents' untimely passing?"

I was bewildered by Eleanor's sudden curiosity as to the care and custody of some heiresses, which seemed to me to bear no relation to the matter at hand. However Abbot Suger now tensed visibly. "Yes," he said. "And?"

"I am thinking," Eleanor continued in breezy fashion. "Would it not be more suitable for the Queen to be made guardian of such girls? After all, with her woman's eye, she could choose husbands for them who would be most likely to make them happy."

Abbot Suger did not answer for several seconds. Then he said, "I suppose, assuming the Queen were a woman of sufficient piety. Marriage is a sacrament, you know."

Eleanor nodded gravely. "Indeed," she said, then looked the Abbot hard in the eye. "Then, do we have an understanding?"

Abbot Suger returned her gaze. "I believe we do," he said solemnly.

"Excellent," said Eleanor. "By your leave Father, this has been a very interesting afternoon, but we must return now to the palace."

"Go with God, my daughter," Suger said.

As we descended the spiral staircase from the Abbot chamber to the yard below, I pulled on the back of Alicia's dress.

"So, what happened? Did she agree to do it?" I asked, unsure of the outcome.

"Yes, Marie, she did," Alicia said, with a tone of taxed patience.

At that moment we reached the door to the yard, and I was struck by the light that fills the world. "Magnificent!" I cried.

*** *** ***

And thus it was that Eleanor achieved her masterstroke, for in one move, she not only seized the glory of the greatest project of all time, but also the power to change our own age.

Chapter 7

Of the Revolution in Poitiers, and Its Threat to the Great Chain of Being

The next day, however, a courier arrived in Paris bearing tidings so dreadful and portentous as to throw all plans askew.

For the news was that the burghers of Poitiers, the capital of Eleanor's own County of Poitiou, had risen up in revolt, and throwing off all legal authority, had declared themselves to be a free commune.

All Paris, and most especially those of the court and of the cloth, were shocked and angered by this affront, and the rage of the high born only deepened as each new messenger brought more information about the radical program of the insurrectionists.

The communards, it seemed, would stop at nothing. Henceforth, they said, they would accept no governor appointed by King, noble, or Bishop. Instead they would elect their own Mayor and town council, with every burgher of legal age and sober repute possessing a good house, or a middling house plus either shop, yard, or horse, and no unpaid debts, having the right to vote. The Mayor and Councilors, themselves chosen from the same class with but thrice the property required of the rest, would draw up all the ordinances of the city, without regard to the will of their betters, and likewise themselves dispense all the appointments, sinecures, and honors among the people. In place of their customary duty to their lords they agreed only to pay taxes of one denier for each sou earned to the King, one to the Count, which is to say Eleanor, and one to the Bishop. Other taxes they might collect besides, but these they would keep themselves to spend within the city on projects and whims of their own. All other obligations, no matter how long enshrined by tradition, were cast aside. No townsman would owe any labor to any noble. No townsman would owe any labor to the Bishop. No townsman would owe any labor to the King. In fact, no townsman would owe any obedience of any kind to anyone outside the commune except that which he agreed to himself in exchange for goods, monies, or favors of equal value. The town would be ruled in accord with the precepts of our Faith and the general laws of the Kingdom, but neither Church nor King would have any role in the ruling. The Councilors would dispense justice themselves, too. Anyone could marry anyone, without any noble's permission, so long as the espoused and their parents agreed. Furthermore, should anyone, even a peasant or serf, escape to the town, and make himself welcome there through his good conduct for a year and a day, then the town would enter him into their commune, and protect him from any recapture by his lawful lord.

This madness sent the entire palace into an uproar. Or perhaps I should say, almost the entire palace. For, dare I say it, though equally amazed as the rest, as a burgher myself and a lass given to adventure, novelty, and the spirit of youth, the crazed impudence of the communards did not at first cause me much distress. In fact, to confess the truth, I even felt some secret sympathy for them, and a corner of my heart warmed with hopeful excitement when I heard of their incredible actions. This though, I did not dare tell Eleanor, for though she did not manifest the outward frenzy of the Frankish nobles, I could see that she was very upset by the rebellion of her countrymen.

"How could they do this?" she kept asking Alicia. "My own Poitevins, loyal subjects to my family for so many generations, they upon whom we have shown such care and kindness, how could they do such a thing?"

In this way she sulked about for nigh on two days. But on the third day, just after breakfast, she finally turned to us.

"We cannot just sit here while this insanity unfolds. We must do something."

"Yes, certainly," Alicia said. "But what?"

Eleanor looked at me so hard I feared she might suspect my feelings. But then she said, "Marie, do you remember the Master scholar who stood beside Abelard on the stage after the debate?"

"The one who held up his arm in triumph?"

Eleanor nodded. "Yes. That was Father Gilbert of Poiree. I recognized him because he has been a retainer of my family for many years. He is a Poitevin himself, and though a cleric, a man of broad education and wisdom. My father would sometimes have him grace our court when we held it in Poitiers. I want you to bring him a message."

"Of course, Your Majesty," I said. "What is it?"

'I'll write it out for you," she replied. Then she gestured to a maidservant who swiftly stepped out through the door and returned in a trice with quill, knife, ink, and parchment and set them down on the table.

Eleanor examined the quill, and it not being sharp enough for her liking, took the knife and made it good with a few expert strokes. Then seating herself at the table, she dipped the pen in the ink and began to write in a hand beautiful and refined. I watched over her shoulder as she set down these words:

"My Dear Father Gilbert:

"Greetings. I hope you are well. How many years has it been since our last Easter together in Poitiers? Such fond memories, I will always treasure them, remembering you, my mother and father, uncle Raymond and little Petronilla, and all the happy times we shared in that beautiful place.

"But alas, catastrophe has struck, and it now seems that all the joy that was Poitiers is now to be consumed by the fires of mutiny and anarchy.

"What has caused this rebellion? I do not know. Certainly my family has always ruled Poitiers with gentleness, mercy, and every kindness, and I have made no changes in laws and customs long acknowledged by everyone to be fair and just.

"Do the Poitevins have grievances? None have been expressed to me. Or are they simply madmen, drunk with pride? Has mindless selfishness and rampant arrogance simply turned them into a pack of lawless thieves, brigands, and deserters from duty? That is what most people here at the palace think, and certainly the evidence supports such an opinion.

"But I, despite this, am not willing to conclude just yet such a verdict against my subjects, people who I still regard fondly as my own countrymen. That they are deluded there can be no doubt. But still, I must believe that there must be some cause for their madness, and if such cause can be discovered, perhaps a cure as well.

"Father, please, I ask you this favor. Go to Poitiers, and walk among the people. Talk to them. Find out what they are thinking. Do they have a grievance? If so, and it is reasonable, then I authorize you to go to the one who calls himself Mayor, his Councilors, and the other principal rebel ringleaders and tell them this from me; that I, Eleanor, as their lawful Queen, Duchess, and Countess, am prepared to forgive all, and will hear their petition, if only they will abandon their insane revolution and return to their senses.

"I know, Father, that in asking you to undertake this mission, which may well prove perilous, I am asking a great deal. However I know that you love me and my family, Poitiers, and its people, and by that love that never faileth, I beg you. Do this for me and I will be forever in your debt.

"Your friend, and countryman, "Eleanor

"Queen of France, Duchess of Aquitaine, and Countess of Poitiou."

Finishing thus, she rolled the parchment, and closed it with wax upon which she impressed the seal of the house of Aquitaine.

She handed me the letter. "Go at once," she said.

I nodded and left straight away.

*** *** ***

Of course, I did not know where Gilbert of Poiree lived. However I reasoned that as a Master scholar of some repute, that he would make his habitation not in the Frankish island of Paris itself, but in the Latin-speaking suburb on the south side of the river. So, with the sounding racket of a hundred river mills grinding the City's morning bread growling away beneath my feet, I crossed the Grand Bridge to the Latin district.

Julius Caesar conquered Gaul some fifty years before the birth of Our Savior, and the Romans continued to rule the province for five hundred years after that. However the Latinate speech that fills the alleys and taverns of the community on the left bank of the Seine is not a holdover from ancient times. Rather, it is a modern development caused by the influx of scholars from all over Christendom whose only common language is that given to the world by the empire-building heirs of Aeneas.

My Latin is excellent, as it must be to allow proper performance of Virgil and Ovid. So I had no difficulty making my way among the Frankish, Norman, Breton, Aquitainian, Spanish, Catalan, Burgundian, Italian, Flemish, Dutch, German, Danish, English, Welsh, Irish, Norwegian, and other assorted nations of young scholars who infested the taverns of the area, and in asking and receiving directions I also received many invitations to stop and drink for a while. Unfortunately, my mission was of such hasteful importance that I could only accept a half dozen such offers, and much good wine and opportunity for good company was tragically wasted.

My diligent search was rewarded with success late in the afternoon, when I spied my quarry leaving an establishment of a type I would not care to specify, except to say that I myself would never go into one.

"Father Gilbert?" I said, approaching the man.

He looked up at me sharply. "Yes?"

"I have a letter for you from Queen Eleanor."

He took the roll, regarding me seriously. Then he said, "Of course. I remember you. You were one of the girls with Eleanor in the back of the lecture hall at Notre Dame on Tuesday."

I startled. "You recognized us?"

"I recognized her." He smiled. "Don't worry. Your little secret is safe with me."

"And yours is with me," I assured the cleric.

"What secret? Oh!" he said, looking back briefly at the establishment he had just left. "I wouldn't worry. But that's kind of you. So, what's in the letter?"

"Open it," I said. "It's about Poitiers. It's very important."

"Very well," he replied. He broke the seal and unrolled the parchment. Holding it up to the failing late afternoon light, he read it carefully, I think at least twice. Then he rolled it up again and turned to me.

"Tell Eleanor I will leave at the first light of dawn."

*** *** ***

That Sunday, Notre Dame was filled beyond capacity, for Father Langres, the Bishop of Paris, had let it be known that he would speak about the Poitiers rebellion at Mass. Every noble, every cleric, every notable burgher, myriads of the middling sort, and even droves of the poor were there to hear the holy man set forth the Church's response to the crisis.

The Mass itself was not unusual, or would have been if not for the size of the crowd and the tension among the parishioners as we waited for what was to come next. Hymns were sung, verses were recited, and communion was taken, just like any other Sunday. But if the Mass was ordinary, the speech that followed it most certainly was not.

"Your Majesties," Bishop Langres began, speaking in plain Frankish. "Lords and Ladies, brave knights, brothers of the cloth, worthy commons, thank you all for staying today to hear my words.

"We live in a fallen world, a world of flesh. And though we have souls

that are the image of God, our flesh is endlessly, helplessly, prone to sin. What is it then, that prevents our world from being destroyed, as flesh devours flesh, and sin devours sin? It is only this, the divine law, given to us by God for our own good and eternal salvation. This law that God in his mercy was so gracious to bestow upon us, known to all of our holy faith as the Great Chain of Being, is the only source of order and harmony in our world. For it is this law that shows us the way to avoid eternal hatred and strife, instead teaching us the duty of each, for we all have a place within the Great Chain. What then must we do to live in accord with the law? It is simply this; to govern wisely those who God has set below us, and respectfully obey those who God has set above us.

"The rebels of Poitiers have broken this law. Nay, they have more than broken it, they have violated it, raped it, burnt it to the ground, and thrown its ashes to the wind. It is not merely that they have deserted their obligations, duly sworn on their behalf by their ancestors in ages past. No, were that the case they would only have sinned in the manner of a runaway serf, and such can always be forgiven after due repentance.

"No, the sins of the communards are far deeper and more damnable than anything like that. For they have not merely fled from the law, they have denounced the law. We've all heard their filthy, lying, unholy, proclamations. They do not have the decency of common brigands who admit that their crimes are motivated by selfish greed. Instead they claim they are just!

"Just! How can they claim to be just when they overthrow God's law? Are they saying that God's laws are unjust, that God himself is evil?"

Here the Bishop paused, and a hushed silence filled the cathedral. He looked about, and it seemed that his burning eyes met each of ours.

"Yes," he said, pausing again. "That is exactly what they are saying, and in doing so, make themselves not only rebels, but heretics, united with the Cathars against their Creator and all He has made."

"Let us be clear then. The communards are not fugitives from God, they are enemies of God, they are slanderers of God, they are the vile minions of the Devil himself.

"Their rebellion cannot stand. This is not a matter of enforcing feudal dues and duties, as important as those might be. No, this is a matter of defending the Great Chain of Being itself. If this mutiny is allowed to triumph, obedience and authority will collapse everywhere, and everything that holds our world together will come apart. Plants will revolt against animals, animals against people, children against parents, wives against husbands, apprentices against masters, and commoners against nobles. Nothing will be safe. Even the angels that move the heavenly spheres will abandon their posts, and the entire universe will dissolve into chaos and anarchy!"

At this last pronouncement I gasped, for I had not thought through these implications of the Poitiers rebellion at all before. Mumbling quietly under my breath, I offered a quick prayer to the Virgin begging forgiveness for my previous foolishness.

Bishop Langres turned towards the royal box. "King Louis," he said. "You are God's appointed defender of this realm. I ask that you take it upon yourself to lead the brave knights of France to Poitiers and put down this accursed rebellion before it is too late. The matter is too important to leave to any lesser man.

"Your Majesty, will you do it?"

All eyes turned to Louis, who seemed momentarily surprised. Recovering himself, however, the King stood up and spoke in a loud if squeaky voice. "Yes, Father, I will do my duty to God, as I am sure my valiant knights will do theirs."

At this, all the nobles, knights, and sergeants in the church stood up, applauded, and stamped their feet in loud approval. The sound was like thunder.

Eleanor turned to Alicia with a shrug. "So much for the communards."

I looked at the Queen. "You'll still accept their surrender though, won't you, just like you said in your letter to Father Gilbert?"

Eleanor smiled. "Of course, that's why I sent him. Marie, there's no cause for worry. The Poitevins may be crazy, but they can count swords as well as anyone else. When they hear about this Frankish horde coming towards them, they'll choose the wiser course and submit to their own Countess instead straight away. They'll have taken a good fright, but learned their lesson. My own knights, vassals, and I will get our lawful rights back, and everything will be fine again, just like it was before all this madness began."

"Oh," I said, both greatly reassured and amazed.

***   ***   ***

Despite all the enthusiasm shown that Sunday at Notre Dame, it took more than a month to assemble the army of knights to put down the communards. But finally they did march off with King Louis at their head, and though it would take some time to reach distant Poitiers, the results of their expedition could hardly be in doubt.

The threat to the Great Chain of Being thus having been averted, calm returned to Paris. In September, Eleanor made her gift to St. Denis, and with silver in hand, Abbot Suger commenced work to turn his dream into a reality.

Chapter 8

The Cathedral Finds Its Maker

Papa was in Paris! I had sent word to him about the Abbot's great project, telling him that without an enginator of surpassing genius the glorious cathedral of light could not be built. Such a challenge, I knew, could not fail to rouse him from his freehold. In due course, then, I received his letter, telling me that he would come to the town within a fortnight, which is to say by that very day, as his letter had spent two weeks traveling from tavern to road post before it reached me. Patrick and Michael would not be coming though, since the one was needed to manage the freehold while the other had to build more wind engines, in accord both with the wishes of the Queen and the clear opportunity for profit.

Still, Papa had arrived! With a gay heart I set forth from the palace in the early morning, my feet stepping merrily towards St. Denis, for it was at the site of the construction work that Papa surely would be found. I was so anxious to see him again that I forswore my breakfast with Eleanor. This did not cause me to starve, however, for despite my recently elevated circumstances, I had by no means forgotten the skills I had learned during my common youth. Thus I found no difficulty in freeing a good bread roll from its captivity on a crowded baker's cart, and dining upon this as I walked, reached St. Denis with both high spirits and a contented enough stomach.

St. Denis already had a church of fair size, and I had taken note of it, along with the nearby stone cutting field, when I had arrived in Paris several weeks prior. Now, however, the working place was filled with life. Multitudes of men were cutting stones, while others lifted them, placed them in hand carts, and shuttled them to their places on the ground line to begin the walls. A small chorus of holy sisters stood nearby in a group, singing together to entertain and uplift the workmen, while two others offered watered wine and old bread to any of the laborers who might want some. Abbot Suger was running about, yelling instructions at the workmen, as happy as a dog chasing a flock of crows from one side of the field to the other. I watched him for a while, for the man's enthusiasm now that his cathedral was underway was a joy to behold.

Then I spied Papa, off to the side of the stone field, standing next to a table among a group of carpenters. I ran to him and gave him a big hug.

"Papa!" I cried.

He took me by my shoulders and held me before him. "Marie," he said. "You look well, my girl. You've gained some buttressing!"

"Yes," I said. "The Queen has been very good to me." Then I hugged him again.

He put his hand around my waist, and turned me to face his friends.

"Brothers," he said, addressing the carpenters. "You all remember my daughter Marie, the crazy one? Well here she is, nearly grown and a companion to the Queen!"

He was so proud of me, and I was so glad to have finally made him proud. For I must tell you that, while being a bard is a noble profession, it does not increase a girl's chance of finding a good match among the families of the builders' guilds. This had given Papa much cause for anguish in the past, for he had feared for my future. But now all was sunshine.

I smiled at him, then at the carpenters. I knew many of them, for, in as much as engines are for the most part made of wood, carpenters are the enginators' constant companions and assistants. This is different than it was in the time of the Scriptures, when those who were called carpenters, such as Our Savior, actually were enginators themselves. It is only the specialization accruing to the greater complexity of technique in our modern time that has caused the two crafts to diverge.

Papa said, "So, Marie what do you think of my plan for the engines to lift the stones of the cathedral of light?" He pointed at the table, and I looked.

There, upon a parchment unrolled and weighted down at its corners by the tool boxes of the carpenters, were drawings not of one engine, but many. There was a watermill, wind machine, a large windlass, and several varieties of large counterweighted lifting cranes.

"You see," Papa said, addressing not only me but all of the carpenters. "We can use these smaller engines to lift the stones up to the middle level, and these others for the levels beyond. These engines here will be used to move these other engines, and these in turn those of the third type, so no stone will be too heavy for us to manage, and no height too high for us to reach."

I scanned the drawings, and gradually Papa's concept started to make sense. In fact, it was amazing, as amazing as the wonderful cathedral of light itself.

No stone would be too heavy! No height would be too high! Such is the power of the noble mind, God's gift to man, which exhibited thus, truly affirms we are made in His image.

My father was a genius. If I had not been certain of it before, at that moment I was. The cathedral of light had found its maker. The marvel would be built. I knew it, and I saw that the carpenters knew it. Nodding their approval, they collected their tools and went to work.

I spent the rest of the day talking with Papa when I could, helping out a little here and there, but mostly watching the work and listening to the singing of holy sisters. For they sang a new and remarkable music of a kind I had never heard before. Instead of singing all as one, they divided into groups, each of its own pitch, and these would sing sometimes in turn, and sometimes together, but always as separate voices. So it was as if different spirits were speaking, each answering the other, each teaching the other, then joining in praise and love of the Lord. The effect was magnificent, for it truly made one think of heaven. I asked the sisters how this wonderful music had come to be, and they said it was the work of one Hildegard, the Abbess of Bingen. This made me very happy, for call me vain if you choose, but it did delight me to hear that, in the noble science of music, a member of my sex had shown herself so masterful as to utterly confound all who might wish to disparage the power and grace of the female intellect.

But I do not think that my pleasure in this matter is vanity, because in as much as the human mind is the image of God, to say that half of all such minds are imperfect would be to say that the mind of God is imperfect, which is evil heresy. Therefore I decree that those slanderers who say that the minds of women are less perfect than the minds of men are heretics, and as such, tools of the Devil, while those refute their lies are heroes of the Faith, and their triumphs should be celebrated by all true Christians even as we celebrate those of saints and crusaders.

It was another week before I could visit St. Denis again, but when I did I made sure to bring with me a box of meat left over from the palace dinner. For though King Louis might say prayers every hour, and seven times at every dinner, at each such well-prayed over meal he and his knights, clerics, and retainers regularly left to waste uneaten as much meat as the men building the cathedral altogether might hope to see in a year. But now, with the King and most of the knights gone to Poitiers, such wastage was doubled, and even with all the dogs running off with their share, there was still plenty left over to fill my box. These choice pieces I passed out first to my father and his carpenter friends, then to the other master builders, and finally to the journeymen, apprentices, laborers, and boys as the amount would allow. This happy task being done, I examined the work, which I was pleased to see had advanced rapidly. The walls of the cathedral were already almost as full fathom tall, several small counterweighted lifting cranes were nearly ready, a large crane with windlass was fairly started, and a half-built wind engine was rising, to the wonder and curiosity of all.

***   ***   ***

Having received his boon, Abbot Suger was also quick to deliver his end of the bargain, and on the first day of October there arrived at the palace three young maidens. These were Katharine of Reims, Anne of Chartres, and Beatrice of Champagne, noble heiresses all.

Eleanor gathered them on her terrace and had them stand in a line. Then walking back and forth before them, she looked them over in the manner of a knight commander inspecting his men at arms. They were not much younger than her, but in the presence of her authority they appeared childlike.

"So," Eleanor said. "You are the heiresses recently under the care of the Abbot Suger. Your names please?"

In response, each recited her name.

Eleanor nodded. "Very good. Allow me to introduce you to my companions. This is the Lady Alicia of Bordeaux."

Alicia smiled at them and opened her hands in greeting. Acknowledging one of their own rank, the heiresses all nodded in return.

Eleanor pointed to me. "And this is Marie," she said.

Katharine tilted her head, eyeing my burgher clothes with some distain. "Marie of?" she enquired.

"Marie of France," I said.

"And what would be her lineage?" Anne asked.

Eleanor said, "She is a descendant of Homer, Virgil, and Ovid."

"And the great King Arthur," I added.

The heiresses exchanged doubtful glances with each other. But they did not dare say more.

"That's right," Eleanor said, although whether she was verifying my claim or approving of their submissive attitude was hard to say. "Now, as to you, you are my wards, and you will take instruction from me and my companions. You wish to be married to noble Lords?"

The heiresses all nodded. This indeed was their one goal in life.

"And that you shall," Eleanor said. "But you shall do it on my terms. The men you seek are nearly all gone now, but they'll return soon enough. When they do, you will follow my every instruction in dealing with them. You will not allow any man to court you who lacks my approval. You will report the content and quality of all such courtship to me, and you will not respond with any favors, until and unless I direct you to do so. Furthermore, under such conditions, you will respond with precisely the level of favor that I direct, no more and no less. Is that clear?"

The heiresses hesitated. They had not expected to be ruled by such an imperium.

A touch of anger appeared in Eleanor's face and voice. "I asked, is that clear?"

Frightened, the heiresses nodded agreement. "Yes, Your Majesty," they all said.

Satisfied, Eleanor concluded the interview. "Very well. Lady Alicia will begin your instruction in the proper use of tableware. Marie, please come with me."

Chapter 9

Suger's Choice

So it went throughout the winter. The walls of the cathedral continued to rise, and more and more pieces were added to the assembly of the intricate, ingenious, and ever grander engines that would make even higher construction possible. With the King and his knights away, Eleanor had a free hand and all the leisure required to instruct the heiresses in all the arts by which noble ladies might make themselves mistresses and idols of men, rather than their chattels. As the girls grew in knowledge, this schooling produced much merriment, especially when upon occasion Eleanor's students were allowed to practice their lessons in assorted experiments upon the hapless clerics who still hung about the palace.

But as Yuletide came and went, and the cold months each passed in their turn, Eleanor began to fret, for she still had not heard from Father Gilbert. Poitiers had been besieged for more than enough time for the communards to see not only reason, but famine. Yet no message of surrender came. Were the Poitevins so mad that they would prefer to have their city sacked by the barbaric Franks, rather than make an orderly submission to their own lawful government? It seemed unbelievable, yet apparently that was the course they had chosen. As March approached, the Queen's alarm grew extreme. For it was clear that the city could not hold out much longer, and though they had been disobedient to her, Eleanor still loved her countrymen, and wished to protect them from the worst that must inevitably follow.

Then, two weeks before Easter, church bells rang out all over Paris. Poitiers had capitulated! Order had been restored! King Louis had been victorious!

I ran to see Eleanor as soon as I heard the news, and found her pacing about the terrace with Alicia.

"At least there was no sack," Eleanor said.

"So all is well now?" I asked.

"Perhaps. I'm not certain." The Queen shook her head. "I wish I had more information."

At this moment, I heard running footsteps in the hall, then a lad burst forth onto the terrace. That he was a messenger   was obvious, as he was carrying a letter. But that he was no royal messenger was equally clear, for he wore the apparel of a burgher of modest means, except for his shoes, which were of better quality of the rest. He was skinny as a stick, but his clothes were big enough for a lad of ample girth. A touch of famine deepened his eyes. A cobbler's apprentice, I readily surmised, but one who had not eaten much for some time.

He knelt and held up his parchment roll, then spoke breathlessly in a Poitevin accent. "I bear a message for Queen Eleanor!"

Eleanor eyed the lad curiously, then walked over and took the parchment. She looked down at the kneeling boy and pointed her finger at his nose. "You stay right there," she said, then handed me the scroll.

"Read me the letter, Marie," she said. Then she folded her arms and looked out on the garden.

"Very well, Your Majesty," I replied.

I broke the seal and examined the letter. "It is a message from Gilbert of Poiree!" I said.

Eleanor nodded. "I know. Please proceed."

"Your Majesty," I began, reading with some difficulty the hand of one who had apparently written too much over the years. "I pray that you are well."

"As I received no reply from my previous messages, I can only assume that they were intercepted by the Frankish host surrounding the city."

Eleanor nodded. "That explains his long silence. Go on."

I continued my reading. "I will therefore apprise you of events as they transpired starting from my arrival here last fall.

"During the first week as I walked around the city, I talked with many Poitevins as you requested, simply for the purpose of discovering their views and uncovering any hidden grievance that might have led to the revolt and whose amelioration might therefore lead to the peaceable reestablishment of lawful order. On the basis of these explorations I was able to arrive at a number of remarkable findings:

"First, that the burghers of Poitiers actually believed that they were as good as any baron, and that under the justice of God they had every right to govern themselves without noble supervision. From the adamancy with which this view was expressed to me, the universality of its support, and the consistent nature of the arguments made on its behalf, I am forced to suspect that these beliefs may be shared by burghers in general, not only here in Poitiers, but all over the kingdom."

Eleanor startled. "What? That can't be." She looked at me sharply. "Marie, do you believe that?"

"Well, Your Majesty," I began. "It all depends. I mean, naturally everyone would prefer to be in charge of their own affairs, but of course, we all understand that some are better suited to rule than others."

The Queen regarded me with a sly smile. "Of course. How interesting. Well, go on with the letter."

I continued. "That said, the Poitevins had been willing to endure your government."

Eleanor erupted. "What! 'Endure?' What was there for them to 'endure?' what better government could they possible have had?"

I said nothing. The Queen calmed herself. "Proceed," she said.

I went on. "However, what they could not abide was the Frankish governor that was appointed by the court to rule over them after your marriage to King Louis."

Eleanor slapped her forehead with her hand. "So that was it. I should have known. Oh, I should have paid more attention to the municipal appointments. Of course the Poitevins would never tolerate being lorded over by a Frank." She waved at me to go on with my reading.

"This man insulted their customs and their women, and comported himself not as they expected a noble to act, but as a crude and offensive lout. It was a particularly egregious example of such behavior, whose details I will spare you, which ignited the rebellion.

"All this being the case, during the first part of the fall, the leaders of the revolt were all heady with success and their new found power, and not inclined to compromise. However, once the news arrived of the Frankish army on the march against them, and the implications of what was to follow sunk in, they were quick enough to beg me to arrange the surrender of the city to you. "

"Hah!" said Eleanor. "Isn't that exactly what I said would happen?"

"I pushed them on this, to make sure they were in earnest, and they swore to me by the Bible, Our Savior, the Virgin, and every saint and holy relic, that if you would only accept them back into your protection, that they would be your loyal subjects forever, and perform for you any duty owed by them, or asked of them, and pray for you always, and thank you, and call upon Heaven to bless you both in this world and the next, for all eternity."

Eleanor nodded. "Reasonable terms. I would have accepted them. Go on"

"This contrition seeming to me sufficiently dutiful, I sent four messengers to you, one after the other, to arrange surrender. No reply was received, however. Then the city was surrounded, and no more messengers could be sent.

"While willing enough to submit their city back to you, the Poitevins vowed to fight to the death rather than give up their town to the ravages of the Frankish barbarians. Pots and kettles and every other piece of iron in the city was gathered up and given to the smiths to be beaten into pike heads. Table tops were sawed up to make shields, and every guild was turned into a battalion.

"They were a strange sight to see, drilling in the marketplace; weavers and cobblers, grocers, smiths, coopers, carpenters, and builders, each grouped by trade, all practicing with clumsy arms to be soldiers. Yet, when the alarm bell rang, they stoutly manned the walls, and bravely beat off the Frankish assault."

"What?" cried Alicia. "That's incredible. Burghers defeating knights. How can that be?"

"Not burghers defeating knights, Alicia." Eleanor smiled. "Poitevins defeating Franks. That explains it well enough." The Queen gestured for me to continue.

"In achieving this noteworthy result, the Poitevins were materially aided by the disorganized nature of the Frankish attack. I pray that you take no offense, my Queen, but I am compelled to tell you that your husband must be the most incompetent general I have ever seen lead, if such a word may be used to describe the prominent manifestation of scatterbrained hysteria, men into battle."

Eleanor looked at Alicia. "Why is that not a surprise?" she said dryly. "Go on."

"Having been humiliated in combat, the Franks settled down for a siege, which, as you know, lasted throughout the winter. Against this tactic the Poitevins could do nothing, for to take the open field against cavalry was clearly far beyond their capacity. They rationed their provisions as best they could, but by February all the food in the city had run out, and the burghers were reduced to eating cats, rats, and grass, then finally sawdust and leather belts. Still, they would not give up."

Eleanor's eye began to tear. "Oh, my Poitevins. My poor, brave, foolish Poitevins."

I continued. "Mothers' breasts dried up and babies began to die, then children and the old. In the end, the sight of their children dying, begging for food, was too much for the communards, and they asked me to arrange a capitulation.

"So setting out under a flag of truce, I met with one of the King's advisors, a monk of St. Denis named Odo de Deuil, to propose terms of surrender. The only term he would agree to, however, was that the city would be retaken without a sack. This being better than nothing, I advised the communards to accept, and after some deliberation, they did. Accordingly, surrender banners went up, the gates were opened, and the Franks entered the town.

"The Mayor and the Councilors were all promptly arrested and strung up on a gallows. This did not surprise anyone, and indeed I must say that these men showed considerable dignity in accepting their fate in order to save their city. But what was shocking to me, was that after distributing some food to alleviate the immediate starvation, the King, acting apparently upon the advice of this same Brother Odo I had negotiated with previously, ordered that all the children of the leading citizens of the town be arrested as well."

"What?" cried Eleanor. "They're arresting the children?"

The messenger lad, who was still kneeling on the floor, now spoke up. "Yes, Your Majesty, they've taken hundreds. Not just the children of the rich, either. My own little brother and sister have been taken! It's horrible!"

"Why are they doing this?" snapped Eleanor. "There must be a reason. Read on."

I gulped. "Apparently, this Odo, in consultation with his Abbot, who serves as the King's Principal Minister, has decided that it would be advisable to collect the children of the burghers to hold as hostages to assure continued good conduct in the future. Accordingly they are all being gathered up for transportation back to Paris, where they will be held as prisoners indefinitely."

I looked at Eleanor. Her eyes were wide agog with horror, but she said nothing. So I continued.

"Your Majesty, I pray you will intervene. This is a crime the like of which has never been seen in the history of Christendom, and which will stain the reputation of this kingdom forever. Whatever offense the Poitevins may have given you, they beg you now, they plead with you. Save them. Save their city. But most of all, save their children."

"Your humble servant, Gilbert of Poiree."

Eleanor took several deep breaths, and her face turned livid with anger. Then she closed her eyes and shuddered, and breathing more deeply, appeared to count under her breath until her rage subsided.

"Clara!" she called out to her lead maidservant The

girl appeared instantly. "Yes, Your Majesty?"

Eleanor pointed at the messenger lad. "Take this boy to the kitchen and see that he is well fed."

Clara bowed, then beckoned to the apprentice, who followed her from the terrace.

Then she turned to me. "Marie," she snapped. "Will Abbot Suger be at the St. Denis construction site today?"

"No," I replied. "He's here at the palace. I saw him enter his office chamber whilst I was on my way over."

Eleanor's eyes darkened. "Good," she said with a voice like ice. "Then let's pay the King's principal minister a visit."

She stormed from the terrace, and Alicia and I followed. Then through the great hall we went, the Queen in front, we two on either side, marching in step like dreadful infantry advancing in the final moment before the charge. Dogs scattered to either side as we tramped by, our double time steps resounding on the stone floor like the pounding of approaching doom.

When we reached the Suger's office chamber, a monk tried to bar the way.

"Excuse me," he said. "Do you have an appointment with the Abbot?"

Eleanor walked past him like he was not there, then threw open the chamber door with a crash.

From behind his bureau table, Abbot Suger started and stood up. "Your Majesty!" he cried as we entered the room.

Eleanor advanced to face Abbot Suger from the opposite side of his table. Of equal height, she looked him straight in the eye.

"So Suger," she began. "What madness is this that you have ordered?"

A look of alarmed caution crossed the Abbot's face. "I am not sure what Your Majesty could be referring to."

"You're not sure." Eleanor's eyes flashed anger. "What, Abbot, are you possessed? I am referring to your decision to kidnap the children of Poitiers."

"Oh, that," Suger said. "I'd hardly call it kidnapping."

"Really," said Eleanor. "What then would you call it?"

"Arresting," said Suger. "I'd call it arresting."

"I'm sorry," Eleanor said in harshly. "Pardon my Frankish."

She continued to stare at him, demanding explanation.

Abbot Suger waved his hand. "In any case it wasn't my decision. It was the will of the King. I'm simply a humble advisor."

Eleanor shook her head. "Don't mock me, Suger."

Abbot Suger returned her gaze for several moments, then nodded. "Very well, I did advise it. What would you have me do? Suffer the Poitevins to revolt again? We need to have some security."

"What about the security that comes from the good will of the people?"

"Good will?" the Abbot scoffed. "From the Poitevins? Rebels who scorned the entire Great Chain of Being, the fundamental principle upon which all society is…"

"Oh, stop it," Eleanor snapped.

The Abbot looked puzzled. "You don't believe in the Great Chain?"

"I believe that the Chain pulls two ways," Eleanor said. "And that is something that you need to learn."

"Your Majesty," said Abbot Suger. "I was born one of the peasantry, so I think I know a good deal more than you about what is required to govern common folk. They must be ruled with firmness, or not at all."

Eleanor shook her head. "The Poitevins are not peasants, they are burghers. They are a new kind of people, and their heads are filled with strange new ideas. They need to be governed with respect."

I was surprised to hear Eleanor speak thus, for she had never voiced such thoughts in my presence before. But hearing her say it made me very happy and proud to be her companion, for in truth most nobles do not think this way.

"I fail to see what you are talking about," said Abbot Suger.

"Precisely," said Eleanor. "And that is why <u>you</u>, dear Father, must bear a substantial amount of the blame for this rebellion."

"I beg your pardon," said Suger, now sounding generally offended.

"Beg all you like," said Eleanor. "What did you think would happen when you appointed a Frank to govern the Poitevins? I thought you were a man of sense! Poitiers is a civilized city, a part of the Aquitaine. Yet you take a crude barbarian baron from Frankdom, a man with no culture or manners of his own, and no regard for those of others, and make him ruler of the town. Tell me, what did you expect to happen?"

Abbot Suger looked at the Queen with sober eyes. "Eleanor," he said softly. "The King's realm must be unified. Until and unless that is done, we will remain weak, prone to endless civil war, revolution, anarchy, and invasion. We must have a united kingdom."

Eleanor raised her eyebrows. "A worthy goal. Yet you propose to do this by appointing the King's own Franks to rule it all."

Suger nodded. "That is correct. That is the only way it can be done."

"And so you would crush all those who resist this plan."

"Regrettably, force is sometimes necessary to achieve great ends."

"And thus," concluded Eleanor, "the fate of the Poitevins is to be the horrid example to force submission from all the rest."

"Yes," said Abbot Suger.

"No," said Eleanor shaking her head. "No."

Suger spoke firmly. "The decision has been made. They have broken every law, and they have forfeited all their rights."

"Perhaps," said Eleanor hotly. "But I have not forfeited mine. They are my subjects, and by God and the honor of my family I'll not see them so abused!"

Suger seemed taken aback. "What are you saying?"

"I am saying," said Eleanor, "that I am their Countess and their Duchess, and under the law of the Great Chain of Being that you like to talk about so much, it is my duty to protect these people, and I intend to do exactly that."

Suger waved his hand dismissively. "There's nothing you can do."

"Really?" said Eleanor with deadly softness, a touch of a smile curling her lips. "Tell me Abbot, this cathedral of yours, is it done?"

After Eleanor said these words, Suger froze like statue, and an absolute silence filled the room for several seconds. Then the quiet was broken by the sound of my gasp, as I realized the meaning of what Eleanor had just said. The Queen was threatening to stop paying for the construction of the cathedral of light!

When Suger spoke again, his voice was much more humble. "Your Majesty, I thought we had reached an understanding."

"We had, Abbot," replied Eleanor, "until you decided to seize the children of my subjects."

"But I have already committed the funds you had pledged to me! Don't you see the position you are putting me in?"

"Indeed I do Abbot," Eleanor said in soothing tones. "I'm sure it must be very distressing."

Suger spoke angrily. "So to avenge these rebels for their just punishment, you would destroy the greatest project ever undertaken in

Christendom, a cathedral that will glorify God like no other, that will show to one and all the true nature of the divine light?"

Eleanor shrugged. "If you force me to, Father, I will. It really needn't be that much of a loss, however. After all, we can always build one like it somewhere else." She turned to Alicia. "What say you Alicia, would Bordeaux be a good place for the first cathedral of light?"

Alicia smiled. "Yes, I should think so."

Now Suger became frantic. "No, you mustn't. Don't you see, it's not a just a question of the form of the cathedral, the place is equally critical. It needs to be in Paris, at St. Denis, because Paris is the capital of France, and St. Denis is the patron saint of France. By building it here, we will endow the idea of France with the grandeur that must have if it is to become a unified and mighty kingdom. The cathedral of light at St. Denis is the essential symbol necessary to realize my entire vision."

"That is unfortunate," said Eleanor. "But I'll have no part in building a temple to tyranny."

Now it was Abbot Suger's turn to stand and shake in anger as Eleanor had earlier. Finally he calmed himself.

"Very well," he muttered. "I'll advise the King to release the children."

"Thank you, Father," Eleanor said brightly. "I knew you would find the right answer."

"Yes, my daughter," Suger said dryly. "God is kind."

"However," Eleanor continued. "As you pointed out earlier, we still need to deal with the issue of preventing another revolt."

"Absolutely," Suger said. "I'm glad you think so."

"Yes," Eleanor went on breezily. "I have given a good deal of thought to this matter, and it seems evident to me that the key to preventing another rebellion is to give the people a government of their own countrymen, rulers who speak with the same accent, who share the same temperament, sentiments, pastimes, and heritage, who understand the needs, and who honor the same customs, as those who they rule."

Abbot Suger's look turned dark, but he said nothing.

"And therefore, in short," Eleanor concluded, "all the Frankish governors need to be withdrawn from not only Poitiers, but all of Aquitaine, and native nobles appointed in their place."

"So that's what this is all about!" shouted Suger. "Sinecures for your own vassals! For that you would destroy the dream of a united France!" The Abbot started shaking again, even more violently than before.

"Now then," Eleanor spoke sweetly. "There's no reason to be upset. No one is destroying the dream of a united France. I am trying to help you unite France. After all, am I not Queen of France? Who then could possibly be better to hold Aquitaine for France than those nobles who are most loyal to me?"

Abbot Suger collapsed back into his chair and held his head in his hands. Eleanor sat herself on the edge of his bureau table, and looked down on him with a soft smile, much as Caesar must have looked down on Vercingetorix, when the latter was brought before him in chains.

***   ***   ***

The great Roman statesman, orator, and philosopher, Marcus Tullius Cicero once famously wrote; "Gifts make slaves." Nowhere could the wisdom of this adage be better proven than in the dealings of Eleanor and Abbot Suger. For in accepting the bounty of her purse to achieve his great project, the Abbot became a captive of her purse, and thus the Queen's chattel, to direct as she wished. And since Abbot Suger was also the King's Principal Minister, by gaining power over him, Eleanor gained the power of the kingdom as well. For though the King would not listen to her, he would listen to Suger, or to monks beholden to Suger. This power, Eleanor knew, would not last forever, for when the cathedral would be done the power would be done. But while it lasted, she used it for much good. She saved the children of Poitiers, and prevented further rebellions by giving the people of all of Aquitaine governors who they could abide. These governors were her own vassals and kinsmen, and thus known to her to be all very fine people, and well deserving of the honors, responsibilities, and benefits that their appointments incurred. And with these trustworthy persons in place, the independence and protection of the Aquitaine was best assured.

I have sometimes wondered what might have happened had the Abbot Suger not given into Eleanor's demand that he release the children of Poitiers. Would she really have destroyed his project of the cathedral of light? After much pondering, my conclusion is, yes. This is not because, as some people say, Eleanor did not care about the church or the need to honor God. No, it is because she cared so much for the welfare of her subjects that she would give up the glory for herself of patronizing such a wondrous project, rather than see them suffer. Furthermore, had St. Denis been allowed to be built by an Abbot and a King with such a hideous crime upon their hands, what then would it have signified? Instead of standing as a monument to the truth of our holy faith, it would have proclaimed our Gospel as mere hypocrisy to all the world. Could any true Christian want such a disastrous result?

No, it was precisely because of the strength and honesty of her faith that Eleanor was willing to wreck St. Denis. I loved the project of St. Denis, and the instant she made it, her threat left me aghast. But I knew even then that there was no other choice; not only to save the children, but to save the cathedral of light itself. A St. Denis constructed in infamy would have been worse than no St. Denis at all.

And even though Abbot Suger raged for a while against Eleanor for the way she had bent him to her will, in time he came to thank her for it, for he realized she had saved him from a mortal sin. For her part, Eleanor, knowing that her power over the Abbot would end someday, used her rod lightly, and did all she could to make him her friend. This also showed her wisdom, for though they came from different worlds – he the son of a peasant, she a descendant of Charlemagne – the two shared a certain greatness of spirit that made understanding between them possible, even if politics sometimes drew them wide apart.

Chapter 10

The New Civilization is Born

Eleanor's power in the Frankish realm was only through Abbot Suger, and this was a frail thing, since the cathedral would someday be completed, and even before that, God might take him at any time. This being the case, she began to wonder about what she might do to gain better security. The response of the Franks to the Poitevin revolt had underscored their savage nature, and she, for one, had no desire to be left a helpless woman amidst a barbarian horde. The King was of no use, since as unnatural as he was, he had no interest in her beauty or charms, and this oddness about him denied to her even such influence as the most ordinary woman might expect to obtain with her husband. Excepting Abbot Suger, who the women of the town tell me was indeed a healthy fellow, most of the rest of the King's monkish advisors were equally strange.

The knights of the court, however, were another matter. For, as rough as they might be, these at least were natural men with natural desires. It was with this in mind that Eleanor had insisted on obtaining the guardianship of the Kingdom's orphaned heiresses as condition of her support for the project of St. Denis, and furthermore devoted so much effort to the training of these ladies to constitute an effective and disciplined cadre.

So now, with the rich and beautiful heiresses at her command, the knights might become Eleanor's to reform, as was clearly necessary if any kind of worthy, gentle, and refined civilization was ever to take root in France. After the knights returned from Poitiers, she made it known that all who wished to court the ladies must wash their hands every day, bathe every fortnight, and change their clothes every month. Furthermore, they must cut off any over-greasy edges of their beards, eat with knife and spoon, and be prepared to serve and defend their ladies in every way that a knight of King Arthur's fellowship would have done. This last catechism it was my duty to explain.

I waited until the first feast day in the month after Easter to deliver my lesson. As we all sat at the King's table, I noticed with pleasure that the appearance of many of the knights had much improved. Their beards were no longer so wild and bushy, their clothes were mostly clean, and   several even attempted, in clear accord with Eleanor's wish, to cut their meat with knife and spoon.

The meal concluding, Sir Bertrand rubbed his hand across his shorter, but still greasy beard. "A fine meal," he said. "Time for music. Let's have another tale of Arthur!"

The Frankish knights started to bang their fists down on the table, chanting "Arthur! Arthur! Arthur! Arthur!"

I looked to Eleanor, and she nodded for me to proceed. So I rose from my chair, took my lute, and walked to my chosen performing area. It took but a moment to give the strings a final test, and then I began.

"I sing of Arthur, whose kingly rules
Rid his court of craven fools
To win each war, by Christ he swore
No coward would stay within his door.

It was a well-chosen beginning, for the announced theme was very much in accord with the knights' taste. Looking around as I proceeded, I could see that I had them all in rapt attention. So I went on, for nearly the length of a candle, until I reached my conclusion, wherein the lesson of the tale was delivered.

"But then Sir Mark, in jest, he said
Let spill some wine on the Queen's fair head.
Red with rage went Guinevere
"Were I man, your end be near!"

Mark laughed, "Lady, you are not a man
So I will tweak you, how best I can."
Then Arthur rose and threw his spear
Slaying he who mocked thus Guinevere.

"Death to you, you craven churl!
Who makes bold insult to a girl.
You'd fight not man, you'd fight not beast
But challenge those who fight the least.

Those who insult maids are craven
And within my court will find no haven.
So swear now, knights, to be ever brave

And defend all ladies, or be called a knave."

And fair maidens came from every land
To bless with love that courageous band.
For damsels choose their men with care
And only the brave deserve the fair.

Finishing thus, I flourished the strings of my lute. Everyone applauded, although I must say that Eleanor and Alicia did so with greater vigor than the knights, who for the most part, seemed slightly confused.

Sir Bertrand said, "That was good. Well, most of it was. Aye, but the ending was most strange. What do you think it meant?"

I answered, "Fine knight, it is simply the true history of the reign of the great King Arthur, and the method by which he rid his court of cowards."

"It was a wise test that Arthur chose," Alicia added, pointing Bertrand's attention towards the moral of the tale. "For when ladies see knights brave enough to protect them from all insult, they feel no fear and come and show them their love. But when all they see are louts and cravens, they wisely stay away."

"I see," said Sir Bertrand. Apparently, considering the matter thus made him think of the orphaned ladies that Eleanor had in training, for he continued: "So, Your Majesty Queen Eleanor, I hear tell you have taken several young heiresses into your care."

"Yes," Eleanor said. "Three maidens of great beauty, sweet temperament, and noble blood, and quite rich too."

Beautiful, sweet, noble, and rich! What more could a knight desire? Sir Bertrand exchanged interested looks with several of his fellows. The he turned back to Eleanor.

"Then why not invite them to dine with us?" the knight asked the Queen.

Eleanor suddenly appeared distraught. "I have, I have," she exclaimed, like a mother complaining of her difficult children. "But they simply won't come. I think they are afraid of something, but I don't know what."

Sir Bertrand looked at Alicia. "You don't suppose...?" he began.

"What?" Alicia said.

Sir Bertrand banged his fist on the table. "This cannot be," he said. "We are not cravens. They should not be afraid."

"But how can we convince them?" Alicia asked innocently.

An expression of decision appeared on the bold knight's face. "Let them know this," he said. He stood, and drawing his sword, raised a salute. "That I, Sir Bertrand, hereby swear, on my honor as a knight, the oath of King Arthur; that I will defend them, and all ladies who should grace this court, and that anyone who dares insult them, insults me, and shall face my sword."

At this, Eleanor gave me a sly look. Then straightening her face, she spoke to the knights. "Well said, brave Sir Bertrand. Are there others who will so swear?"

Several more Frankish knights then stood and drew their swords. "I so swear! I so swear! I so swear!" each said, one after the other.

Then the rest of the French knights all rose, saluted their swords, and spoke as one. "We so swear!" they said.

I looked at Eleanor and strummed a chord of triumph on my lute.

***   ***   ***

The oath thus taken, the heiresses were brought to the table, and with these gentle lasses acting upon Eleanor's instructions, it took no time at all to generate a challenge between Sir Bertrand of Tours, defending the superior beauty and honor of the heiress Lady Katharine of Reims against Sir Michel of Orleans, supporting the incomparable fairness and quality of Lady Beatrice of Champagne.

Our plan, however, nearly went amiss, for instantly the challenge was delivered, the two knights drew their blades and made as if to slay each other right there in the dining hall. This was only prevented by Eleanor, who seeing the peril, leapt to her feet to command the two to hold fast before they could deliver their deadly blows.

We thus had to make clear that the issue needed to be settled not with an immediate fatal assault, but with the more polite form of combat styled the tournament. Of this they had never heard. The rules we explained, however, and the knights were much delighted to discover, that under the Code of Arthur, he that unhorsed the other in tournament would not only be declared the victor, and gain the favor of his lady, but the armor and horse of his opponent as well. This promised great sport, and other knights rushed to join in.

In a trice, we had not one knight to represent each of the offended ladies, but five. These numbers being ample, Eleanor declared that that five months following, at the harvest fair, Paris would have a tournament.

***   ***   ***

At midsummer the cathedral walls were ten feet high. The number of holy Sisters had grown too. When the work had started the previous year there had only been six singing, now the choir numbered nearly a score, and the sound of their voices as they sang out the magnificent music of Hildegard of Bingen was such as to thrill the hearts and lighten the labors of the workmen, and make the day of those able to spend their time idly watching and listening a pleasure not to be matched. I was thus able to induce Alan and several other excellent and handsome young scholars to join with me in this pastime, especially as I always brought plenty of good meat from the palace to dine upon as we harkened to the holy concert. By this time many of the small counterweighted cranes were in action lifting little platforms holding cut stone up to the workmen on the walls. Now that the walls were so high, the larger windlass cranes would soon be needed. Fortunately, one was ready. We watched as Papa directed it to be wheeled close to the wall, and then unreeled the windlass so as to let the rope down to be tied to a large platform that the workmen had already loaded with cut stone. Papa signaled, and two laborers started to push down on the outer perimeter of a windlass wheel, which was some two fathoms in diameter, to get it to reel in the load rope which was affixed to the engine's central axel, whose diameter was but a foot.

Now the secret of the windlass is this: the more the outer diameter dwarfs that of the inner, the easier it is to lift heavy loads, but the slower it is that the loads will rise. So with a wheel as large and as narrow an axel as this one, it was possible for two men to lift a ton of stones, and this was a marvel to behold, yet the slowness with which the stones rose was an agony to endure.

But there is a remedy for this, and I knew it. So, taking my scholar friends in tow, I ran to the wheel. There was a goodly sized wooden crate nearby, and taking proper advantage of this, I had the lads place it next to the wheel so we could use it as our step. Then climbing up the crate, we mounted the wheel, and by running upwards upon it from the outside, so sped its spin that the load of stones rose from the ground like a bird taking wing. The workmen waiting on the high walls cheered. I looked at Alan. He looked at me. We laughed, and ran even faster.

***   ***   ***

But the construction of the cathedral was not the only great work that was advanced that summer. For fine nations need not only fine buildings, but fine men as well, and it was these than Eleanor, Alicia, and I sought to create through our work at the palace.

The knights, having taken the pledge of Arthur to protect ladies, were made to understand that protection included not only from the violence of others, but of themselves, and that therefore, if they were to win the heiresses, they had to do it not by conquering their bodies, but their hearts. To do this, they had to learn the same refinements and courtesies that the great King Arthur ordained for the knights of the Table Round for this very purpose. As we were the experts in the true history and form of this famous etiquette, we three, perforce, became their instructors. Now, I grant that not every detail of the courtly customs prescribed by Arthur is known today with documented exactitude from well-preserved chronicles. However in as much as these practices were designed by the wise King precisely for the purpose of allowing his knights to please the ladies whose love they hoped to obtain, we three, using our powers of rational deduction, were able to determine with great accuracy what those customs must surely have been, simply by pondering what practices would have been most pleasing to us.

It was clear both from history and logic that every knight of King Arthur had to be able to dance. Accordingly, we so informed the knights, and offered instruction so that they might not remain deficient in this regard. Sir Bertrand, Sir Michel, and several other notable knights accepted our offer on this account, and it must be said that if they were not elegant men, they were rugged ones. For in learning the dance they frequently tripped one leg behind the other, and in so doing, endured more toppling upon the ground then they ever would have in a hundred battles.

We had also to teach them to stand when we stood, to pull our chairs out for us when we arrived at the table, and in general to observe all such customs as are followed by the polite knights of Aquitaine today, and which therefore surely must have been observed at least as strictly by the noble knights of the great King Arthur in the days of yore.

But above all, of course, they had to learn the proper style of courtship as it was practiced by the brave and mighty knights of Arthur. This, we duly informed the Frankish swordsmen, involved inviting the lady to stand upon an elevated circumstance, and then the knight should kneel on one leg before her, and praise her beauty as if she were a goddess standing upon a pedestal.

However, as the knights of King Louis knew nothing of goddesses, praise, or pedestals, it was necessary to perform a demonstration. So gathering Sir Bertrand, Sir Michel, and our other most intrepid students in a private room, I had the Lady Alicia stand upon a chair, while I, wearing my troubadour hat to provide a boyish simulacrum, knelt on one leg before her and pronounced the following praises:

"Your eyes are like sapphires
Your hair is like gold
Your teeth are like pearls
Your cheeks are like roses"

I had the knights all kneel in a row in my place, and then, as I snapped my fingers to provide guidance as to the proper rhythm of delivery, had them recite until they had full mastery of the required lines.

Now this poetry of love may seem very commonplace today, but that is only because it is so good that every knight perforce chooses to use it upon all occasions where he seeks to court a lady. However all things, before they are widely known, must first be introduced into the world by a single creative soul, and in the case at hand, it was I who played the role of Prometheus, bringing from heaven to Earth, through these eternal lines, the divine power to set hearts aflame. Let those who claim they are tiresome come up with something better.

Of course, the knights themselves might have found all this instruction tiresome, had we not entwined it with that part of court ritual of Arthur which truly interested them, which is to say the tournament. So as the midsummer turned to August, we frequented the fairgrounds outside the city, where in accord with the instructions of Eleanor rows of benches were being erected, with the ones in the back higher than the rest. Upon these benches, many people would be able to sit and bear witness as, before them upon the field, the valiant knights dashed back and forth upon their mighty steeds. Targets were placed upon three-legged stands at each end of the field, and during the late summer the knights with their lances would charge these and knock them down, winning many approving shouts from the bench makers if their blows were well aimed.

The men of Sir Bertrand and those of Sir Michel spent many a hot afternoon practicing in this way, with each band taunting the other with promises to take good care of their horses and armor after they won it in the coming tournament.

Chapter 11

A Lesson in Strategy

In October came the harvest fair, with it, the long awaited tournament.

Eleanor, Alicia, and I walked through the festive gathering accompanied by a few knights. Everywhere merchants were selling foods, wines, linens, crockery, pots, pans, tools, and arms by the cartload. Traders of horses and cows paraded their fine beasts about, showing them to anyone who evinced interest, as well as many who did not. There were jugglers, magicians, puppet shows, and troubadours everywhere, offering free entertainment to any who might stop long enough to have their pockets picked. The crowd was enormous, and included people of every rank and condition; priests, nuns, scholars, tradesmen, burghers, peasants, knights, and ladies, all walking about and mixing like fellow guests at a tavern.

As we approached a vintner's cart, I discerned the scholars Alan of Cherbourg and Thomas à Becket leaning upon it and sipping from goblets. The vintner called out to us. "Wine for a pence. Fine wine for a pence."

Eleanor looked at the man. "Fine wine, you say," she answered. "Then let's have some."

The Queen then beckoned to Alicia, who gave vintner a coin, receiving three goblets of wine in return, one for each of us.

Becket eyed us curiously. For we were wearing palace clothes, and so at first he did not perceive we were the same three he had met in burgher guise. But then, of a sudden, I saw his eyes open in dawning recognition. Alan appeared amazed as well, for though by this time he knew me better, it was as the daughter of the enginator of St. Denis, a social rank not inconsistent with that I had manifested at our first meeting.

Becket hesitated, then spoke. "Begging your pardon, ladies, but aren't you…?"

Eleanor smiled mischief at the bewildered man. "Master Becket, scholars, well met."

The scholar's astonishment was now complete. "Then you are the Queen?" was all he could say.

Eleanor shrugged.

"That would appear evident."

Becket turned to Alan, and each opened and closed his mouth without saying anything. I found this piscine gaping so amusing that I could not resist imitating it, obtaining a good laugh from Eleanor and Alicia for my effort.

"Methinks they are learning to be fish," I observed.

"Ones out of water," Alicia replied.

Eleanor looked at the two scholars with merry eyes, then lifted her goblet and drunk it down. "Yes," she said. "Well, we must be off. The tournament is about to begin."

Eleanor and Alicia and the knights promenaded away. But Alan held me in place for a moment with his gaze.

"Who are you, really?" he said to me.

"I'm her bard," I answered.

Thomas à Becket gazed at the retreating Queen. "And to think I knew her when she was but a scholar," he mused.

Alan laughed. "Then perhaps there's a royal future for you as well, Thomas à Becket."

Becket smiled and quaffed from his goblet. "Not likely," he said.

I finished my cup off and hurried after Eleanor.

***   ***   ***

The elevated benches were filled with fairgoers of every condition. But between the two rows of benches there was a shaded pavilion reserved for the royal party and their closest retainers. In addition to our party, Louis, Odo, and Abbot Suger were also seated there, as were the ladies in contention, Katharine of Reims and Beatrice of Champagne. As a courtesy of consolation, since she was not represented in the tournament, the lady Anne of Chartres was also given a place, along some guards, heralds, and several other notables.

Since it was a festive day, Eleanor was dressed her best, and looked every inch a Queen. Alicia was also in finery, and I had been lent some courtly clothes as well. Abbot Suger and Odo were dressed as a churchman, which was understandable, since that is what they were, but the Queen was plainly annoyed, although not surprised, to see that, even at such a festival, King Louis chose to manifest himself as a joyless monk. Katharine wore a dress of silken sky blue, while Beatrice had one of summer orange, and both had instructed their supporters to sport clothes of like color. Accordingly,

76

Anne dressed herself completely in verdant green.

A line of seven trumpeters and seven drummers stood before the pavilion. The trumpeters lifted their horns and blew out a fanfare in unison, or what in the kingdom of the Franks passes for unison. Since the instruments were not all of one pitch, the effect was quite discordant as well. These deficiencies notwithstanding, the performance did prove adequate to achieve its intended purpose, and the noisy crowd on the benches quieted down.

King Louis spoke to the Queen. "Eleanor, this tournament business is your affair. Why don't you make the proclamation?"

This suited Eleanor. "Very well, as you wish," she said.

Eleanor then rose to her feet and addressed the crowd.

"Loyal subjects," she proclaimed. "Welcome to this field of valor. On this day, we shall witness the courage, skill, and gallantry of the greatest knights in Christendom!"

The vast crowd cheered.

"Let the herald announce the knights!" Eleanor commanded.

The herald stood forth. "On the left, wearing the blue colors of Lady Katharine of Reims whose supreme beauty they espouse, Sir Bertrand of Tours, and his gallant companions."

The trumpeters blew another fanfare, and Sir Bertrand and his knights, all in chain mail and helmets of Norman-style, and wearing blue tunics and capes, galloped before the benches. The drummers drummed their kettles, the people shouted their cheers, and then the knights took their position at the east end of the field.

The herald spoke again. "And on the right, wearing the orange colors of Lady Beatrice of Champagne, whose fair beauty they defend above all others, Sir Michel of Orleans, and his brave knights."

Again the trumpeters blew, and Sir Michel and his men, armed and armored in equal manner as those of Sir Bertrand, but wearing tunics and capes of orange, galloped the field to the cheers of the crowd and the drumming of the drummers. Then they took their position at the west end of the ground opposite Sir Bertrand.

For the third time, the herald spoke. "May God defend the right," he shouted. "Let the combat begin!"

The trumpeters now blew their mightiest blast, the drummers beat like thunder, and the two parties of knights charged at each other at full tilt. It was such a sight to see! Everyone rose to their feet and cheered as the bold chevaliers in armor collided, their lances turning to splinters upon each other's shields. The force of their blows was so great, that it was impossible to imagine how any of them could remain in their saddle.

Yet, when the dust had cleared, we could see that only one knight from either party had been unhorsed, although several on each side had sustained some injury. As I watched, I saw several of the knights upon their horses kneading bruised shoulders where they had taken a blow. One of the companions of Sir Bertrand was coughing blood.

I heard Sir Bertrand call out to him. "Are you wounded, friend?"

"I can manage," the man said bravely.

The knights continued their ride forward and assembled again at the far ends of the field, where they were greeted by squires who rushed out with new lances to replace the ones now broken.

The trumpeters blew. "Then at them again, lads!" Sir Bertrand shouted. The bold champion and his heroes in blue turned and charged. Sir Michel and his remaining four men did the same. Again the drummers beat and the crowds yelled, and in the ensuing crash, one more knight of either side was unhorsed.

Now it was Sir Michel and his men who passed close by me, their bruises and bloody wounds evident, and their winded horses breathing spittle. Then each party rallied at the end of their run, to have their lances replaced as before.

"The teams seem well matched in strength and skill," Eleanor said to Alicia.

"Yes," Alicia said. "But now comes the test of wind. I'll wager you a penny on Bertrand."

"Done," Eleanor said. "Michel's endurance is worth a penny's sport."

With that, she withdrew a penny from her purse and handed it to me. "Here Marie," she said. "You can hold the wager." Alicia gave me a penny as well.

I held the two coins tight, a treasurer to nobility.

Again the trumpeters blew, the knights charged, and one more of each party was unhorsed. Now but three were left to each band, with horses exhausted and the men themselves clearly the worse for wear.

Alicia said, "Surely, this next must be their last charge."

"Indeed," replied Eleanor, observing the contestants with an expert eye. "They look ready to fall without a touch."

The merciless trumpeters blew once more, and the remaining knights, reeling in their saddles, began a slow lumbering charge towards each other.Suddenly, from behind the benches, came a new party of six knights, all dressed in chain mail and green.

"For Anne! For Anne!" the green knights shouted.

Eleanor turned to the Lady Anne. "What's this?" she inquired crossly.

But Anne, who had been without expression during the entire contest so far, now had a big smile upon her face. "Strategy, my lady," she said. "Strategy."

The exhausted knights upon the field turned to face their fresh assailants, but their cause was hopeless. In a single smashing encounter, they were all thrown from their saddles, leaving the green knights triumphant on the field.

Their leader trotted his steed up to the royal pavilion and removed his helmet. I recognized him as Sir Pierre, a warrior who also had studied Arthurian etiquette under our tutelage.

Eleanor nodded to the man. "Sir Pierre," she said. "You are victorious."

"Thank you, Your Majesty," Sir Pierre replied. Then he shouted to the crowd. "And as victor this day, I declare that Lady Anne of Chartres is the most beauteous of all!"

The crowd cheered their approval. I slid the two pennies into my pocket.

Eleanor said, "Very well, Sir Pierre, come forward and receive your favor."

Sir Pierre rode up to the pavilion, bringing himself to a place just below Lady Anne. Eleanor gestured to the triumphant noblewoman, who took her cue.

"Sir Pierre," Anne said, so all could hear. "For defending my honor so well this day, I pronounce you the strongest and bravest knight in Christendom."

Anne leaned down and kissed Sir Pierre gently on the forehead. The knight smiled with glee, and waving his lance, galloped off to the cheers of the crowd. Eleanor looked to Alicia and shrugged. And thus it was that the great Queen Eleanor and I brought chivalry and elegant civilization to France.

Book the Second

Of Faith and Reason

Chapter 12

To the Street of Strangers

When November came, the leaves of the trees had all fallen away. The walls of the cathedral had climbed to more than three fathoms, and several thick buttresses had been built out along their sides.

On the fifth of the month, word arrived from Papa that his grand engine was ready for its first trial. Of course I had to witness this, and Eleanor and Alicia, inspired by my obvious excitement, decided to accompany me to see the extraordinary event for themselves.

We arrived at St Denis in the hour before noon. A new crane, larger than any I had ever seen before stood by, its lifting platform heavily loaded with cut stone. There was a good crowd gathered eyeing it from every side, including my friend Alan and many of the other scholar lads. All the onlookers wondered how it could possibly be made to work, because it was much too big to be operated by climbing its windlass wheel.

But the wind engine was now completed, and its sails were spinning rapidly. Papa had created an intricate wooden gearing, and through that and a belt of rope, the motion of the wind was conveyed to a water screw, which spinning thus without the labor of human or animal, drew water upwards from a large tub on the ground to pour into a smaller basin elevated upon a tower. This tub in turn had a pipe that would allow it to flow the water to a series of hinged troughs that were attached to the perimeter of the huge windlass wheel that worked the giant crane.

Papa let the small basin on the tower fill up. Then, when it had reached capacity, he signaled to a workman to pull out the plug, and in a rush, water flowed down the pipe and gushed into the windlass trough. It only took seconds for the trough to become heavy enough to make the windlass turn. It moved, and as it turned, the second trough moved below the water pipe and filled as well, causing windlass rotation to speed up. With that, the rope attached to a pulley at the top of the crane was reeled in. The rope to the load tightened, and strained with enormous force. The platform began to lift.

Suddenly from above there was a sound of splitting wood. I looked up, and saw that on top of the tower, the pivot that held the crane beam out   in its horizontal position was beginning to break loose from its platform. Only two iron spikes still held it down. As I watched, they started to pull out and bend. Below the crane beam a group of town waifs stood, oblivious to their peril as they gawked at the rising load.

Papa saw all this too, and he ran towards the children, shouting at them to flee. But they either didn't hear or understand until it was near too late. Then they began to run, but one little girl was too frightened and froze. Papa dashed towards her, and threw her aside, even as the beam broke loose and crashed down upon him.

"Papa!" I cried, as I ran towards the scene of the disaster. "Papa!"

I reached the fallen beam. There, crushed below it was my father, his eyes bulging and blood running from his mouth.

"Come on, help me get this off of him!" a voice shouted. It was Alan, yelling at two of the workmen.

They lifted the beam, and I gasped as I saw my Papa, bent, twisted and broken, panting painfully like one soon to expire.

I knelt down to help him, but what could I do? "Papa," I wept. "Oh Papa! Oh, Virgin, save him, Save him please" Then I felt an arm on my shoulder. It was Eleanor, kneeling down beside me.

"He needs a surgeon," Eleanor said. "Have him taken to Paul of La Rochelle at once. He's the best in Paris."

"Paul? Who?" I whimpered, confused.

"Paul of La Rochelle," said Alan. "I've heard of him. He lives on the Street of Strangers and offers lessons in Galen and Avicenna. But he takes no patients of his own"

"He will if you tell him I sent you," said Eleanor.

Eleanor handed me five silver sou and a ring with the seal of Aquitaine upon it.

"Here's money for a hired carriage, and my ring to show Doctor Paul," she said.

"You're not coming?" I asked.

"No, I can't," she said. "But go now. He may be able to help."

Some of the workmen brought a wounded body carrier, and with Alan's help, I gently moved Papa on to it. Then Alan and his friend John of Salisbury each picked up an end and carried it to the road, where Alicia was waiting next to a carriage she had stopped for us. We went aboard.

"To the Street of Strangers!" Alan said to the teamster. The horses were whipped, and we set off fast down the bumpy roads, Papa's already contorted face wincing with every jolt.

I cradled his head in my lap. "Don't die, Papa," I pled. "Please don't die."

***   ***   ***

We reached the Street of Strangers in less than half an hour, and asking about, it took little time to find the house of Paul of La Rochelle.

As I ran to the door and knocked, Alan and John followed me up the walk with Papa upon the body carrier.

The door opened, and a little old man looked out upon me.

"Are you Paul of La Rochelle?" I asked, breathlessly.

"Yes," he said, glancing at my stricken father. "But I don't practice medicine any more. I only teach it."

I draw Eleanor's ring out from my pocket, and held it before his   face. Instantly, his eyes went wide.

"All right then," he said. "Come in quickly."

We entered the house, which was dimly lit by a few candles.

"Can you manage the stairs with him?" he called to the lads.

"Yes," said Alan, who was a tall, broad shouldered fellow. "I think so."

John was not as strong a lad, so I helped him lift his end of the body carrier, and with Alan leading and the two of us following, we trailed Paul up the stairs. Reaching the second floor, the old physician beckoned us into a large room with good bright windows. At one end of the room was a bed, at the other was a big table with at least five books set on it, and many piles of loose parchment.

"Put him on the bed," Paul said to the lads.

They did so, and then backed away. I stood next to Paul as he gently moved Papa's limbs to stretch him upon the bed. With each movement, Papa gasped with pain, but afterwards, seemed slightly less contorted than before.

Paul reached his hand under Papa's back, and started slowly feeling down his spine. "I see, I see," he said softly. "You've taken a nasty blow." As the doctor did these things, I observed him carefully. His clothes were those of a wealthy Christian burgher of Aquitaine, but his accent rung of Aragon, and his features bespoke an origin even further south. Paul was definitely not from La Rochelle.

"You there," he said to Alan. "You seem like a stout lad. Come here, I need your strength."

Alan approached. "What would you have me do?"

"First, help me sit him up some." Paul said. Alan obeyed.

"Right," said Paul. "Now I am going to put my hand in place. You put yours over mine. When I squeeze my fingers, you reinforce me."

"Very well," said Alan, moving into the required position.

"And you, my lass," said Paul. "You hold the patient from the front so that does not move whilst we make the adjustment."

I knelt down on the bed, and held Papa to my chest, my cheek touching his.

"Is everyone ready?" Paul said.

I nodded and mumbled a silent prayer to the Virgin. "Then push now!" Paul cried.

Suddenly, Papa gasped, and his arms flailed wildly as he spasmed again and again. I hugged him tight, praying for a miracle. Then his twitching stopped, and I felt his chest breathing evenly against mine.

"All right, then lay him down," I heard Paul say.

We lay Papa down on his back. His eyes were shut, but his face was peaceful, and his breast slowly rose up and down.

Paul stood up. "He's fainted, but it's just as well. He'll live now. He's got some broken bones that will take some mending, but now that his joints are back in place he should be out of danger."

I looked up at him and wiped my eyes. "How can I ever thank you?" I held up the three silver sou I had left from Eleanor's gift. "This is all that I have."

Paul smiled at me. "There's no need for that. The knowledge that I have rendered some assistance to Eleanor is sufficient recompense for me. Who are you, by the way, and what is your connection to the Queen?"

"I'm Marie," I said. "I serve Eleanor as her bard. These scholars, Alan and John, are my companions, and this is my Papa, Peter of Nantes."

Paul looked at my medallion. "I see you are of the builders."

"Yes," I said proudly. "Papa is the Master Enginator for the construction at St. Denis."

"The very man who would build the cathedral of light," Paul said. "That might explain Eleanor's special interest, although perhaps she had an added reason." He looked at me with a smile.

I brushed away a tear. "She is my friend," I said.

Paul put his hand softly upon my arm. "Well don't worry. It may take a while, but your Papa will recover. Trust me. This enginator has not yet built his last machine."

At this point, John walked over with one of the parchments that had been lying on the table. It was covered with a foreign script which I could not read, but which I did recognize.

"This is Hebrew, isn't it?" said John.

"Yes, certainly," Paul replied.

This confirmed my earlier suspicions. However John would not leave matters there.

"Are you a Jew?" he pressed. This, I thought, was rather impolite, since it obviously was a matter that Paul did not care to have widely known. Paul, however, surprised me with his answer.

"No," he said. "But I was once." He looked down at Papa, sleeping on the bed. "We have a lot of time to pass before he awakes. Would you like to hear my story?"

"By all means," said I.

Chapter 13

The Story of Paul

"I was born Joseph of Valencia," Paul began. "My father Nathan was the leading physician of the town, and both my brother Samuel and I were brought up to follow in the same profession. This was in the days when Valencia was still part of Al Andalus, and the Emir ruled the city."

Alan startled. "So you grew up under Moorish government?"

"Yes," said Paul. "Although the townspeople included as many Christians and Jews."

"But," John was shocked. "To be ruled by Muslims!"

"What was it like?" I asked, both curious and horrified by the possibilities.

"Well," Paul said. "There are those, especially among my people, who say that Al Andalus was a land of wonders, and others who call it a world of horrors. In truth, it was both. In terms of material culture, it far outshone anything I have seen in Christendom, with fountains, baths, book houses, ornamented palaces, and markets filled with spices, scents, and finely crafted objects from all over the world. In terms of law and justice, however, it could be harsh."

"Under Moorish law, Christians and Jews were tolerated, but kept underfoot. We had to pay three times the taxes of Muslims, and were not allowed to own a weapon or ride a horse. Nor could we testify in court against any Muslim, and so were helpless against any private injustice that such might commit against us. To mark us out for easier abuse, Jews were made to wear yellow stars sewn upon their clothing, and Christians had to wear yellow crosses."

"How shameful," I said, "that anyone should be treated that way." Then a thought crossed my mind: the Cathars use the yellow cross as their symbol. Were they saying that they lived among us as Christians did among Moors?

"Yes. However compared to other regimes we Jews had faced over the centuries, it was no worse than most, and we were able to live with it. The Christians, however, had greater problems, for many refused to understand that they had to keep their faith to themselves. Instead some would go to the market and preach to the Muslims, and the penalty for doing this was decapitation."

I gasped. Had I been there, this might have been my fate. For I also think that everyone should be saved. It is for this reason that I have often tried to explain the truth of our holy faith to the Jews that I meet. And though my efforts have never been successful, the worst punishment the Israelites have dealt me in return has generally consisted of patient smiles followed by invitations to examine merchandise. But among the Moors I would have been rewarded by a scimitar through the neck.

The example of Our Savior compels us to spread the words of truth, love, and light that will someday free all mankind from darkness and sin. But the religion of Mohammed commands his followers to murder all those who would liberate them. How then can there ever be peace between our two peoples?

"But all in all," Paul continued. "Things were not too bad provided you kept your mouth shut. In fact, many of the Moors were quite friendly to the Jews and the Christians, and would look the other way when some of these regulations were violated. In fact, they had even adopted many Christian ways themselves."

"Really," said John. "How so?"

"Well," said Paul. "First and foremost, they had taken up wine, and even stronger spirits. These pleasures are forbidden by the Koran."

"Wine is forbidden to them?" Alan asked. Apparently, he had not known this.

"Yes," said Paul. "Their prophet Mohammed has proclaimed that God has ordered that it be shunned completely, on pain of damnation."

Alan shuddered at the thought of this heresy, just as I had when I first learned of it.

Paul continued. "However, after living among Christians, fear of hell was not enough to keep the Moors abstaining from wine, or from music, for that matter, which is equally forbidden. Seeing how the Jews and Christians lived, many Moorish fathers would refuse to betroth their daughters to any man, unless he agreed that she should be his only wife. The brides thus made had much more say in their house than is customary under Islam, and began to run their homes like Jewish women, and dress themselves like Christian ladies. Not only that, many Moorish girls and women, observing how their Christian and Jewish counterparts would go about the town and market without chaperone or veil, insisted upon doing likewise, and there was   no stopping them in this. In fact, the Moorish men came to enjoy the custom, and compounded the sin by inviting such females to join them in the taverns for wine, song, and dance, just like Christians."

"These all seem like happy improvements," I said.

"Yes," Paul replied. "You might think so, but the more orthodox Muslims visiting from outside Al Andalus were horrified. They returned to their homeland in Africa, and told everyone there that the Muslims of Al Andalus had become apostates. Upon hearing this, a group of fanatics called the Almoravids decided that it was their duty to invade Spain and restore the rule of pure Islam by crushing the apostate Moors and their upstart Dhimmis."

"Dhimmis?" Alan asked. "What are those?"

"Christians and Jews," said Paul. "Non Muslims whose existence may be tolerated, as opposed to polytheists, atheists, star worshipers, and spirit cultists, who are to be killed.

"It sounds like a term of derision," John said.

"It is," said Paul. "So, to continue, when we heard that the Almoravids had invaded Al Andalus with a mighty host and defeated the Emirs of Cordoba and Seville, the town quaked with fear. Then the news arrived warning that the fanatical horde was marching on Valencia, and the entire city panicked.

"The Emir was a fat and lazy man, in love with pleasure, and lacked the spirit to fight against the Almoravids. So it surprised no one when we awoke a few days later to discover that he had absconded with his harem, his kinsmen, his captains and guards, and the city treasury, leaving us totally defenseless.

"A meeting was held in the market plaza to decide what to do; Moors, Jews, and Christians mixed together in the comradeship of shared impending doom. All seemed lost, for while everyone filled the air with words and imprecations, no one had any useful ideas. Some counseled flight, but this was no option because we had nowhere to go. Even if we had, the Almoravid horsemen were already close at hand and would slaughter us all upon the road should we try to escape by land, and, anticipating the imminent sack, all shipping had abandoned our harbor.

"Others called for negotiation, but with what did we have to negotiate, and with who?

"The city's women were there too, both low and high, all pleading, shrieking, desperately pleading, the Moorish women most frantic of all, crying out for us to find some way to save them from rape and slavery.

"Then, in the midst of this incredible clamor, a Christian nobleman rode silently into the marketplace, followed by a lady of distinction and some sixty mounted knights and sergeants. This took us by surprise, for so great was the chaos in the city that no watchman had been left at the gate. At the sight of this lord and his warrior band, the mob quieted and an eerie stillness filled the plaza.

"I will never forget my first sight of that man. His hair was gray, for he was well on years, nearly as old as I am today. His shoulders, though, were broad, his back straight despite the weight of his full armor, and his proud scarred visage presented a countenance of calm resolution that commanded immediate respect.

"My father was the first to find words to address him. 'Who are you, Sir knight, and why have you come to Valencia?'

"The noble looked briefly at my father, then lifted his eyes to address the entire crowd. 'My name is Sir Rodrigo Diaz,' he said. 'I know your peril. Acknowledge me as your lawful Count, swear to me your fealty, loyalty, and obedience, and I will save your city.'"

My mouth dropped in amazement upon hearing these words, for the name Paul had spoken was known to every bard. "Rodrigo Diaz?" I asked in a hushed tone. "You mean, the Cid?"

Chapter 14

The Arrival of the Cid

"Yes," Paul replied. "It was the Cid himself, who even then was renowned throughout Spain for his deeds of valor."

I exchanged glances of wonder with Alan, and saw that the words of the old doctor had lit a fire in my scholar friend. As well they might. the Cid! We were sitting in the same room with a man who had seen and heard the Cid in the flesh! It was like meeting someone who had known King Arthur.

"Well, as you can imagine," Paul continued. "The Cid's statement sent the whole marketplace ablaze. Some, especially the Moors, and, I must admit, also many of the Jews, were alarmed at the prospect of the city being taken over by a Christian lord, and called upon the people to refuse. Even some of the Christians were opposed, because the Cid was a rebel against King Alfonso of Castile, and should we accept Sir Rodrigo as our lord, we would make his enemy our enemy as well. Most of the Christians though, were swayed by Father Jerome, the chief priest of the town, who implored his flock not to refuse this God-given chance to reunite the city with Christendom.

"My father had heard of the deeds done elsewhere by the Cid, and believed that, despite being a Christian, that he was a just and honest man." Here John interrupted. "What do you mean 'despite being a Christian,' that he was just and honest? What kind of thing is that to say?"

Paul sighed. "I'm simply conveying my father's assessment as he saw it at the time. Being a Jew of Al Andalus, he was somewhat leery of the idea of Christian government."

"I see," John said in a sour tone. "And what was your viewpoint?"

"Well," Paul said. "Being his son, instructed by him, and merely eighteen years old, I naturally thought the same way."

"Naturally," John mocked. "So, now that you are older, and supposedly no longer a Jew, what…"

"John," Alan said. "Let the man tell his story." Alan looked at John for several seconds until the latter calmed himself. Then he turned back to Paul and said, "Go on."

I was very proud of Alan for doing this, for after what he had done for my Papa, I felt we should treat Paul with every kindness in return, whatever his faith might really be. Besides, I truly wanted to hear his tale.

"Thank you," Paul said. "In any case, my father recognized that there was clearly no choice. So he asked the Cid a question that would draw him out in a way that might reassure the non-Christians of the town. 'Sir Rodrigo,' he called out. 'Why do you ask us to agree to be your subjects? You are here inside our walls with all your armed men. We have no soldiers. The town is yours already.'

"The Cid looked my father up and down. 'You ask a good question,' he said. Then he delivered the rest of his answer to the crowd. 'Yes, of course, I could take this city right now, were that my purpose. But without your loyal support, worthy Valencians, I could not hold it against the oncoming Almoravids. And hold this town is what I mean to do.'

"'Valencians, I need you not just to accept me, I need you to fight for me. Why should you do this? I am a Christian. For those of you who are Christians, that should be sufficient answer. For the rest, who may be wondering which foreign master is preferable, this is my promise to you; That though I shall put this city under Christian government and law, each of you shall retain the right to live here as before, observing your own customs and religion, so long as you fulfill the duties of loyal subjects. Can you expect as much from the Almoravids?'

"Here he stopped and looked about, giving the people a few seconds to take in the import of his remarks. Then he said, 'the odds may seem impossible. But I know war, and I can make you into soldiers. I will demand much of you. But this I swear, by God, the Virgin, the saints, and this my great sword Colada and my own right hand: Make me your lord, obey me in all things, and I will lead you to victory!'"

"Saying this, he pulled his mighty sword and held it high in the air. Then he called out; 'Now, Valencians, choose!'"

"Instantly, everyone in the plaza was shouting. 'The Cid! The Cid! We choose the Cid!' Moors, Jews, Christians; men, women, and children; even the dogs were shouting. I can still remember that moment like it was yesterday. What an uproar. We waved our right hands in the air, in salute, as if we were holding swords too. 'The Cid! The Cid! We choose the Cid!'

"The commotion went on for several minutes. Finally it quieted down, and the Cid spoke again. 'You have chosen wisely. Now here are my first orders; go to your homes, and gather everything made of iron; every pot, every pan, every tool, and every shovel, and bring them here to the market plaza. We also need table tops or other large boards, and every horse, ox and wagon in the town brought here at once.'"

"We obeyed immediately, and by afternoon, large assemblages of these crucial war materials were visible in the plaza. The pots and pans were given to the smiths to make pike points, and the table tops to the carpenters to make shields,"

"Just as the Poitevins did," I commented, remembering the tale of the cobbler's apprentice.

"Yes," said Paul. "But the Cid was far more practiced in war than the Poitevin leaders. For that night, we lads of the town set out from the city with all the wagons horses and oxen, and accompanied by the Cid and his knights, visited all the farms in the district. By the light of the Moon, all the peasants were rounded up, together with all their animals, foodstocks, and farm implements, and transported back to the city. Everything left behind was burned to ashes. By dawn, there was not a scrap of food to be found for miles around Valencia."

"Why did the Cid do that?" I asked.

Alan answered me. "The food was gathered to prepare the city for a siege."

"I know that," I said, annoyed that Alan should not credit me with sufficient wit to perceive the obvious. "I meant why did he devastate his own country?"

"The farms were destroyed to deny them to the enemy," said Alan. "Without the availability of local foodstuffs, the logistical difficulties faced by the Almoravids would be greatly magnified, the more so as their army was reportedly quite large. This would compel them to either attempt victory through immediate assault, or disperse most of their forces, either of which would be disadvantageous. "

The precise military lexicon Alan used in this discourse took me by surprise. I blinked. "Alan, how did you come by this? I didn't realize you had studied war."

Alan seemed embarrassed. "Well actually, before I became a scholar I was trained as a knight. In fact, I was nearly ready to be knighted."

Paul seemed intrigued. "Really, and you gave it up for scholarship?"

"Yes," said Alan.

"Just like Peter Abelard," John chided.

"I make no such claims to greatness," Alan said modestly. "However it seemed to me that the world could do better with more scholars and fewer knights."

While my heart warmed to hear Alan make such a wise statement, at the same time it was stricken by the rest of what he had said. Alan had been trained for the knighthood. That meant he was of noble blood, and that meant… Well, I was a young girl, and Alan was a young and handsome lad, very kind and merry of spirit, and even somewhat intelligent, and it was only natural that I had come to entertain certain hopeful thoughts about him. But if Alan were a noble, then none of those dreams could ever become a reality. I turned my head away from him so he would not see my face. Then I sighed, and pushed the sadness into a corner to be dealt with later. There was no use mourning for something that never could have been.

"Perhaps," said Paul. "But it might be best of all if we had more knights who were also scholars, and more scholars who were also knights."

That thought was very novel, and it pulled me out of my sad meditation.

"Why?" said John.

"To give force to reason, and reason to force," Paul replied, then regarded us for a moment until we nodded our understanding.

"Anyway," Paul continued. "Master Alan's explanation for the Cid's action is completely correct. With no food to be found in the nearby countryside, and the city amply stocked, the Almoravids could not besiege us. They would have to take us by storm or not at all.

"But the Cid's preparations were even more thorough. For the same night that we had foraged the countryside, he had set all the men and women of the town to digging pits outside the walls. Hundreds of these were dug and staked, then before morning roofed over cleverly with sod to form multitudes of deadly hidden traps for our assailants.

"The next day the first part of Almoravid cavalry showed up, some one thousand strong, denying us access to the country, but presenting no threat yet to our city's stout high walls. Day after day, though, more thousands came, and then their infantry, until a vast host of ten thousand horse and fifty thousand foot encircled the town.

"In the face of such preparations, what hope did we have? Valencia was a good sized city, with a population of over thirty thousand, but still the enemy had two veteran warriors for every one of us, men, women and children included.

"Yet the Cid remained calm, and kept all of us too busy to panic. Aside from his own band, the only trained soldiers in the city were Moors, for the laws of Al Andalus denied to Dhimmis the use of both horses and weapons. But nearly every Moor had been trained from boyhood in the use of the bow, their grown men all had swords, and all of wealth owned and were skilful riders of horses. This last group, nearly two thousand in number, the Cid formed into a troop of cavalry, and trained them to act with forceful discipline, so that they might, as it were, comprise the shaft of a lance whose iron point would be formed by his own invincible knights. The Moorish boys were formed into companies of archers, and their men lacking horses deployed as swordsmen to guard the walls.

"Every Christian and Jewish boy and man was given a new forged pike and a wooden shield. We were taken to the market plaza, and taught by the Cid's sergeants how to thrust and how to block, and how to lock our shields together and charge at a run, pikes level and deadly. Back and forth we charged, from dawn till dusk for three days, shouting, thrusting, jabbing, and blocking. Then we were sent to the walls as well.

"While this training was going on, the Lady Dona Jimena, who was the wife of the Cid, organized the women of the town into companies which set about breaking up buildings and bringing the stones to the walls for use as projectiles.

"I mentioned this woman earlier, as the lady riding at the side of the Cid when he entered Valencia. She was rather younger than him, perhaps two score years in age, but of an equally resolute nature, and it soon became clear why he had chosen to bring her with him to battle for the city.

"The first building she chose to have broken up was the Emir's bath house. Then she selected several other remarkable buildings owned by the old ruler and his kinsmen to be wrecked. Dona Jimena chose these structures because their absent owners were clearly resented by the people of the city, and being wise, she knew that the women would take to their task with more alacrity if they found pleasure in their work. Also, being made of fine stone, the pieces of these buildings would serve the military purpose better than the soft mud brick that comprised the houses of the poor.

"Acting as true leader does, Dona Jimena assigned to each part of the town's female population the task to which they were most suited. Thus the women of wealth and distinction were given the job of directing the work. The actual task of breaking the buildings to pieces was given to the women of the middling sort, who took to it with gusto. After teams of these had knocked the walls down and apart with battering rams, the women of the laboring class would take the stones upon their backs and carry them up to the top of walls.

"Thus by the end of the second week after the Cid's arrival, we were ready for combat. This was well, for the Almoravids were finally ready too.

"It was on that fifteenth day of the siege that we woke up to discover that the Almoravids had drawn themselves up in battle array on two sides of the city. Both the west side, where the main gate faced inland, and the south side facing down the coast towards the Almoravid camp would be assaulted by massed troops with ladders, towers, and rams. As the cock crowed, the alarm bell rang.

"The battle for the city was at hand."

Chapter 15

The Battle for Valencia

Paul looked at us. "You cannot imagine the fear that gripped the city at the sound of that alarm. I ran to my post, which was on the west wall near the gate, and joined my company of mixed-faith Valencians, commanded by sergeant Diego, who was one of the Cid's men.

"For a while nothing happened, and we had time to catch our breath. An hour went by, during which women brought us breakfast, which we ate at our posts. Then a lone rider dressed in black rode up to within thirty fathoms of the gate and called out to us.

"'Rebel slaves of Valencia,' he cried. 'Your lord, the supreme Caliph Bucar, chosen by the will of Allah the compassionate as your master and owner, commands that you lay down your puny arms, surrender, and abase yourselves before him. Submit now, and he may be merciful.'

"The Cid then stood up and addressed Bucar's messenger. 'Tell your master Bucar that he is Caliph of nothing, and that his false claim to that title makes him a rebel and a heretic, to be scorned and spat on by Christian and Muslim alike. But thank him, from me, the Cid Rodrigo Diaz, by grace of God Count of Valencia, for coming here. For we are a poor city, and we rejoice in the opportunity he has given us to enrich ourselves by looting his camp after we strip the arms off his corpse and the bodies of all his slaughtered soldiers after the battle today.'"

"At these bold words, a cheer went up from our battlements. 'The Cid! The Cid!' we shouted, banging our weapons against our shields.

"The Almoravid messenger waved his fist in the air. 'You shall regret those words, infidel slave,' he called out. 'For such impertinence, my master will have your head removed, and your skull cleaned and gilded for use as his chamber pot.'

"To this, the Cid laughed. 'Then you have brought gold with you? How thoughtful! Now I know I shall enjoy the spoils of your camp. Please thank your master again, for I shall not be able to thank him myself after I split him from head to groin.'

"Duly enraged, the messenger spat and rode back to his lines.

"The sound of drums was then heard, thousands of them, banging deep and slow. Across the plain, huge masses of Almoravid infantry, all sinister in black, began their steady advance. There were companies of archers, and masses of swordsmen, with ten ladders to every battalion. They also had ten wooden towers on wheels, each as tall as our walls, with a drawbridge at the top to provide a ramp for their troops. These were pushed from behind by gangs of whipped slaves, as was their battering ram, which was roofed over with iron sheets and aimed squarely at the main gate. The sight of them all coming on together was one to chill the soul, for they seemed utterly unstoppable.

"When they reached fifty fathoms from the walls, they halted. For a few seconds silence reigned, which was even more terrifying than the din that had preceded it. Then, from the Almoravid ranks, a thousand trumpets sounded forth, and with a mighty shout, their entire army ran towards our walls.

"I crouched behind my parapet, shaking with fear. Beside me I could see all my companions were equally stricken. From behind, I heard sergeant Diego say, 'Here they come men. Steady now, lads, steady.'

"Our Moorish archer boys started to let fly with their arrows, but they were so few, and the onrushing horde so numerous, as to have little effect. I saw an Almoravid tower hit one of our traps, and topple over as its wheel went through the sod to crush a score of their foot soldiers in its fall. This evoked some cheers from our side, but only for a moment, as an instant later their infantry started throwing ladders up against our walls. The top of one slammed right next to me. Looking over the wall and down, I saw a stream of well-muscled swordsmen climbing fast, coming straight up at me with death gleaming in their eyes.

"I picked up a stone to throw down upon them, but as I rose, a cloud of arrows came flying up over the parapet, causing me to duck back down in terror. It was not just one volley; the Almoravid arrows kept coming in thousands. It was death to stand up. Looking down our battlement, I saw our entire company hunched down behind the parapets, doing nothing while death ascended to meet us from the other side.

"'Stand up and fight, you cowards,' sergeant Diego shouted. But no one would move.

"From the other side I heard a grunt only a few feet below. The enemy was almost to the top. My glimpse of the Almoravid swordsman flashed before my recall. The murder in his eyes, the arm muscles as thick around as my thighs. I knew if he came over the wall there was no chance I could fight him. So I looked up to heaven for a second, drew a deep breath, and rose to the top of the parapet with a twenty pound stone held in both arms high above my head.

"There, but six feet below me was the Almoravid. In that instant, our eyes met, and I saw fear suddenly flash in his. Then he surged up at me, and

I threw the stone down, catching him straight in the face. His leering countenance turned in a blink into a bloody pulp, and he fell off the ladder to one side, sending the ladder itself into a fall in the opposite direction. There it collided with a second ladder, which also fell to knock down a third.

"Instantly, our entire company stood up and cheered, and ignoring the arrows, taunted the Almoravids thrown into confusion below. Sergeant Diego grasped me by my shoulders, and turned me about and shook me. 'Joseph!' he shouted. 'Joseph, my lad! Joseph!' He faced me to the others and called out. 'Three cheers for Joseph!'"

Paul paused. "Now I must say that I felt strange to be so acclaimed by Sergeant Diego, who had always treated me like dirt before. He had no regard for Jews in general, and even less for me, what with my small size and skinny frame. Suddenly he was hailing me like a second Roland."

"Because you had performed an act of valor," Alan explained. "In the warrior's code, that is the measure of a man."

Paul shrugged. "All I did was throw a rock."

"No," said Alan. "What you did was put aside the danger to yourself and stand up and fight for your city. In that moment, you became a man"

"I suppose that's one way of looking at it," Paul said doubtfully. "Anyway, a moment later more Almoravid ladders were thrown up against the wall. But the men had lost their fear, and stood amidst the flying arrows hurling down stones with abandon.

"We killed many, but there were so many more that followed. And the arrows kept coming. An archer boy standing next to me took one right through the throat, and Daniel, my best friend since childhood, was hit in the chest. I pulled the arrow, but it had gone too deep, and he died.

"The battle was pitched in desperation. As good as our position on the wall was, we just didn't have enough numbers to stop the waves of enemy warriors climbing up towards us like a deadly tide. Seeing this, scores of townswomen ran to join the defense, and ignoring all peril, threw down mad volleys of stones like driven furies.

"In the midst of this havoc, the enemy towers made their final advance in concert. We were barely holding the walls against the ladders alone. With this new menace added, we were doomed.

"But as they approached, one after another the towers fell prey to our hidden pits. Some toppled over, others just stuck hopelessly in place. All but one were thus stopped. But that one was enough to destroy us.

"I heard the thunder as the tower drawbridge crashed down upon our battlement. Then as I turned to watch in horror, a horde of Almoravid swordsmen came pouring out of the tower and over the bridge into the heart of our defenses.

"Total chaos reigned on the battlement as the Almoravids and Valencians slashed and stabbed in all directions. There was no chance to form up in any order. I had barely time to grab my shield and lift my pike to level when an Almoravid was upon me. Without hesitating for an instant, he ran himself upon my pike, rendering it useless. Then the fanatic following him smashed his sword down upon me, splintering my wooden shield and knocking me to the ground. Sergeant Diego stabbed him, saving me from the death blow, but before I could get up, I was trampled by two Almoravids advancing upon Diego.

"When I looked up, I saw the Cid in the midst of the fray, hewing all about him with his mighty two-handed sword. In five seconds he killed as many Almoravids. Then he turned his back, and one ran at him from my direction to kill him from behind. I grabbed this man's feet as he passed me, and he crashed face first into the stone battlement. Hurling myself upon him, I knocked his face against the floor again, then grabbed a rock and finished him with a blow to the base of his skull.

"I snatched the dead man's sword and shield, and stood up, finding myself by the side of the Cid. Then Sergeant Diego was there, and others of our company, and with the Cid and Diego doing the killing, and the rest of us guarding their flanks, we advanced upon the tower footbridge.

"From every side Moorish boys shot arrows lit by fire rags at the tower, and the wooden structure began to catch flame. Those inside must have felt their peril, for they hastened outward onto the footbridge, even though the Cid, with our band to help, now had the ramp exit well blocked. The Almoravids on the bridge became a dense packed mob, with those behind pressing those in front to their deaths. Then the weight of them all broke the flame-weakened hinges joining the ramp to the tower. The bridge fell away beneath them, and screaming to Allah, they all fell with it to their deaths.

"How madly we cheered at the sight of their doom! The Cid patted me on the back. As he did so, I saw that he had taken a wound on his left arm. "The Almoravids yet on the battlement were now cut off among too many defenders. They ran down the steps into the city to create havoc, only to be stoned by mobs of oldsters and children hurling tiles from the roof tops, or knifed in the alleys by packs of lurking urchin boys.

"I turned to the Cid. 'Let me bind your wound, my lord,' I said, for my father had trained me in the medical art, and even then I had great skill.

"The Cid looked at me curiously, then observed the medallion indicating my family's profession. 'Very well, lad,' the Cid said. 'But make it quick. For we have much work yet to do today.'

"I did as he asked, using a rag torn from my own shirt as a bandage. Alas, he was right. By the thousands, the Almoravids were still coming up at us by ladder. Their losses were many times ours, but so were their numbers. Even our stones were beginning to run out. And though I did not say it, I could see that the Cid has lost much blood. How long could he fight on so weakened? And how could we fight without him?

"I had just finished the bandaging, when I heard a mighty crash at the town gate. The Almoravid ram had made it to our door. Roofed over with iron plate, it was immune to the heavy stones our people were desperately casting down upon it. The ram smashed away again, and this time I heard the sound of cracking wood. The gate was not going to hold. Looking down from the wall, I could see the Almoravids mass themselves just outside the gate in preparation for their fatal breakthrough. They had thousands of foot and horse all packed together, a devastating force that would be unstoppable once it came through our gate.

"The Cid observed them too. 'So,' he said. 'The time has come. Diego, assemble the town militia companies in the plaza.'

"'But my lord Cid,' Diego said. 'The walls! We need to hold the walls.'

"The Cid just shrugged. 'For the brief time remaining, the archers and women will have to hold them.'

"The Cid's words filled me with alarm. 'For the brief time remaining!' Alas!

"With the rest of my company, I followed Diego and the Cid down from the walls into the plaza. Massed in front of the town gate were the Cid's knights. Right behind them were the Moorish equestrians of our town, armed and armored upon their fine Andalusian steeds. We took our position behind these. With some difficulty, the Cid mounted his charger and joined his knights. Father Jerome, now wearing the insignia of a Bishop, came and blessed us; Christian, Jew, and Moor alike. Then he mounted horse and joined the Cid's knights.

"The ram crashed at the gate again, which splintered in response.

"'Open the gate!' the Cid cried. I gasped in amazement. The failing gate was our last defense!

"The gate opened, and scores of Almoravids came pouring through. 'Allah Akbar!' they cried, waving their swords about.

"'Charge!' shouted the Cid. A bugle blared, and, shouting madly, we charged.

Paul's eyes glinted. "I was told later by my sister Rachel, who was among those standing on the wall above the gate and thus could see the action from the front, what happened there.

"The Cid and his knights dashed their mighty steeds forward, but did not so much as attack the enemy as leap over them, knocking them to the ground. The Moorish horse that followed then trampled them to a pulp. I'm pretty sure that is the way it happened, because as we followed the cavalry forward over the field of carnage they left in their wake, we found few sword wounds among the stricken enemy. We stabbed those that were still alive, and ran on.

"When we reached the gate and looked down the gentle slope that led west from the city, we saw an amazing sight. The Cid and his men were still riding their horses over the Almoravid infantry, crushing them in droves. To the sides of their path of destruction, the enemy had turned to flee, and the rearmost ranks of these were being slaughtered from behind by our Moorish horsemen, who wielded their scimitars like scythes reaping wheat. The retreating enemy ranks more distant from our forces were crushing themselves in a mad press into their advancing countrymen, who attempted momentarily to block their escape before joining the panicked mob themselves.

"As we charged down the hill finishing what our cavalry had left behind, I saw the Cid riding his great horse Babieca over the Almoravid infantry, steering directly towards Bucar. This King and his horsemen were trying to stop the rout by laying about with their scimitars among their own fleeing rabble, who killed a good many of them in return. Then Bucar saw the Cid and Babieca coming at him, trampling the falling ranks of the footmen like giants, and he turned to flee himself."At the sight of their leader fleeing, the Almoravid cavalry bolted. But it was too late for Bucar. Breaking through the last of the enemy footmen, the Cid took off after him at a gallop. Bucar's horse was fast, but Babieca was like lightning. Stabbing the would-be Caliph through from behind with Colada, the Cid lifted him out of his saddle, then held him aloft as he screamed his last.

"With that deafening scream, any semblance of Almoravid resistance evaporated. What had been an incipient rout now turned into a hopeless stampede. Their army attacking our western wall just dropped their weapons and scattered towards the hills, driven and slaughtered from behind by our Moorish horsemen. But we pikemen, following orders from the Cid's knights, wheeled left to take by the flank those battalions of archers who had been decimating our wall defenders but moments earlier.

"Against our massed pikes the archers were helpless. They had no shields, armor, or swords, and within seconds of our onset they were so packed together they could not even draw their bows. We stabbed them without mercy, and all they could do was push back on those behind them in a futile effort to escape. So we drove the mob before us, herding them around so that they crushed the Almoravid ladder assault swordsmen between themselves and the walls. The women on the walls, no longer menaced by enemy arrows, looked down upon the helpless swordsmen and shrieked with mocking laughter as they dropped stones to massacre those who would have been their rapists.

"A few contrived to escape by hurling themselves into the sea. These were left to drown, or, if they ventured to come back, cut down in the shallows by the Cid's mounted men. The rest we slaughtered. Never, I think, has so much carnage ever been wreaked in so small a space.

"Our returning Moorish cavalry fell upon the now undefended Almoravid camp and commenced the looting. Not to miss out, we hastened to join them, and found enough gold and jewels there to make many a poor man rich, at least for a while. Then we marched back to the city in triumph, taking with us not only our valuable prizes, but all the wagons of rations and all the livestock the enemy had assembled to supply their host. Thus, not a scrap of food was left outside the city walls to feed any Almoravids who might have fled the battle, and these were left to starve amidst the desolate countryside."

Paul's eyes shone. "What a sight we were as we entered the city gate, marching in proudly with the Cid at our head. How the people cheered! Was ever there such an army! Was ever there such a victory!" Paul sighed. "Was ever there such a day!"

Chapter 16

The Ruin of Cordoba

I let out a deep breath, for Paul's tale had left me, quite in truth, breathless. "We bards have sung of it ever since."

"Yes," said John. "But your account differs from theirs in many respects I find difficult to credit. For one, I find it difficult to imagine how a great Christian hero like the Cid should have been willing to place himself at the head of a force mixed with so many unbelievers as you describe."

"Yes, I can see that," Paul smiled ironically. "But that is because you have no understanding of how things were in Spain in those days, and also, if I may speak plainly, because you do not think the way the Cid thought. In any case, I was there, and that's how it was."

"If you say so," John said skeptically.

Paul dismissed this remark with a shrug. Then he looked at me and smiled. "I still have it, you know."

"What?" I asked, puzzled.

Instead of answering, Paul stood up from the bed and walked over to a shelf, upon which rested a long low wooden box. He picked up the box and sat down with it in front of Alan and me. Then he opened the box, revealing a scimitar.

"It's the sword I took off the Almoravid that day on the battlement," Paul said.

A sword taken at the famed battle of Valencia! I gazed at it in wonder. It was not a rich man's weapon, for its handle contained no gold or jewels, but the blade shone like silver. I touched its edge gingerly. It was very sharp.

"May I hold it?" asked Alan, his eyes aflame.

"Yes," said Paul.

Alan picked up the sword and stood with it, testing its balance in his hand like an expert. Then he thumbed its edge, and peered closely at it. "An excellent blade," Alan said. "Damascus steel." He lay it respectfully back in its box.

"Did you give it a name?" Alan asked.

"Yes," said Paul. "Maccabeaus."

John snorted.

"So I suppose you know the rest," Paul said. "The Cid died of his wounds the next day. We gave him a great funeral, and every person in the city placed a flower upon his tomb. Donna Jimena took upon herself the government of the city, and ruled it well for three years. But then word came that the Almoravids were assembling an army for another attack, even more mighty than the first, and she lost heart. She felt there was no way she could defend the city herself, so she called in her husband's old enemy, King Alfonso of Castile for help. This mighty man arrived at the town with a considerable force of knights and men at arms. But as soon as he had taken control, he declared the town to be indefensible, and ordered that all should leave."

Paul looked at as with a pained expression. "Three days he gave us to leave. Three days! 'Take what you will and depart where you will,' he said, but do it in three days. After that, his soldiers would loot the town and destroy what remained, for it must not fall into the hands of the Almoravids.

"Thus the glorious victory won by courage of the townspeople and the daring of the Cid was undone by the treachery and cowardice of his enemy."

Yes, I thought, and by the guilelessness of Donna Jimena. Eleanor would not have made such a mistake.

Paul continued. "Like most others, my family decided to travel back to Castile with Alfonso, for there seemed to be no place else to go. But I could not stomach the thought of making myself the subject of such a King, and swearing loyalty to him, after he had so foully betrayed us. So instead I went to Cordoba."

Here I interrupted. "But didn't you say that Cordoba had already fallen to the Almoravids?"

Paul nodded. "Indeed, it had. But its Emir had been defeated in the field, and the city was surrendered without a sack. The great Moorish aristocrats of the place had then used their fantastic wealth with cleverness; bribing this Almoravid subaltern here, corrupting that one there, so as to preserve their luxurious way of life in private, even while the fanatics patrolled the streets. Thus in Cordoba, beneath the surface of Almoravid rule, a semblance of the old Al Andalus, with all its pleasures, still lived on. And, most important to me, the great library of Cordoba still stood."

Paul looked at Alan, then at John. "What is it that Aristotle says that all men by nature desire?"

"To know," said John. "Correct," said Paul, with the tone of a Master acknowledging the successful response of a scholar. "It was the second year

106

of this century, I was one and twenty years old, and I wanted to know. I wanted to know everything; about Nature, about Man, and about God. My father had introduced me to the world of thought. Now I wanted to explore it for myself. I had no home to hold me back. In Cordoba there was a library of over ten thousand books. What young man of spirit and curiosity would not want to discover what secrets they held?"

"Ten thousand books!" exclaimed Alan.

Even John was impressed. "Were there really so many?"

"Yes," said Paul. "The place was amazing. It held all the books of the Greeks and the Romans, of the Mohammedans, of course, but also of the Jews, the Christians, the Arians, the Persians, and even of the Carthaginians."

"The Carthaginians?" John asked.

Paul nodded. "Yes, the people of Hannibal. They had once ruled Spain, before the Romans, but in their downfall there were not so completely destroyed as they were in Africa. Their tongue and writing were much like Hebrew, so I could read their books. They were bold sailors, and the things they recorded were incredible."

Paul looked about as if making sure no stranger was listening. Then he spoke quietly. "According to them, there is a vast unpeopled land hidden across the western ocean, with forests abounding in game animals, and rivers filled with fish."

John shook his head. "There is no mention of any such place in the Bible."

"Nor is there any of Norway," Paul countered.

"It could be Eden," I offered.

"Maybe," said Paul. "Or perhaps Atlantis. Who knows? Anyway, that was but a small sample of the amazing knowledge that was to be found in the place. So I stayed there studying for seven years, reading book after book, gladly enduring the indignity of life as an Almoravid Dhimmi in exchange for a chance to acquire such learning."

"How did you live?" Alan asked, naturally curious, as finding means to maintain wherewithal for food and roof is frequently a matter of great interest among scholars.

"That was not so hard," Paul answered. "For I already had some medical skill, which increased greatly with the reading of the works of Ibn Sina that the library held."

"Ibn Sina?" asked John.

"You may know him as Avicenna," said Paul

John nodded. "Certainly we've heard of Avicenna. He was an Aristotelian, was he not?"

"Yes," said Paul. "But more than that, he put Aristotle's philosophy into practice, searching for natural causes for all things, most notably human ailment. In consequences, he was able to find medical cures that seem miraculous, but in fact are simply the product of knowledge. For example, it was his instructions for the proper positioning of bones that I was able to use to help this good man here today."

I marveled to hear this. My father had been saved by the discoveries of a Muslim!

"So," continued Paul, "I was able to make some income through occasional medical practice. Beyond that, I had other sources, for I was not the only foreigner studying in Cordoba. There were other Jews, and Christians from many countries, including some from as far away as Aquitaine, France, Italy, or even Flanders. These boys could not read Arabic, which was the language in which most of the books were writ, so I helped them with the translation, in return for a fee. Of course, most scholars had little money, but a few had rich parents willing to support their quest for truth, and it was among these gifted individuals that I shared my time. Charles of Bordeaux was one such. A lively younger son of a baron of Aquitaine, he gave me much business. But he also loved to hear my stories of old Valencia and the Cid, especially over cups of wine drunk secretly from Almoravid spies, and in time we became good friends.

"Thus it went, until the ninth year of this century, when one Almoravid chief seeking power discovered that his rival had allowed such unholy practices to go on in the city, Cordoba, the very capital of a new Caliphate that must someday embrace all the world within a realm of pure Islam. So he roused the mob to destroy the apostates and blasphemers and all their temples of heresy and impiety. This, of course, included the library.

"It was nighttime when they broke in. There were hundreds of them, carrying swords and torches. We scholars had been warned, of course, for the call to put an end to the library had been proclaimed all day from every mosque in the city. Most of the boys had fled, but a score of us remained to offer what defense we could. I had Maccabeus there with me, and Charles, being a noble, had a sword of his own as well. Four of our number were Moors from old and wealthy families. Two were Jews, that is I and the son of a Rabbi of Granada. The rest were Christians, mostly from outside

Spain."

Paul sighed. "It is strange to think that when the hour struck to defend the last light of old Al Andalus, most of the defenders were foreigners. But that is how it was."

"Still," Paul went on. "Given the disparity in numbers, our main hope lay with the Moors. The foremost among these was a man named Al Rahman, a distant descendant of he of the same name who had once governed Al Andalus in its time of united glory, and whose ancestors in turn had long ago ruled all Islam from Damascus.

"Al Rahman's voice was refined, and his posture was regal. He stood in front of our line and faced the leader of the Almoravid mob, a brutish Berber chieftain named Abu.

"'Why have you come here, brother?' Al Rahman asked Abu.

"'We have come to destroy the works of the enemies of true faith,' Abu replied.

"'But,' Al Rahman said, gesturing to the books that lined the rows of shelves behind us. 'These are not works of the enemies of our faith. These are the books containing the writings of the greatest thinkers of Islam.'

"This was true enough," Paul commented. "For the library was divided into rooms, and this first room held the works of the Mohammedan philosophers, with other rooms each holding the works of the Romans, Greeks, and so forth."

"Abu, however, was skeptical. 'Show me,' he said.

"So Al Rahman swiftly walked back to the shelves and selected three volumes, which he returned to display to Abu.

"'You see,' Al Rahman said. 'Here are the books of Al Kindi, Al Farabi, and Ibn Sina, devout Muslims all, and famous for their wisdom.'

"'They are Mutazelite heretics,' Abu answered abruptly. 'Their books should be burned.'

"'No,' pleaded Al Rahman. 'You don't understand. These man are heroes of our faith, for as a result of their philosophy, Islamic thought is admired by all the world.'

"'What should we care what the non-believers think?' countered Abu. 'The fact that the infidels admire these books is proof enough that they should be put to the flame.'

"Abu spoke to his followers. 'These are impious books. Put them to the torch.'

"'Wait!' Al Rahman said, and there was still sufficient command in his voice to halt them, at least for a moment. He grabbed another book and laid it open before Abu.

"'I understand,' said Al Rahman. 'Why you might have concerns about thinkers like Ibn Sina, who seek to find the causes of things within Nature, rather than the will of Allah. But not all our books are of that type. Here is a book by Al Ghazali, the most orthodox of men. Look here, he condemns Ibn Sina himself, and all the other Mutazelites. See this part, he says in no uncertain terms that truth can be obtained only from the Koran, and no other source. Surely you can have no objections to books such as this.'

"'I agree with that author,' said Abu. 'Truth can be known only from the Koran. That is why we don't need any of these books, including his.' He turned again to his followers. 'I told you to burn the books. Now burn them! Burn them all!'

"With that, the mob rushed forward. Al Rahman spread both his arms outward, and cried out, 'Stop! You know not what you do!'"

"Like Jesus upon The Cross," I said, amazed at the vision of such an apparition in Muslim form.

"Yes," said Paul. "But more quickly dispatched. For even as he said these words, Abu slashed him across the stomach with his scimitar, and the last of the great Moors of Al Andalus fell to the ground. Then the mob was upon us.

I swung Maccabeaus and cut one, but then his fellows started battering away at me with their scimitars, forcing me to block and parry, and step back again and again. Charles was more skillful, and did in several with quick and forceful stabs and slashes. But there were too many assailants, and most of the boys had nothing but knives for their defense. In seconds we were pushed back into the book stacks, which the mob quickly set alight. The room was filled with fire and smoke, yet still they forced themselves upon us.

"Backward, ever backward, step by step, we retreated, and with each step scores of volumes of some of the greatest erudition ever put to parchment were put to the flame instead. Such a loss, books on optics, the entire encyclopedia of Ibn Sina's medical researches, knowledge so valuable and gained at such cost, all turned to smoke! We tried to slow them by tumbling shelves of books upon them. We hurled flaming volumes in their faces. How priceless those projectiles were! How ineffective.

"Soon we reached the back of the hall. Before our eyes, all the intellects of Islam were disappearing into ashes. Then they pushed us through the door, and forced us back thorough the next hall, which contained the books of the Jews, Christians, Persians, and Carthaginians. You would not believe what was in those books: centuries' worth of poetry by my people, as well as that of the Persians; lost gospels authored by Peter, Stephen, and Mary Magdalene; the theological speculations of Philo, Origen, Arius, Pelagius, Zoroaster, and Mani; the profound philosophy of Ibn Gabirol; and the histories and charts of the Carthaginians. How much I wanted to save the secret knowledge left behind in the last writings of that lost race! But there was nothing for it. Barely twelve of us were left, and we could not hold them.

"Back we went, ever back, fighting for every step, but losing ever more ground, until we were thrust into the next hall, which contained the works of the Romans. On one side of this hall there was a statue of Julius Caesar, on the other stood Augustus. How these two must have looked on as we fought to save the words of their glorious nation! If only we had had their legions to help us.

"First to now fall to the fire were the plays of Horace, Seneca, Plautus, and Terrence. With the next shelves went the science of Galen, Lucretius, and Pliny. Then volumes of statecraft and oratory by Cicero, so deadly against the clever Cataline and his conspirators, proved helpless against the flames. Last to surrender were the heroic histories of Livy, recalling the valiant lives of Scipio, Cincinnattus, Brutus, Horatius, and Romulus to instruct the virtue of a noble empire. All this was turned into smoke.

"Our desperate retreat brought us to the final door, this leading to the hall that contained the works of the Greeks. Only three of us now remained; myself, Charles, and a Moor named Suleiman, the last of a family of notable warriors of Seville. For a moment we three stood side by side, swords in hand, defending like the Spartans of Leonidas the pass to the precious treasure of Hellas. Then I heard a sound behind me, and saw that three Almoravids had entered by the far window and were coming to attack us from the rear.

"Suleiman saw them too. 'Take them, Charles,' he said. 'And get Joseph out of here. I'll hold the door.'

"For a moment, Charles hesitated. Suleiman insisted, 'Go now. Save yourselves. My world is lost.'

"Charles saluted Suleiman with a slight nod of his head, took a final slash at the opponent before him, and shouted, 'Joseph, follow me!' Then he turned and charged the Almoravids coming from behind. Swinging his sword, he killed the first with a blow, then battled back the next. I confronted the third, dueling for a few seconds until Charles, having finished his second opponent, dispatched mine for me. We heard a shout from the door. Suleiman had fallen, and the mob was charging in.

"Charles pointed to the window. 'Let's go!' he cried, and headed for it. I took one last look around. The hall was filled with the books recording the greatest thoughts ever thought. Pythagoras, Thales, Anaxagoras, Socrates, Plato, Aristotle, Chrysippus, Cleanthes, Zeno, Herodotus, Thucydides, Xenophon, Demosthenes, Homer, Hesiod, Aeschylus, Sophocles, Euripides, Hippocrates, Hipparchus, Aristarchus, Archimedes; In seconds, they would no longer exist. What could I do? There was only time to save one book, just one out of all those thousands! Thinking quickly, I grabbed it, and ran for the window.

"When I dropped outside, I found myself in a small courtyard to the side of the library. There were three horses there, apparently the possessions of our late assailants. Charles was already mounted. He beckoned me to get on another. Having been brought up a Dhimmi, I had never ridden before, and I hesitated.

"Charles saw my difficulty. He said, 'Just get on and hold on tight. I'll lead her for you.' As I mounted with some difficulty, he came by and took the rope fastened to my horse's bridle. Then he kicked his mount hard, and with me fiercely clutching my horse's neck, we galloped through the darkness and out of the city.

"When we reached the hills outside of town, we stopped and looked back. Not only the library, but all over Cordoba, fine buildings, bath houses, and villas were burning. It was the end of Al Andalus.

"'Where to now?' I asked Charles at last, at a loss for what to do next.

The night was dark, and the stars of the two Bears glittered the sky in the direction opposite the dying city. Charles lifted his hand and pointed at Polaris.

"Aquitaine is that way,' he said."

Chapter 17

The First of the Troubadours

"Aquitaine!" Paul exclaimed. "He was inviting me to come with him to Aquitaine!"

"My head swam with the thought. It was exciting, but terrifying too. For I had never been out of Spain, and the reputation of the lands to the north of the mountains was that of wild barbaric places filled with danger and lacking all refinement.

"But Charles assured me that Aquitaine was different. He said that Duke William was a very great man, of broad and noble outlook and liberal views, who was seeking to create in Aquitaine a realm within Christendom that would match in splendor and civilization anything that had ever existed in Al Andalus. He said that Duke William was a patron of poetry and the arts, and in fact was a great poet himself."

I interrupted. "This Duke William, was this William IX of Aquitaine, the grandfather of Eleanor?"

"Yes," said Paul.

"Then," I said. "Charles did not overpraise him. For he is still known to all bards today as First of the Troubadours."

"And deservedly so," said Paul. "Charles said that I should fear nothing in Aquitaine, that there was a large Jewish community in Bordeaux who were well and fairly treated by Duke William, but that moreover a man of my learning would be welcomed by the Duke at his own court and table, regardless of my faith. I told Charles that I found this difficult to credit, but he insisted, saying that Duke William was a man who wore his own religion lightly."

"That was certainly true," John said harshly.

"What do you mean by that?" I asked.

"He was excommunicated, you know," said John.

I was shocked to hear that.

"Yes, well," said Paul. "Charles told me that too. He told me how Duke William had laughed at the Church when it tried to tell him how to order his own life and realm, and had dismissed as absurd its demands that he use his might and power to crush the Cathar heretics who found such a friendly home in his domain. 'Live and let live,' was the Duke's motto. For this, Charles said, they had excommunicated him."

That put a different face upon the matter, I thought.

"I found this both fascinating and reassuring," continued Paul. "So I agreed to Charles' plan."

"I see," said John in his sour voice. "In other words, far from being put off by Duke William's outcast status, you decided to come to Aquitaine precisely because it had an excommunicated ruler."

Paul shrugged. "You can put it that way if you like. So, to continue, we trotted our horses north all that night, and made fifty miles before dawn broke. As the Sun came up, I saw that we were traveling through a valley. On the hilltop to our left, there was a small castle, and it flew the banners of Castile. At that moment, Charles turned to me. 'So, Joseph,' he said, pointing to the yellow Dhimmi Star of David that defaced my clothing. 'You won't be needing that anymore.'

"I tore the damn thing off and threw it to the ground. You could not believe how good it felt.

"We traveled on, camping by night and finding food in the forest, until we reached Toledo. My family had resettled there, and urged me to stay. But I still hated King Alfonso, and my heart was set on the prospect of the adventure of Aquitaine. So after a visit of a week, we pressed on. My father gave us sufficient money for the road, allowing us to travel the rest of the way with good food and tavern beds to comfort us every night. Without further difficulty, we reached Bordeaux less than a month later.

"The town of Bordeaux may not have been quite as refined as Charles had claimed, but certainly it was much better than anything I had expected to find in the north. The remains of fine Roman civilization were still apparent, if not quite so preserved as had been the case in Al Andalus. The main roads were covered with stone, and if there was no water in the houses, at least the old aqueducts still brought it to the public fountains in the squares."

"Excuse me," John said. "Are you implying that the Moors of Al Andalus actually had fountains inside their houses?"

"Yes, of course," Paul answered. "Didn't I make that clear?"

Alan, John, and I exchanged glances. Fountains inside of houses!

"But," Paul continued. "Beyond that, there was something new in the air. People were wearing clothes with new cuts and colors. New kinds of music could be heard in the market and the taverns. New songs were being sung, new stories were being told, new foods were being cooked, and new thoughts were being thought. It was like everyone in the town was young.

"And nowhere was this more true than at the court of Duke William himself. Here novelty competed for novelty. I tell you that Duke feasted on novelty; New poems, new dishes, new jokes, new ideas, new dances! If ever there was a place and time that it was a joy to be young, it was at the court of Duke William. All the men there were brave and cultured, the ladies were beautiful and witty, and they mixed, sparred, loved, and deceived in an endless dance of merry courtship and secret liaisons."

"Such a place," Paul sighed. "Such a time. And Charles was right. I was made welcome there. For the Duke, did indeed value knowledge, and loved to question me of all I knew about the world around, the starry spheres above, the past, and the future. He wanted to know about the plants and animals of every land and clime, and the thoughts, deeds, and poems of every nation. About the Cid, there was no end to his curiosity, and this was true of all the rest. So many an evening they had me hold forth on the battle of Valencia, like some kind of bard whose every repeated word they waited for with anticipation and delight. They were all Christians, of course, and some joked with me about my faith, which seemed to them anachronistic and silly, but beyond that they did not press. For the men, my courage shown in battle at Valencia, which Charles vouched for as well, was sufficient proof of my worth. For the women, well, I may have been short, but I was twenty eight, handsome, witty, and able to dance like a true Spaniard. They all insisted on me showing them the steps, and for a while at the court of Aquitaine, Spanish dancing became all the rage."

"My popularity was only increased when it became apparent how skilled a physician I was, and soon I was welcome not only at court, but in many a noble home, and I developed a medical practice that earned me sufficient wealth to maintain an adequate appearance among such company.

"I spent some time among the Jewish community of Bordeaux as well, for as Charles had said, this was quite sizable and prosperous. But I found that, aside from a common love of the poetry of Halevi and Ben Ezra, I shared few interests with them. Their endless disputations about the Talmud bored me, and when I tried to open their horizons by teaching a class in the philosophy of Ibn Gabirol, the Rabbis intervened and shut me down." Paul shook his head. "Can you imagine that? They didn't want the boys to know anything about Ibn Gabirol, the greatest Jewish thinker of modern times."

"Well," John said in a snide tone. "Perhaps he wasn't so great. I've never heard of him."

"Of course you have," Paul snapped. "You know him as Avicebron."

John looked dumbfounded. "Avicebron was Jewish? How can that be? True, he never states his religion explicitly. But his thoughts are so wise, he is taught in all the cathedral schools. You expect me to believe that he was Jewish?"

Paul looked at the ceiling and mumbled something I couldn't hear. Then he took a deep breath and continued. "Anyway, the point is that, strange as it may seem, I found myself more at home among the court of Duke William then among my own people. So increasingly, that is where I chose to reside.

"Thus six happy years went by, during which time I gained still greater favor with both Duke William and his wife, Phillipa of Toulouse, by assisting in the difficult birth of their second son, a fine little baby boy named Raymond."

That, I thought to myself, would have been Eleanor's uncle Raymond. She was always talking about him.

"Then," said Paul. "I met Christina."

I startled at the name. "Christina? Who was that?"

"She was the daughter of a rich merchant of La Rochelle, and she was…" Paul paused, closed his eyes, and sighed the sigh of a man who is still in love with a woman long gone. "She was beautiful. Her figure was slim and graceful, her hair long, brown, and smooth, so that when she walked, beholding her was like listening to soft music. Yet her eyes, which were brown as well, sparkled with life, wit, mischief, and merriment. And her voice," Paul paused again. "Her voice was like that of an angel, so sweet, so kind, that even when she lightly made fun of me, I could but adore her for it. So beautiful, she was, inside as well as out; her heart was filled with warmth and friendship, her soul with hope, her spirit with light. In truth, she was a woman made out of love, and I fell madly in love with her."

"Did she love you too?" I asked.

"Yes," said Paul. "By some miracle, she did. She could have chosen anyone, for any man gladly would have been hers. But she chose me, and talked to me and gazed at me with such affection, that when I was in her presence, I felt like I was in heaven. And when we walked together in the Duke's garden, her hand in mine, looking at the flowers or discussing the shape of the clouds, I truly was."

"But," said John, impolitely bringing up the obvious problem.

"Exactly," said Paul. "Our love for each other was such as epics are sung of, yet she was a Christian and I was a Jew. What could we do?"

"Christina's father was a kind hearted man, and seeing her passion for me, and observing in me but that one objectionable quality, let it be known to me that he would consent to our marriage if only I would convert.

"Now I'm sure you can see, as even I did then, how big a leap this was for him. I was, after all, a stranger, with no family in Aquitaine, and a member of a race which many about him held in low esteem. Yet still, he would entrust his darling daughter to me, were I simply to drop my separateness, and make myself one with their faith. This seemed to him to be a very generous viewpoint.

"It seems that way to me too," said John.

"Yes, no doubt," said Paul. "In a way it was. Yet you must understand how hard it is for a Jew to agree to convert."

"Why?" said John, with both anger and real curiosity. "It obviously is, but I'd really like to know why."

"Well," said Paul. "For some it is theological, in that Christians and Muslims both come to them and demand that they believe in various supernatural occurrences that are not to be found in our scriptures, and therefore seem simply fantastical. They therefore refuse to join such faiths because they find them, quite literally, unbelievable.

"But for many others, and I counted myself in this group, it is obvious that the miracles which are reported in our holy books are equally strange, and that if the one can be accepted, either as reality, or if necessary, allegory, then so can the other. The difficulty in converting, therefore comes down to a matter of dignity."

John seemed puzzled. "Dignity? I don't understand."

"Look," said Paul. "Use your imagination. Try to imagine yourself a member of a race of people who have been besieged by one set of oppressors after another for thousands of years, all demanding that you kneel down and abase yourselves before them and their gods. Pharaoh, Nebuchadnezzar, Antiochus, Vespasian; one after another they come with deadly force and demand obeisance. But no matter what the odds, no matter what the cost, your ancestors had the courage to resist, and for generation after generation continue to hold their sacred trust. After all of that, are you then, going to be the one who surrenders?"

John seemed thunderstruck. "Are you saying that the Jews look upon us as Pharaoh?"

"Yes," said Paul.

117

Alan was fascinated. "So then really, it's more like a matter of your family honor."

Paul gave a half nod. "That is one way you might understand it."

"But then," Alan shook his head. "Seeing the world, that way, what could you do?"

"I thought about it long and hard," said Paul. "I knew my father would be deeply upset if he ever received word that I had converted. But the more I thought about my own beliefs, the more I realized that I did not actually believe in Judaism, and that while there were certain Jewish contributions to culture and thought that I valued highly, there were many more from other people, notably the ancient Greeks, that I found far more interesting. The Jews of Bordeaux did not consider me one of them, and with good reason, because in fact I was not. I no longer saw the world with their eyes. They longed for Jerusalem, but I yearned for Athens. Why should I give up Christina to maintain a fiction? Was it really a matter of dignity, or had it simply become a question of pride? Christina was no Pharaoh. She had greeted me not with oppression, but with love. And that love now moved me towards dropping my pride and accepting her faith as my own."

"Christina saw how torn I was, and did not cajole me, but spoke to me tenderly with every sympathy. She even offered to travel with me to Toledo to speak to my father herself so as to gain his understanding and lessen my pain. Then one night, as I sat out in the palace garden contemplating my dilemma, she came and sat beside me.

"The night was soft, for it was Maytime, and the Moon was up. She took my hand, and for a long time we just sat together, looking at the Moon and the stars, smelling the fresh scent of the flowers, and listening to the sounds of nature. Then she spoke softly to me.

"'You know, Joseph,' she said. 'When a woman chooses a man for a husband, she must show great courage, for she is entrusting her life to another. You are a stranger here, Joseph, yet I would and will entrust my life to you. You can be my husband and my governor in all things, if you but let me be your governor in this. Gentle wanderer, let me be your soul's shepherdess and I will show you such happiness.'

"Her words evoked an odd comparison. 'You sound like the Cid,' I said

"She smiled at me and laughed. 'Oh really, how so?'

"I raised my right hand like the Cid holding Colada. 'Make me your Count and I will lead you to victory!' I proclaimed in a deep voice.

"Christina's eyes glinted mischief. She grabbed my upraised arm with

118

one hand, and put her other on my shoulder. 'Yes!' she cried. 'Make me your Countess and I will lead you to Heaven!'

"Then she pushed me off the bench and into the flowers and showed me exactly what she meant.

"So I allowed myself to be baptized and became a Christian."

Hearing this, I practically broke into tears of joy. "Oh, I am so happy for you," I exclaimed.

Paul appeared puzzled by my outburst. "Er, why?"

"Because now you will be saved," I said, practically sobbing with happiness. Paul was such a good man. It would have been wrong for him to end up in hell.

"Oh," said Paul. 'Well thank you. That's a very sweet thing for you to say. In any case, having converted, I took 'Paul' as my Christian name, and Christina and I were wed at the cathedral of Bordeaux. Charles was my best man, the whole court attended the ceremony, and afterwards Duke William threw a grand feast in our honor at the palace. Then we went to La Rochelle to make our home, as that was the residence of Christina's family, and she did not want to live far from them.

"So we passed some happy years together in a fine house overlooking the bay, with Christina's relations and many other friends and visitors for company. For my medical practice not only brought us ample wealth, but a celebrated reputation throughout all of Aquitaine. And each year, when the festive season opened in Bordeaux, we would travel there and spend some months at the court of Duke William, enjoying the feasts, the music, the dances, the gaiety, and the laughter.

"Christina gave me three children, two boys and a girl, and I could not have been happier in my new life. Thus Joseph of Valencia was reborn as Paul of La Rochelle."

"So," said John. "While you were enjoying your new life as a Christian, did you take the trouble to publish a polemic to urge your former coreligionists to make the same happy choice?"

"What?" said Paul. "You mean write a dialogue against the Jews like that of the former Moses Sefardi?"

"Yes," said John. "Precisely. Such documents from converts are of immense value."

Paul shook his head. "No," he said somewhat disdainfully. "I have no interest in that sort of thing."

"Why not?" pressed John.

Paul seemed frustrated. He paused and took several breaths. "It's just not my way," he said finally.

"I see," said John. "Some convert. Doesn't it mean anything to you that..."

Alan turned and put his hand on John's shoulder, silencing him with a firm look. "John, please," said Alan. "This man fought at the side of the Cid. That is good enough."

I was so happy that Alan did this. I rewarded him with a big smile, then shared it with the old man to reassure him and encourage him to continue.

This seemed to work, for Paul recovered himself instantly.

"Now where was I?" Paul said. "Oh, yes. Then it happened. It was December of the eighteenth year of this century. We had arrived in Bordeaux after Christmas to attend the Duke's New Year feast. On the day before this occasion, Duke William called me into his office chamber for a private talk. After I sat down, and he had poured me some wine, he said 'Paul, I would like to ask you to do me a service.'

"'Anything, my lord,' I replied, meaning it in earnest, for I much admired the Duke and was grateful for all that he had done for me.

"Duke William looked at me and nodded gravely. 'Thank you Paul," he said. 'I knew I could count on you.' He paused for a moment, then continued. 'You know my younger son Raymond is now five years old.'

"I was seized with alarm, for I had delivered this very child. 'My lord,' I said. 'Is the boy ill? By all means, take me to him at once and I will do everything I can for him.'

"The Duke waved his hand to calm me. 'No, no,' he said. 'It is nothing like that. It is just that now that he is of an age where he can be taught, I wish him to have the best teacher in the world.' He looked at me sharply. 'Paul,' he said. 'I want you to be Raymond's teacher.'

"I was astonished at this request, of course. 'This is a great honor, my lord,' I said, stalling for time to think..

"The Duke looked at me calmly. 'I know you must have many questions,' he said. 'So let me explain my reasons to you. My older son, William, is already eighteen, and too old to be taught. He's a sound lad, brave in battle, and he is my heir. His future is set. He will be the next Duke, a reasonably good one I should think, and that is that. But Raymond is an extraordinary child. He's only five years old, but he's so clever. He rhymes, he draws, he makes jokes, and tells stories. He's curious about everything.

I tell you, a man like you could teach him so many things, that when he got older, he would be utterly brilliant.'

"'Now, to be clear, the last thing I want is for him to become some kind of pallid cleric who spends his life locked away in a chamber scribbling unread commentaries on unread books. He is to become a prince, and I myself will teach him the arts of authority, arms, and amour that will suit him to such a station. But he is born into the world a prince without a realm, and he will need every piece of knowledge and wisdom you can teach him in order to win one for himself, and even more to keep it afterwards. For a man who takes power without inheriting it needs to win the loyalty of his subjects through the wisdom and justice of his rule. That is the kind of man that Raymond must become, and to become that, he needs a vaster education than I alone can give him. He needs to know about the Greeks and the Romans, and why they rose and why they fell. He needs to know the arts of oratory, and understand the way men of many nations think, and have thought in the past, so he can say the words that will move their hearts. He needs to know so many things, and you are the one who can teach him.

"'You know, Paul, you are the last of a breed. I sent Charles to Cordoba to try to learn some small part of the ancient knowledge of the Moors. Instead he came back with you, and in you we have it all. Now I am asking you to take that light that you have saved and share it with my son.'

"Then he smiled at me knowingly, and said, 'Think of it as your chance to create a philosopher king.'"

At this, John startled. "Philosopher king? What did he mean by that?"

Paul raised his eyebrows, then he stood up. "Come," he said. "I'll show you."

He walked over to his study table, and we followed it. In addition to the several sheets of Hebrew writing John had found earlier, there were several books with leather covers. Most of these had Greek or Latin writing on their spines, but one very thick volume had a cover inscribed in Arabic. Paul opened this book upon the table, revealing pages filled with more Arabic script inside.

Paul pointed at the tome. "You will recall I mentioned that I saved a book from the great library of Cordoba? Well there it is."

None of us could read Arabic, but the boys were too proud to readily volunteer that. So I broached the obvious question. "What is it?" I asked. "Plato's *Republic*," answered Paul.

John was flabbergasted. "What?" he said breathlessly. "This is Plato's Republic, right here on this table? Saint Augustine refers to this book repeatedly, but no one has ever found a copy. This is actually it? Complete?"

"Yes," said Paul.

John stared at the book, awestruck. Again, it was I who broke the silence.

"What does it say," I ventured to ask.

"Well," said Paul. "In it, Plato says a great many things, some of which are intensely profound, and others quite bizarre. But overall, the thing that makes this book remarkable is the way he attempts to define a science of Justice, and then discusses ways in which an ideal state might be ordered to correspond best to such rationally derived laws."

"But," said John. "What is the purpose of such a discourse? The form of the ideal state is already well understood. It is described by the Great Chain of Being."

Paul shook his head. "Plato would disagree with that. He would say that in accepting the Great Chain, that you are simply accepting society as you find it, without considering its inequities. For Plato, Justice is an absolute, knowable by human reason, and reason may therefore be used to judge, correct, and improve any social order, no matter how well established in custom, in order to achieve a truly just world."

My mind soared with the thought. A truly just world achievable through human reason! What a noble mind Plato must have had to conceive such a thing! How fortunate it was that Paul had saved his book, so that such a grand idea should be saved from oblivion to illuminate our age.

Paul went on. "In any case, to get to the point of Duke William's remark. Plato says that in order to actually create such a just and rational order in the real world, philosophers must become kings, or kings become philosophers."

Alan nodded. "To give force to reason and reason to force," he mused. "Just as you said earlier regarding knights and scholars."

"Exactly," said Paul. "I had on several previous occasions enthusiastically described this interesting philosophy to Duke William, and now he used it to summon me to his purpose. Under the circumstances, there was no way I could refuse, even though it meant forgoing the lovely company of Christina for many months of the year. For my duty, not just to Duke William, but to my own most deeply held beliefs, was now clear,

"When I explained the situation to Christina, she was not happy, but she understood.

"I took the post, and effectively became a part of the family of the court."

Chapter 18

How Eleanor Came to Be

Paul looked at us as if he were about to confide a secret. "Now," he said. "If Duke William was an extraordinary man, as indeed he was, then his wife, Phillipa, Countess of Toulouse, was even more unusual. For this woman was not only learned and curious about all things, but of such mind and intellect as was willing to derive original ideas or otherwise adopt novel concepts at great variance with the general opinion of mankind, and then hold to such views strongly without regard to custom or the disapproval of all around her.

"Thus it was that when Robert D'Abrisil came to Aquitaine, she invited him to come to court, and became an early and ardent advocate of his teachings"

"Who was that?" said John. "I don't think I've ever heard of him."

Hah! I thought to myself. The supposedly very learned scholar John of Salisbury had not even heard of the brilliant Robert D'Abrisil, perhaps the loftiest and most penetrating mind of modern times! This must be any candid person's opinion of him, even were he not a Breton, although the fact that he was certainly adds luster to his name and immortal fame to my nation. I have known about Robert D'Abrisil since I was ten, although I must admit learning much more about him since joining Eleanor, as she was indeed a true and enthusiastic student of his great and noble philosophy.

"Oh," said Paul. "He was this eccentric lay preacher from Brittany who believed that women should have precedence over men in the Great Chain of Being. His doctrine was so crazy that the Church didn't even bother to condemn it as heretical." Paul laughed. "But I must admit it earned him quite a following with some of the ladies. They came to his lectures in droves and applauded him like he was a second Cid whenever he would say something, or even when he would say nothing. Then afterwards, they would descend upon him and crowd about touching him as they questioned him, and offering so many warm invitations for private instruction that I would wager the man had more children than the Caliph."

"How bizarre," Alan said.

"Indeed," said John.

These comments annoyed me, for a great thinker like Robert D'Abrisil should be treated with more respect. Paul had not presented his views well or completely, with due account to their intricate and logical reasoning, nor proper attention to their subtle nuances, highly developed complexities, or solid foundations. I therefore found it necessary to intervene in the discussion to correct Paul's crude vulgarization.

"That is not an accurate description of Robert D'Abrisil's philosophy," I said.

Paul looked at me amused. "Oh, no?" he asked. "Then please   explain it."

"Well," I said. "He began from the premise that kindness, mercy,   and love are the greatest virtues celebrated by our faith." I looked at John. "You would agree with that, would you not?"

"Yes, of course," said John. "It is stated explicitly in Corinthians, 1-13."

"Very well then," I continued. "He then asked the question, who is   it, men or women, who most generally and often exhibit these virtues?"

None of the men said anything.

"Women, obviously," I answered for them. "Therefore, it is women, and not men, who are most truly Christlike in thought and deed, and thus it would clearly be best if as much as possible of the leadership of the world were entrusted to us."

"You forget," John said. "That it was Woman who caused Adam's disobedience to God, and thus our expulsion from paradise."

An oft-repeated canard, refuted long ago by the brilliant Robert D'Abrisil. "Oh," I replied. "Are you then saying that men lack free will?"

That shut his mouth.

I continued. "No? So then Eve was no worse than Adam. But consider; It was a woman who bore Christ, women who were with Him last upon The Cross, and Women who saw Him first when He rose. Therefore, what scripture clearly shows is that it is women who are most suited to bear Christ, to remain with Him, to perceive Him, and to imitate Him. If then, we wish the teachings of Christ to prevail on Earth, who can best serve as his appointed representatives?"

Having proven the case, I folded my arms and awaited any further futile attempt at refutation.

John and Alan shook their heads.

Paul, however, burst out laughing. "I see you have been talking with Eleanor! Indeed, the acorn does not fall far from the oak. In any case,

Phillipa, having deeply inhaled these strange ideas, became very difficult for Duke William to deal with. For though he was a great admirer of women, it was not in this sense that he wished to worship them. This estrangement was driven further, when Phillipa conceived the mad project of proving the validity of her philosophy by sponsoring the creation of a community which would fully put it into practice. Thus she used her wealth to build a great Abbey at Fontevrault, populated it with brothers and sisters and lay men and women, and established the rule that the government of the place should remain entirely in female hands."

"What insanity," commented John.

He could say that if he liked, but I had been to Fontevrault, having been taken there on a visit by Eleanor, who continued the sponsorship of her grandmother's great project. "Why?" I asked. "There is no better managed manor in France. I have been there. Every field is well planted in the best and most modern way, with wheat in the first part, beans in the second, and fallow pasture in the third, and good hedges between them so the animals never wander and waste the crops. All the animals are well treated, particularly the horses, who are so strong and happy as a result that they pull the plow twice as fast as other horses do elsewhere. There are flowers and vegetables in every garden. No weeds may ever grow that are not immediately plucked, and nothing is ever broke that is not instantly fixed. The chamber pots are dumped and cleaned the first thing every morning, so that the air is free from vapors and there is hardly any sickness. Everyone has enough to eat, but no one is allowed too much to drink. There is a shoe for every foot, and a cloak for every back. They have plenty of bread, but no one ever has to grind the grain, because their river mill is never left idle. Everything grown is carefully stored, so that nothing good is ever allowed to rot, and each granary has its own cat to keep away the mice. Prayers are said every day, but only twice, so they never become tiresome. At nighttime, everyone who can read spends some hours copying books, so that dozens of beautiful volumes of the best and most famous authors are produced every year."

"The Abbess and her sisters of the Order of Fontevrault manage all this so carefully and well, that come harvest time they have three times as much as they need. The extra part they send to market, with their most clever bargainers, who know just what to say, and to who, and when to strike the sale, so that they always come back with a good sized sack of silver to safeguard the commonwealth against any future necessity."

I let this sink in, then I threw down my gauntlet. "All this has been arranged and accomplished by a government of women. How then, can anyone doubt our capacity?"

Alan and John said nothing.

Then Paul spoke up. "Be that as it may, Phillipa's obsession with Fontevrault drove Duke William to seek other company. Now there was frequently at court a beautiful Viscountess, who went by the exotic name of Dangerosa. With this fair dame Duke William fell passionately in love, and wooing her ardently and artfully, won her love in return. The two then decided to wed."

Alan interrupted. "But wasn't the Duke already married?"

"Yes," said Paul. "As was the Viscountess Dangerosa. But such considerations mattered little in Aquitaine in the court of Duke William. If two people were in love, they would just marry each other and tell their old spouses, 'sorry, but that is life.'"

Hearing this, John's jaw went slack. I could forgive him for this, because even though Eleanor had tried to explain this Aquitainian attitude to me many times, I could still not understand it myself.

"But didn't the Countess Phillipa or the Viscount object?"

"Actually, no," said Paul. "The Viscount just shrugged and found himself a younger bride, and Phillipa was far too taken up with her Fontevrault project to care who Duke William spent his nights with. Her one concern, though, was to make sure that her sons by William should not lose their titles or inheritances to any child he might conceive by Dangerosa. "Dangerosa, on the other hand, absolutely wanted to make sure that her blood should indeed become part of the House of Aquitaine. But she was far too smart to want to make an enemy of Phillipa by trying to displace her son, young William, who was clearly the Duke's intended heir in any case. So she arranged to meet with Phillipa, and the two came to an agreement that young William should marry Dangerosa's daughter by her previous marriage to the Viscount. This girl's name was Aenor, and she was beautiful, noble, intelligent, and refined, and, at this time, possessed of exactly the same nineteen years as young William. Phillipa was immediately delighted with Aenor, as was young William himself. So the match was arranged, the wedding was held, and they all got on splendidly with each other after that.

"This is unbelievable," said John.

Paul shrugged. "That's how it was in Aquitaine. Anyway, a year after the wedding, Aenor was got with child. She was a very slim lass, so that it appeared the birth would be too difficult for the skill of the midwives alone. Therefore, as had been the case eight years before with Raymond, I was the one to deliver the child.

"It was good I was there, for the baby was a bit too large for Aenor, and was filled with such fierce fighting spirit as to endanger the life of the mother. Still, even as I pulled the babe from the womb and looked down on her for the first time I could see that this infant girl was one of the most extraordinary creatures that I had ever beheld. Her features were perfect, nearly angelic, yet her body was strong and lively, and when I sprinkled the water on her to wash away the birth blood, she smiled, as if enjoying the bath but planning a bit of clever mischief to play upon the world in return.

"Two days later, I went with the Duke's family to the church and stood by as she was baptized. They named her Eleanor."

I spoke up. "The future Queen."

"Yes," said Paul.

At this moment, we heard a sound from downstairs of a door opening, and the bustle and voices of several women entering the house.

"Oh," said Paul. "That must be my housekeeper and the servants, returning from the market."

Footsteps resounded upon the steps, and then a woman perhaps twenty five years of age looked in upon the room. Her eyes were dark, her features sharp, and her hair brownish-black, yet she might have been considered attractive, or even striking, if not for the dowdy burgher clothes that she wore.

"What's this, a patient?" she said.

"Yes," replied Paul. "They were sent by Eleanor."

The woman arched her eyebrows. "Really? Well, I'll be back as soon as I get some soup started." She looked around the room and frowned when she saw the table. "In the meantime, I'd appreciate it if you would put away the books that you are not using."

Then she left.

Paul looked at us, shrugged, and offered an amused smile. "That's Kate, my housekeeper." He paused for a moment, then continued. "Now where was I? Oh yes, the baby Eleanor." He laughed a little laugh. "That tyke was quite a handful."

"Eleanor walked early, and in no time at all was running all over the palace, picking up and playing with everything, for her curiosity was

127

endless. But she didn't speak a word until she was two. Then, one day, when she was playing in the courtyard, Duke William rode in. She looked up at him, then spoke; 'Grandpa, let me ride the horse.' Can you imagine! Those were her first words. 'Grandpa, let me ride the horse!'

"The old Duke was so delighted. He jumped off his horse and lifted her onto the saddle. Then he mounted up behind her, and trotted around the courtyard, the child laughing and proud upon her high mount. I tell you, that little girl was fearless. By the time she was four, she was riding her own pony, and not just in the courtyard, but galloping and leaping it all over the meadow. How she loved to chase after Raymond. He was eight years her senior, and more like an older brother to her than an uncle. She copied his moves in the saddle, and was so ardent to impress him, that soon she was riding more like a young knight than a little girl. When she saw him practicing with lance or sword, she would demand to be taught those as well.

"She was fascinated by chess. I had taught Raymond the game, for being a Spaniard, I was expertly practiced in it, and a strong believer in its value for training a young mind.

"It is originally a Moorish game, is it not?" asked John.

"Well," said Paul. "The Moors brought it to Spain, and it may be their invention, although some think that they learned it from the Persians. That is the theory I hold to, since in chess, when you threaten the opposing king you say 'shahk,' and 'shah' is the Persian word for king. But everyone in Al Andalus played chess, and the Jews most of all.

I nodded to myself, for I had observed this in Toledo.

"So," Paul continued. "Little Eleanor would sit and watch carefully as Raymond and I waged our battles upon the chessboard. Soon she was playing the game herself, and defeating many an adult with the grasp of strategy that was astonishing to behold within one so young and pretty.

"And she wanted to know everything. She would listen in for hours as I instructed Raymond, her eyes wide, her ears taking in every word. History especially interested her. I had focused my instruction of Raymond on the works of the Greeks, because they were the wisest of the ancients, and also because their language is still spoken in the disputed lands of the overseas east, where, as a younger son, Raymond might most likely be able to someday carve out a domain of his own. So, when I read from Herodotus, she was unquenchable. Her favorite character was Artemisia, Queen of Halicanarsis, a Greek who saved her city by leading a squadron of warships to join the Persian cause, then turning her fleet on Xerxes in the midst of the battle of Salamis. Sometimes she would dress up and pretend she was Artemisia herself, and wooden sword in hand, stand in the prow of a boat on the palace pond, issuing brave commands as one of the servants rowed her about.

"I was not her only teacher, of course. Duke William himself was the one to introduce her to the arts of poetry and song. Her father, William the younger, a brave and skillful warrior if ever there was one, gave her first lessons in arms. Dangerosa and Aenor were ladies of refinement, and they taught her how to walk, how to dress, how to move gracefully in a flowing gown, how to pose, how to throw a glance to stop a heart, and above all, how to dance. And when they had shown her all the dances of Aquitaine, they pointed her at me, and she became my most demanding and accomplished student of the Spanish dance.

"Then finally, there was Phillipa, who taught her to consider herself more than equal to any man."

John interrupted. "The Duke did not object to this?"

"No," Paul laughed. "Not at all. The very willful strength he found so difficult in his former spouse was exactly what he hoped for in the character of his granddaughter. And his son, her father, felt the same way. For Eleanor was of the House of Aquitaine, and would be the bearer of its interests within any marriage she might contract. So, in her instance, they wanted the wife to be the greater power, and were grateful to Phillipa for any instruction she might give the girl that would allow her to become such.

"This was always their inclination, but it became their imperative after…" Here Paul stopped and looked about sadly. It almost seemed like he was about to cry.

"After what?" I urged softly.

"After the pestilence," Paul said finally.

Then he gathered himself and continued. "It happened when she was eight years old. A pestilence hit Aquitaine at midsummer. People would wake up in the morning and find their skin had turned red, and their throats were parched. Then they would feel themselves hot, then hotter, and no river or bath could cool them off. They would start coughing phlegm, then blood, and would gasp about in great pain. Some would go mad from the agony, and drown themselves in the bay. Others would just sit and clutch themselves, and curl up until they died. Neither rank, sex, nor age was spared.

"Aenor was among the first to die." "Oh no," I cried out.

"Yes," said Paul. "Then Eleanor's little brother, William XI, the presumptive eventual heir to the Duchy caught sick, and expired quickly. He had been Aenor's only son.

"That made Eleanor the heir, for in Aquitaine, women inherit if there is no son. But then she fell ill too.

"The Duke, Phillipa, Dangerosa William, Raymond, indeed everyone at court was mad with grief as they watched her cough and fade. I was beside myself, for you cannot imagine how special that little girl was to me. The Duke begged me to do something, anything, but what could I, for the most part a fixer of wounds and bones, do for such a case. I searched my memory, then recalled an obscure reference Ibn Sina made in one of the books lost in Cordoba. He discussed how it is rumored that in Greece of old, the priests of Apollo used a potion made from the green mold that grows upon old bread to cure themselves of pestilence, thereby convincing the populace that they possessed special favor from the god. Lacking any other hope, I made such a potion, and poured it into Eleanor's mouth, for she was too weak even to hold a spoon. The next morning she was well enough to sit up and smile.

"It must have been a miracle!" I cried.

Paul shook his head. "I don't know what it was. At the time, I thought it was a medicine of immense saving power. So I mounted a horse and made for La Rochelle as fast as I could, for I reasoned that the pestilence would soon reach the town, and I wanted to be there to save Christina and our children.

"I made it in time, but just barely, for the morning after our arrival, Christina and the two boys woke sick. So I gave them the potion."

Paul looked at me sadly. "They died within the hour. Christina's last words to me were, 'it's not your fault.'" Paul closed his eyes, and covered them with his hand.

I reached out to touch Paul, for he seemed completely stricken. "I'm so sorry," I said.

Paul breathed softly for several seconds. Finally he rallied himself, and continued.

"Charles found me sitting by the side of her bed three days later, and brought me back to Bordeaux. It took a few months for me to recover my sanity, but I eventually did. When I returned to the world, I discovered that Christina's parents had claimed guardianship of our daughter, and sent her off to be educated in a convent.

"So I gave up practicing medicine. Instead, I threw myself into the project of educating Eleanor, for she was all I had left in the world."

"What about Raymond?" Alan asked.

"Raymond was now sixteen," Paul said, "and getting too old to spend much time taking lessons from me. But more to the point, he had to leave Aquitaine. For if he stayed, being so much younger than his elder brother, he might be seen as a competing heir to Eleanor. This of course would also be a threat to Dangerosa and the younger William, both of whom would have their blood lines cut out of the inheritance, should Raymond succeed in such a usurpation. Still, given that Raymond was such a promising young leader, and Eleanor but a little girl, he might have found plenty of nobles willing to support a claim that after young William, the Duchy should pass to him. But he loved Eleanor far too much to wish to make himself her enemy. So rather than do so, he left for England to offer himself as a knight to King Henry, and let fortune lead him on from there. He continued to visit now and then, so he and Eleanor remained very close. Eventually, though, much as I had anticipated, he found his way to the east, and made himself Prince·of Antioch."

"Shortly after Raymond left, the old Duke died, and the younger William became Duke. With Eleanor now direct in line, all hopes now centered on preparing her for her future role. Her father taught her to fight as well as most men. I taught her to think better than any man. Phillipa taught her how to use her character to stand up to a King. Dangerosa taught her how she might use her charms to bewitch one.

"With her younger brother dead, and Raymond gone, Eleanor became lonely, for the only child left in the palace was her younger sister Petronilla, who was still just a tot. But Charles, now a married baron, had a beautiful daughter who was just Eleanor's age. This girl was not as brilliant as Eleanor, but she was equally spirited, and even more wild about horses. The two became fast friends, and again the palace was filled with laughter, as we happily endured or heard reports of their many mad and mischievous adventures."

"Was that Alicia?" I asked.

"Yes," said Paul. "Well, with Eleanor now heir to Aquitaine, it wasn't long before the court starting hearing from Abbot Suger, the principal minister to old King Louis the Fat of France. This rather grotesque monarch had a son named Phillip, tall, strong, and valiant, who was his lawful heir and but five years Eleanor's senior. Why not, said Suger, betroth the two, and through the wedding of France to Aquitaine, create the mightiest kingdom in Christendom.

"While the offer had much to recommend it, William, Phillipa, and Dangerosa were all reluctant to accept. Because while warrior enough, Prince Phillip was known to be coarse, cruel, and brutal, and they did not feel at ease subjecting their precious Eleanor to life with such a man. They sought guarantees from Suger, but could obtain no satisfactory answer.

"The diplomatic impasse, however, was eventually resolved by the intervention of one of Paris' humblest yet most noteworthy inhabitants, to wit a pig whose name, if he had one, has escaped the chroniclers. This fine creature, seeing fit to cross the road at just the moment when Prince Phillip was cantering through the town, caused the great man's steed to lose its mind. Unhorsed by the intrepid pig, the divinely appointed heir to all of France fell and broke his neck. This made Phillip's younger brother Louis the new heir.

"Now Louis was a boy known for his mild and pious disposition. Indeed, he had been destined for a career in a monastery, a vocation that might have suited him well, until his older brother's untimely demise summoned him back into the world. Since it would not do for Eleanor to marry a corpse, Suger, of course, immediately changed his offer. Instead of Phillip, Eleanor could now marry Louis.

"This put a different face upon the matter. As it became apparent to William and the two grandmothers how weak and dull a lad Louis actually was, and most especially so in comparison to Eleanor, they conceived the idea that through such a match the two realms might not only be united, but that it would be Aquitaine rather than France that would emerge ruler over the whole. As I'm sure you will understand, this thought delighted them no end.

"One problem, however, threatened the accomplishment of this plan, and that was the willfulness of Eleanor herself. For the girl was now a spirited and imaginative maiden just approaching marriageable age, and raised as she was upon the romantic tales of her grandfather, she dreamed of a husband who would be a glorious and noble chevalier; valiant, strong, handsome, courteous, witty, and brave. To put the matter softly, Louis did not fit this description.

"Fortunately for the would be matchmakers, however, Eleanor did not know this. So Dangerosa, who perhaps of the three knew Eleanor's heart the best, drew for the girl such a portrait of the young Prince as might have induced Guinevere to forgo Lancelot. Informed thus, Eleanor enthusiastically gave her consent to the betrothal.

"How strange the world is," Paul sighed. "For within a month of arranging the betrothal, both old Louis the Fat and young William were taken by God. So Eleanor came to Paris not as an heir, but as a Duchess to marry a Louis who was already King. She insisted that I come too, for she felt unsafe living in such a filthy town without a competent doctor nearby. Alicia came too, of course, as did Petronilla, although the latter refused to stay after she saw what the place was like.

"So here we are."

Chapter 19

A Cathar's Tale

As Paul concluded thus, we again heard sounds on the steps. Kate reentered the room, followed by a servant girl. Each bore trays that between them held six steaming bowls of soup, with a spoon in each bowl.

"Supper," she said, then passed the bowls around to all present, keeping one for herself and placing another on the little table nearest where my father was resting his head. Then she dismissed the servant who returned downstairs to eat her own.

I said a silent grace and took a sip. It was thick bean soup, with diverse other vegetables mixed in, but no meat. Not palace fare, certainly, but no worse than what we got many nights in my own family.

When we had finished supping, Kate collected the bowls, and stacked them on one tray. Then she spoke to Paul.

"So," she said. "These guests have brought us a patient from Eleanor. Did she also send money for the treatment?"

Paul sighed. "Kate please. Accepting a fee from Eleanor would be…"

I held up the three silver sou. "She gave me these to pay expenses. Are they enough?"

Kate snatched the coins out of my hand, examined each one swiftly to check for clipping, then dropped them into a little leather bag tied to her belt. "They'll do," she said happily.

"Kate," said Paul. "I did this job as a special favor for a friend. I really would prefer to give the money back"

"Yes," said Kate. "I'm sure you would. That is why it is fortunate that I manage the money in this house." She looked at me and smiled. "The old boy apparently thinks that the food I buy for him in the market falls from the sky. Here we are, living hand to mouth, and he doesn't want to take three sou from Eleanor. Three sou! Enough to feed us for a month, and not offered as a handout mind you, but as a fair fee for work well done. Yet the little fellow is too proud to accept it." She shook her head. "Men."

Then she looked around the room, and again noticed the pile of books and papers upon the study table. "My, my," she said, as she got up. "Haven't we agreed that you would put away your books when you are not using them?" Arriving at the table, she neatened the pile of loose papers into a single stack, then picked up the books and started to put them back on the shelf.

"Kate," Paul called out to her. "I was using those books as references for my translation."

Kate waved her hand, dismissing his remark. "Really. You know you only need to use one book at a time," she said, her voice like a caressing hand that softly moves aside what it wills, and continued with her business.

Paul sighed and shrugged, then explained to us quietly. "Kate is a product of Fontevrault."

"I heard that," Kate called out with a hint of gaiety in her voice. Then as she returned towards where we were sitting, she saw the long box containing the scimitar of Valencia next to Alan.

"So, old man," she said with a smile. "I see you've been telling your war stories." She opened the box and gave the sword an affectionate rub with her rag, then closed the box and put it in its proper place on the shelf. "Ah, Valencia," she said in friendly mockery, and I could see that beneath her haughty manner, Kate held a tender regard for old Paul.

"So," Paul said to us, with an amused laugh. "This is my reward for all I have done for Eleanor. I, who pulled her from the womb, who saved her from the pestilence, who taught her chess, and Spanish dancing, who gave her an education such as few possess, and who accompanied her here to Paris to be available to assist her if needed. What does she do in return? She installs me here in this house and gives me for a housekeeper this crazed Cathar from Fontevrault who thinks herself my caretaker!"

Kate laughed. "Yes, well, that is how she described the position to me. In any case, you must admit I do it well." She glanced at Papa asleep on the bed, and fondled again the coins in her purse bag. "You know, old man, you should take in more patients. They pay a lot better than those penniless students of yours."

"You know why I can't do that," said Paul.

"It wasn't your fault," Kate responded softly.

Paul seemed about to reply, but John interrupted. "Excuse me, but did you say that this woman is a Cathar?"

"Did I?" Paul asked. "Well yes, she is." Then he winked at me. "That is why she was thrown out of Fontevrault."

Kate seemed a little flustered by this. "I was not thrown out. I was asked to consider leaving by the Abbess for the good of the Order. She explained to me that Fontevrault was only accepted by the Church on condition that it diverge no further from orthodoxy than it already had through embracing the teachings of Robert D'Abrisil. Furthermore, she said that our patroness Eleanor had need of me in Paris to manage the household of a little old scholar dear to her from past acquaintance, whose mind had become so addled with age that he could no longer fend for himself.".

"So," Kate concluded with a mocking smile. "I took the post of the old boy's caretaker as a sort of sacred trust."

Paul rolled his eyes and looked up through the ceiling to heaven for guidance. Then he turned to Alan and John. "As you can see gentlemen," he laughed. "She's quite mad."

Kate reddened for a moment, then looked at me, winked, and gently slapped her coin bag, as if to let me know, just between us, how good such madness might be.

"No doubt," said John. "But she is also a Cathar." He turned to Kate. "Is that so, are you truly of the Yellow Cross?"

Kate surveyed John up and down, taking in his priggish and pale appearance more thoroughly that she had done so before.

"Are you studying for the priesthood?" she asked, avoiding his question in the process.

"Yes," he said.

"You certainly look like a future priest," she said, casting me an ironic glance to secretly share her opinion of such men.

"Thank you," said John, fortunately oblivious to her meaning. "I take it from your refusal to answer my question directly that you are, in fact, a Cathar. How can you defend such absurd, heretical, and horrendous views?"

Kate smiled and ran her tongue over her teeth. Apparently she had some experience disputing views with priests and the like, and she relished the prospect of dueling with John. "Oh," she said softly. "Like our view that the Church hierarchy is corrupt? How could any rational person possibly defend such a position? I wonder. Could it be the large estates that so many Bishops seem able to buy for themselves these days? Or perhaps it's the prostitutes who appear to live on such estates, covered with jewels, and bearing children with such amazing resemblances to the holy men themselves?"

John reddened. "I concede that there are grounds for complaint about the moral behavior of some individuals who have achieved high clerical office. But the way to deal with the problem is to work to reform the Church organization from within, not to start a new and heretical religion."

He shook his head and turned to Paul.

"Sir," said John. "I fail to understand how you, a former Jew no less, can allow a Cathar to serve as your housekeeper."

"Well," said Paul. "She manages most things well, and is a fairly good cook. Although your point is well taken in that the lack of meat in her dishes can grow rather tiresome."

John seem flustered. "I'm not talking about the Cathar diet. I'm talking about their theology. You know what these Cathars believe. They assert that there are two gods, one good, the other evil, and that the god we read of in the Old Testament, the god of the Jews, the god who created the world, was evil. How can you tolerate such blasphemy?"

"That is not what we believe," said Kate.

"Oh no?" said John. "That is how I have heard Cathar doctrine described to me."

"By Cathars themselves?" Kate enquired.

"No, of course not," John said. "You are the first Cathar I've ever met. But that is how Catharism is described by the most noted Church authorities on the subject."

I thought it remarkable that John had never met a Cathar, or thought he hadn't. While not as numerous as in Aquitaine, there were more than a few to be encountered in Paris, both in the market and the taverns, and especially among the musicians who played in the streets. The man had to be walking through life with shuttered eyes.

"Well," said Kate. "You are deceived by your own slanders. In fact, you simply don't know what you are talking about." She smiled, and laughed lightly in the manner that clever women do when they wish to undermine a man's confidence. "It really makes you look very foolish."

Again John reddened. "Very well," he said folding his arms. "Explain your doctrine."

Kate nodded. "Thank you. I appreciate the opportunity to do so. Who knows? Perhaps I can show you the light."

"Just get on with it," John said, obviously irritated.

"As you wish," said Kate. "Yes, it is true that we perceive two supernatural forces at work in the world, one good, the other evil. To use your terminology, there is God, and there is the Devil."

I thought to myself; this is not very different from what we Christians believe.

Kate continued. "Now it is clear to any rational person who studies the scriptures, that some of the actions ascribed to God in that book are clearly evil."

"Some?" asked John, perplexed. "You are saying that some of God's actions are good and some are evil?"

"No," said Kate. "God is always good. I am saying that some of the actions ascribed to God are not good, and in fact, manifestly evil. These actions must therefore have been done not by God, but by the Devil disguised as God."

John hung his mouth open in shock.

"For example," Kate continued. "The being who created the world and the Garden of Eden for us to enjoy was clearly good, and therefore God. But the being who expelled us from Eden and condemned all humanity to eternal torment because Eve desired knowledge, was evil, and therefore could only have been the Devil pretending to be God. The being who warned Noah of the coming flood was the good God, but he that carried it out was the Devil. He that ordered Abraham to sacrifice his son was evil, but He that stopped it was good. The God who rescued the Israelites from bondage was good, but He who told them to slaughter the Canaanites, men women, and little children, except for the virgin maidens who He ordered raped and turned into harlot slaves, that being was clearly utterly evil." Kate paused and studied John for a moment. "How can you even dispute that?"

John shook his head. "God moves in mysterious ways. Although it may not be apparent to us, every act, deed, and word reported of God in the scriptures must necessarily be good. You have no business setting yourself up as the judge of God."

"Is that so?" said Kate. "Then what do you say of the god who spoke to Mohammed, ordering him to go forth and destroy Christendom?"

"That could not have been God," John said.

"My point exactly," said Kate, folding her arms.

"I think that Mohammed was just a liar," said Alan.

"You might choose to say so," said Kate. "But the Koran is too big a book to be written by a desert bandit without some kind of inspiration. And consider the way his followers so readily suicide themselves in battle. Truly there must be some supernatural spirit moving such men."

"But suicide is a mortal sin," I said.

"Yes," said Kate. "And what being is He who seeks to increase the population of the damned?

"Look at the other teachings of the Prophet of Islam," Kate continued.

138

"Christ protected the fallen girl from the mob, but Mohammed calls upon them to destroy her. From which spirit could such a cruel and evil creed emanate?"

"I don't see what you are getting at here," John said. "You are suggesting that Mohammedism was diabolically inspired. That seems fairly clear. But in what sense does that in any way undermine the precepts of our faith?"

"Well," said Kate. "Do you think that Mohammed, when he heard the voice, thought he was listening to the Devil? Do you think that he, and all those millions inspired through him, know they are obeying the Devil, and therefore willingly embracing eternal damnation?"

"No," said John. "They are obviously deceived." Suddenly John seemed to grasp Kate's point. He looked at her, then at Paul, in utter horror.

"But," he said, with true desperation in his voice. "But if the Devil can so perfectly impersonate God, how then can we distinguish between the two and avoid damnation ourselves?"

"Use reason," said Kate.

. John's mouth gaped open like a captured fish gasping for air.

"At last," said Paul. "Two intelligent words to illuminate an otherwise inane discussion. Lux sit."

Lux sit, I thought to myself. Let there be light. The first words spoken by God.

John, however, had begun to shake. Alan touched him gently on the sleeve.

"John," he said. "I think it is time that you and I went home."

***   ***   ***

I spent the night at Paul's house, sleeping on the floor by the side of Papa's bed. When I arose, Papa was already awake, and had eaten the soup left for him the previous night.

"Marie," he said. "What is this place?"

What could I say?

"Papa!" I cried, and hugged him harder than I should have. "You are in the house of a great healer. Don't try to move. I'll fetch you more breakfast."

I ran down the steps to the kitchen, as happy as if I had entered Heaven.

Chapter 20

In Which I Meet the Famous Bernard of Clairvaux

I spent another two weeks living in the house with Paul and Kate, taking care of Papa. The Cathar and the Philosopher provided considerable amusement with their endless sparring. In this struggle, Kate would appear to hold the advantage, as in addition to her sharp wit, she possessed the purse, the keys, and the undisputed loyalty of the servant girls of the house, and these latter facts allowed her to have her way in all things and trifle with him in any way she pleased. Yet so great was the power of Paul's intellect, that such teasing affected his ability to scatter her metaphysical opinions no more than birds flying over a battlefield influence the outcome of a charge of armored knights upon a weak line of opposing infantry. Each thus prevailed in their own sphere, she in the real, he in the ideal, and obtaining victory in all the world that mattered, each emerged from every encounter unscathed, and able to regard the other with the lofty friendship of a merciful conqueror.

I had met Cathars many times before, but this was the first time I had lived in the same house with one. I pray I will never have to do so again. For though there be many fine and virtuous people among the Cathars worthy of every friendship, and Kate was certainly such a one; and though many of them are wonderful musicians and troubadours with whom you can spend an excellent and merry evening in a tavern, they all possess one heretical belief that makes them absolutely insufferable to live with for any length of time.

This is their refusal to eat meat.

I have no problem going without meat in my soup for a day, or two, or three. Indeed, in the course of my family's many travels upon the road from one piece of building work to another, this has frequently been necessary. Nor do I ever require as a matter of necessity such huge slabs of meat as are given out every night at the palace King Louis. But to go without any meat at all, day after day and night after night, when plenty is to be had at the market, is a mad penance that neither I, nor any sane person, can possibly abide.

Our Savior liberated us from the mistaken law of the Jews which denied to mankind the enjoyment of pork. How then should we regard this precept of the Cathars, which would deny us not only pork, but meat of every type? Do not mistake my meaning. I am of the free builders, and willing to be a friend to anyone who bears no malice to me. If the Cathars wish to hold to this heresy, I say peace be upon them, for such people deserve not our hatred, but our pity. They certainly have mine. But no one should ever be forced to live under this impious law.

Furthermore, it should be clear that no matter how clever Cathars may sometimes appear to be in disputation concerning matters of faith, their arguments for changes in Christian doctrine should be viewed with amused skepticism. For how wise can anyone be who willfully gives up meat? There are monks who choose to live this way, I know. But our holy Church has provided monasteries so that these people may be safely shut away and not inflict themselves on the rest of mankind, and for this I give thanks to the blessed Virgin, and to her son, Our Savior, who certainly ate meat, as well as fish, as clearly reported in all the gospels.

I wondered how Paul was able to survive under such a regimen, and eventually he told me in confidence his method. To wit, when going out to give lessons to scholars, he would offer them alternative venues of cold church or warm tavern. Being sensible scholars, they naturally always chose the latter, and showed their appreciation for such a good Master by paying for his wine and beef once they were there. I don't know if this subterfuge escaped Kate's knowledge. However, if it did not, then she wisely chose to pretend ignorance, as it no doubt served to encourage Paul to expand his pedagogical endeavors, with excellent benefits to the income of the domestic commonwealth thereby resulting. But unfortunately I had no excuse to go out foraging for my own suppers, and it would have been unkind to Papa for me to desert him for such convenience as well. So I was left to share with him, twice a day, the dreary and heretical meals of the Cathars.

However, just as it is said that every dark cloud has a lining of silver, in this instance the horrid diet that Kate imposed on the household of Paul of La Rochelle had a salutary and blessed effect. For my father, not being one willing to endure such circumstances for a day more than necessary, speeded his recovery, and was able to leave the home of the good doctor barely a fortnight after his arrival.

Having thus made his escape, Papa returned to the job at St. Denis, and avoiding for a while any heavy work, devoted himself to a study of the causes of the failure of his great engine and the design of a successor which would be safe against future disaster.

Yuletide now being nearly upon us, I returned to the palace to recommence my life with Eleanor. The Queen had been bored stiff in my absence, and gladdened by my return and by the news of Papa's miraculous recovery, planned some excellent celebrations for the season.

And, so it was, that at the end of that year, we finally had a truly merry Christmas, with good revels, fine music, excellent drink, and even dancing. For upon Eleanor's invitation, our court was visited by the handsome Duke Geoffrey of Anjou, a most accomplished gentleman, courtly and neat, and unlike the boorish French nobles, quite willing and able to dance properly with Eleanor and her ladies.

Our frolics on that occasion, however, were not a source of universal pleasure, for, as I observed at the end of Eleanor's final turn with Duke Geoffrey on the fourth feast night, King Louis, Odo, and a sour faced monk had entered the hall, and were watching the festivities with expressions of horror.

The dance ending, Eleanor walked away from Duke Geoffrey to pick up a cup of wine from the table set near our blazing fire. Alicia, who had also found a worthy dance partner among Duke Geoffrey's retinue, followed her, and I ceased my strumming to join them as well. We were all enjoying our cups, when Louis and his two companions approached.

"Eleanor," Louis said. "If you will allow me to interrupt your very important dancing, I would like to introduce you to the most holy Abbot Bernard of Clairvaux."

The sour faced monk nodded to Eleanor. He wore a white robe and had only a simple wooden crucifix, with no ornaments. I looked at him curiously, for I had heard of the famous Abbot Bernard. He was reputed to be a very holy man, and this explained his face, which was so gaunt as to only be the result of much self-mortification through fasting. Indeed, if one wishes the wide repute of holiness without venturing its accomplishment, there is no surer method.

Odo spoke to the Queen. "Abbot Bernard is the head of the devout Cistercian order, and is renowned among true Christians everywhere," he paused and raised an eyebrow, before continuing with an insulting tone.

"It would be good if you became acquainted with him as well."

Eleanor bristled. "I am a true Christian," she said. "And I certainly know of Bernard. Greetings, Abbot."

Bernard bowed a shallow bow. "Your Majesty, I am honored that my small repute has reached even your attention," he said, his tone belying any sense of modesty in his words. "But tell me, since you call yourself a true Christian, why do you neglect your duties in favor of such frivolous dissipations?" Here he pointed to the dance floor.

Eleanor was not one to be cowed by a monk, even Bernard. She said, "I think that God put joy in life as a gift, and that it is our duty as Christians not to reject it."

Precisely as I would have put it, I thought.

"Perhaps," said Bernard. "But you have more serious duties. Such as giving France an heir."

Here Louis chimed in. "Yes Eleanor," he said. "Instead of wasting yourself with such useless pastimes as dancing and chess, you should really focus on producing a son. That is what God and France require of you."

Eleanor stared at Louis astonished at his words, as indeed Alicia and I were equally amazed. For in truth, the failure of the royal couple to produce an heir was entirely the fault of the King, a fact that would have been known to him had he possessed a knowledge of the ways of Nature equal to that of any peasant lad or lass above the age of ten.

Louis continued. "And what I really can't understand is your spending so much time consorting with scholars, even attending lectures of this heretic Abelard."

Eleanor would not let a good man be so foully slandered. "Abelard is not a heretic," she said. "Unorthodox, perhaps, but no heretic. Just the opposite. He seeks to reinforce faith through reason and understanding."

Bernard raised his hand. "Unorthodoxy is the first step towards heresy," he said. "Rome is quite concerned, and has authorized an investigation."

Now Eleanor was horrified. She looked at Bernard with fire in her eyes. "What?" she said. "Is that why you have come to Paris? To prosecute Abelard?" Then, not waiting for Bernard's answer, she turned to the King. "Louis, you cannot allow this."

"Why not?" Louis drawled, as if the matter was of no consequence. "I have no wish to see our schools as fountains of heresy. If Abelard is innocent, Abbot Bernard will surely affirm that. If not…"

Eleanor looked about like a drowner seeking a stick to snatch. "But it is an invasion of the power of the crown!" she cried.

"Hardly a material one," Louis shrugged. "In any case, it is not a matter you should concern yourself with, especially since your primary duty to the realm remains unfulfilled."

It was at this point that Abbot Suger entered the hall. He immediately approached the royal group, and nodding briefly to the others, proceeded to greet Bernard of Clairvaux with a light kiss on either cheek.

"Ah brother Bernard," Suger said. "So good to see you again. How do things go at Clairvaux?"

"Well enough," said Bernard in his usual; sour voice. "So Suger, I see you have been busy with this new cathedral of yours."

"Yes," said Suger. "The work is going quite well."

Bernard frowned. "I heard you had an accident. Some children and a worker were almost killed."

I was very upset to hear my father described as a mere "worker." He was a master enginator. How could Bernard be so disdainful?

"The good Lord protected them," Suger said.

"It was a warning," said Bernard. "You are placing human life in danger for this vanity. How many must perish for your Tower of Babel?"

"The new church at Saint Denis is not a Tower of Babel," Suger said. "It will be a cathedral of light that will glorify our faith, our patron saint, and Our Savior."

"And, of course, you," Bernard concluded. "Oh vanity, vanity, all is vanity! How great is your pride, Suger, yet how callous. How much are you spending on this bauble, that might otherwise be spent to feed the poor? Would that not be a much better way to glorify our faith? How many must starve to feed your pride? How many must perish to please your vanity?"

Abbot Suger looked at Bernard and opened his mouth to reply, but no words came out.

"You should know," Bernard continued. "That I intend to write our holy Father in Rome and ask that this vainful, wasteful and dangerous project be halted at once. I know he will listen."

Bernard was going to stop the building of the glorious cathedral of light! I could not let this happen.

"Father Bernard," I said, daring to speak beyond my place. "I am the daughter of the Master enginator who was injured in the accident of which you spoke."

Bernard turned to regard me, and as his eyes lit upon the builder's medallion that hung upon my neck I saw his lips curl for just an instant in that subtle frown that many of noble birth display when they discover a burgher in their presence. He quickly replaced it with an overwarm smile, however.

"My child," he said to me. "I am so sorry to hear about your father. I pray that the good Lord will heal him. But if he does not, you may be consoled that his loss will have given us the warning to save many of his fellows from a similar fate."

"Thank you, Father," I said. "The good God has seen fit to mend him, so he has now returned to help continue the great work at Saint Denis. I pray that you will not be the one to halt this project, for which he and his brother builders have labored so hard, risked so much, and given so fully of their hearts and hopes."

Bernard was taken aback. "But my child," he said. "Can you not take warning? Cannot your father and his comrades take heed? Is paid work so dear that they prefer to endanger themselves so fatally, and leave their children to starve as orphans? I would think that, as builders, they would at least know how fantastic this project is, with ever worse catastrophes inevitable as the walls rise higher than any before. Suger hopes for the false immortality of earthly fame. But what awaits them but crippling injury and painful death?"

"We all die, Father," I said. "It is what we do during our lives that is of account. The cathedral of light is a grand work. It will be a wonder for all the ages. To have a hand in that, to even have a chance to be part of an enterprise so glorious, is something for which we hope and pray all our days, and for which we would gladly hazard all. You must not take this away from us."

Bernard frowned. "You builders seem to fancy yourselves like knights seeking eternal renown through glorious feats in battle."

There it is again, I thought to myself. The contempt of a noble for the aspirations of burghers. I decided I would ask Eleanor later what she knew about Bernard's blood line.

Bernard continued. "But fame is a false reward for knights, and will be even falser for builders. Even if they succeed, no one will remember the names of those who built the cathedral."

This was true. For even though I am a bard and might compose a song honoring their builders, no one else would sing it after me. Battles and love affairs, by their nature, make far better stories than do construction projects, and if a bard wishes to hold her audience, she must tell the tales that entertain. But still I had an answer for Bernard.

"Yes, you are right. The world will not know our names. But we will know them, and God will know them. If future generations will not know who we were, at least they will know what we did; and we will not have passed through the world like the beasts that perish without a trace, but leave a record for all to know that once we were, and that we were noble men."

Bernard shook his head. "You're as mad for glory as Suger is. If only you would learn that salvation cannot be obtained through fame, but through humility and trust in God. In any case, regardless of your folly, I cannot, and will not, allow the Church's resources to be wasted on this vain project when there is so much suffering in the world crying out for our attention."

"But Brother Bernard," Abbot Suger pleaded. "The cathedral will alleviate suffering. It will give the royal authority here in Paris the prestige necessary to put down the anarchy that has ruined France. These endless wars of one Count upon another, that have caused so much wreck, death, and destruction, can only be ended when France has a King with sufficient power to command it to stop, and grandeur is the key to power. Grandeur brings wealth. Grandeur brings respect. And the cathedral of light will bring grandeur. It will turn Paris into a great capital city that will be famous around the world."

"Nonsense," said Bernard. "But I thank you for revealing your true motives. They make this project all the more reprehensible. In any case, it's over now. You would do well to tell your workmen to seek other employment. For come spring there will be nothing further to pay them."

Abbot Suger turned desperately to the King. "Your Majesty, I beg you..."

"I'm sorry, dear Father," Louis said. "But if Abbot Bernard says the Church is opposed, then I can go no further."

"But I can," said Eleanor.

Abbot Suger faced her in some surprise. "Queen Eleanor," he began. "I am grateful for your support, but the amount you have been providing by itself would be insufficient to carry on the work."

"I can give more," Eleanor said.

Bernard's eyes blazed at her. "You would overthrow my decision?"

The Queen smiled. "With pleasure, Father."

Bernard stormed from the room in anger.

Eleanor watched him go, her eyes twinkling with mockery.

My heart soared. Was ever there such a Queen?

146

***　　***　　***

Why did Eleanor so act to open her purse further to continue the Cathedral at Saint Denis? Was it, as some say, because she needed to keep her power over the Abbot Suger, which would have ended if his project had? Or was it because she, in her own way, shared the Abbot's dream of great France united with Aquitaine, that would be able to impose peace upon all the unruly Counts and barons of her own forebear Charlemagne's former realm? Or was it for the magnificent cathedral of light itself, and all that it stood for, and the good she might do for her own salvation by endowing it so generously?

All of these may have had some consideration, for Eleanor was never one to decide things lightly. But afterwards she told me that the element that tipped the scale were the words I used in my own plea to Abbot Bernard. For she said I had stated a true calling for great and humble alike, and that she, for one, would not desert it.

"Leave a record for all to know that once we were, and that we were noble."

Chapter 21

The Trial of Abelard

While Bernard of Clairvaux could not obtain his will to halt the cathedral of light, on the matter of the prosecution of Abelard he was not so easily confounded.

And so it was that in the next spring, May of the year of Our Lord one thousand, one hundred, and forty, that a trial was to be held, and the great philosopher forced to defend himself in person on charges of heresy before a panel of the leading prelates of the land. Bernard would be the prosecutor, and debate Abelard face to face. Only now the stakes of the verbal contest would not be the applause of school boys, but the life and liberty of the great sage himself.

Paris is in the see of Sens, and so it was decided to hold the trial in the cathedral there, with ten bishops and a papal legate serving as judges. The stakes being so great, and the match itself bringing into direct contest the two giants of the age, the trial became an event that was not to be missed. Sens is but two days journey from Paris, and during the week before Pentecost, Eleanor, Alicia, and I traveled thence, amidst a road crowded with scholars, nobles, monks, nuns, and curiosity seekers of every type. There were also many peddlers with much merchandise, including both necessaries and curiosities, for with the gathering of such a crowd there was good business to be done. King Louis also went, along with Odo and Abbot Suger, but we did not travel in their company, because the King was a bore and Eleanor preferred to avoid his conversation whenever opportunity permitted.

At Sens a mass was held in the cathedral for Pentecost, after which Abbot Bernard gave an outdoor sermon to all the assembled multitudes wherein he asked them to pray for the soul of an unnamed unbeliever who had cast his lot among us. This was a very clever thing for Bernard to do, for it led everyone to think of Abelard as a lost atheist, while casting the Abbot of Clairvaux as a man too polite to even name his antagonist, and so merciful and kind as to wish upon him only salvation and the rewards of Heaven.

As we were leaving this event, we encountered the scholars of our acquaintance, Alan, John, and Becket. These, along with many of their fellows, had also come to Sens to witness the trial of the great man.

"Marie," Alan said. "Well met. Have you heard about the dinner for Abelard?"

I shook my head.

"Well," Alan said. "Tonight is the feast of Pentecost, and a number of us who are his friends are joining Abelard for his final supper before trial."

A last supper for Abelard.

Alan went on. "It will be held in the Tavern of the White Lion, on the Street of Latins, just west of the cathedral. You," and here he bowed to Eleanor, who had just approached closer. "And of course, you, Your Majesty, would be most welcome."

I turned to Eleanor. "Your majesty, I wish that we could go."

Alicia looked doubtful. "It would be most unseemly if we were seen in such company."

"We could go in disguise," I said.

"None of us would give you away," Alan said, and Becket and John nodded their agreement.

"Well," said Eleanor. "I do have an invitation to a formal event this evening at the bishop's chateau, but I think this could be much more memorable."

She turned to Alicia. "Alicia, please be so kind as to convey to the King my regrets. We're dining in town tonight."

The Tavern of the White Lion proved to be a dark place, located downstairs beneath a potter's shop. But it was large enough to accommodate Abelard's many friends. In order not to press the fortune of our burgher disguises too far, Eleanor, Alicia, and I took a table to the side. This table we shared with Alan, Becket and John, who all, being of no special account, further shielded us from excessive attention.

At the head table, by Abelard's side, there sat a holy sister. She was perhaps two score years of age, and those years had taken their toll. Yet it was not hard to see that she had once been very beautiful. This, I quickly realized, was none other than the famed Heloise, the great love of Abelard's life, come from afar to be with him on the night before his ultimate trial. When the eating was done, these two joined hands, and sat quietly together, softly touching, while all about the comrades of the sage saluted him with raucous toasts.

The chief among these friends, Abelard's closest peers, were also at the head table. Some of these I recognized, for they included Gilbert of Poiree and several other Master scholars I knew from my travels in Paris. Two other very famous ones John named for us. These were William of Conches and Arnold of Bresica, after Abelard the most noted scholars in Christendom. There was also a vacant chair. Who could it be for?

I found out, when, halfway through the dinner, there arrived in the tavern none other than Paul of La Rochelle. How he got there, I do not know. Indeed, the trip to Sens must have been very difficult for him, but there he was, and upon his entrance immediately invited to a seat at the head table by the side of Gilbert of Poiree. Surveying the room, his eyes instantly lit upon Eleanor, and something wonderful flashed between them. Regarding her, an expression grew on his face as tender and proud as that of an old knight greeting a favorite son who has just proven himself brave and worthy. Then he turned to join in the conversation of the other sages at his table.

I watched them talk, and it was like witnessing Our Savior at his ultimate meal, together with Mary Magdalene and the Twelve Apostles.

Finally, William of Conches rose for a last toast. "Friends," he said. "We gather here tonight to celebrate our comradeship with the greatest man of our age. He stands accused of damnable heresy. For what? For his immortal words that have inspired us all, that 'man should through reason seek the hidden causes for all things.'

"How could anyone condemn such words? They that do so condemn him because they are patrons of ignorance. They know not the forces of nature, and in order that they may have comrades in their ignorance, they suffer not that others should search out anything, and would have us believe like rustics and ask no reason. But we say that in all things a reason must be sought, and we must seek it with the same intrepid courage of those who sought the Golden Fleece, because we are Abelard's Argonauts.

"Peter Abelard," William said. "You have shown us the way. No matter what happens on the morrow, you may be certain of this: that we who you have thus inspired shall never give up your cause. Your torch has lit ours with the sacred flame, and come what may, we will carry it forward, until all may see the light. We will not fail you Abelard. Your fire will not be quenched. Your spirit will never die."

William held his cup high. "To Peter Abelard, Hero of Reason!"

We all stood up and saluted with our cups. "To Peter Abelard, Hero of Reason!"

Heloise reached over and hugged Abelard. As they embraced in their likely final parting, tears dripped from both their eyes. Then they kissed.

There was no need for us to salute him as a hero of Love.

The next morning, the cathedral was packed. On the dais stood the ten bishops and the papal legate, all in their full regalia. On either side of the main aisle were packed row upon row of scholars, monks, nuns, nobles, and wealthy commoners. I stood with Eleanor and the royal party, on the right hand side near the front, adjacent to the judges' dais. Before us, between the two rows stood Bernard of Clairvaux, his simple white robe and wooden crucifix lending him an air of sacredness and saintliness markedly superior to that of the ornately bejeweled bishops. Abelard was not visible.

The papal legate advanced to the podium. "Is the accused present," he called out.

Dressed in a black priestly robe, Gilbert of Poiree stepped forward from the ranks of the scholars. "Not yet, your reverence," he said. "However he is expected shortly."

No sooner had Gilbert said this than the doors of the cathedral opened at the far end of the hall, and in stepped Abelard. Moving with a jauntiness that belied his three score years, he marched boldly down the aisle towards his judges.

The scholars in the hall started to cheer. "Abelard! Abelard! Abelard!" Acknowledging their applause like a victorious Roman general at a triumph, the great sage waved to his supporters as he advanced. Even when he reached the front to stand beside Bernard, the cheers still did not stop. Finally, annoyed with this extended tumult, the legate banged his staff upon the dais, until the scholars quieted their shouting.

"Peter Abelard," the legate said. "Are you ready to stand trial on charges of heresy?"

"Yes," said Abelard, pointedly omitting any honorific in his answer to the legate. "Let the debate begin."

Again the scholars broke into cheers. "Abelard! Abelard! Abelard!" I wanted to shout too, but standing so close to Odo and the King, I did not dare to do so. So instead I cheered him under my breath. There he was, the champion of reason, and master of the dialectic. There was no way that Bernard would be able to out debate him.

The legate banged his staff for order. Eventually obtaining the required degree of quiet, he spoke again. "Very well. Abbot Bernard of Clairvaux. Please state the case for the prosecution."

"Noble bishops," Bernard began. "Worthy legate of our most holy father in Rome. You have all read the writings of the accused, Peter Abelard. How do you judge them?"

"We judge them to be heretical," the legate replied. "We therefore condemn the accused and all of his writings."

"What!" cried Abelard. "Is there to be no trial? No presentation of evidence, argument of point and counterpoint, and no disputation?"

"You have had your trial," the legate said patiently. "All the evidence has been considered, and fair judgment has been made. Disputation would be pointless. However, if you choose, you may now recant and beg the court for mercy."

"I refuse to be thus judged like a guilty clerk," Abelard shouted, and turned to march back down the aisle towards the door.

"Seize him!" snapped the legate. Some constables stepped forward to execute the order, but before they could lay hands on Abelard, mobs of scholars barred their way. For a moment, it seemed as if the whole cathedral would dissolve into a bloody riot, for the constables had swords and the scholars always carried knives.

But before they could draw, Bernard yelled out; "Peace, let him go. He won't get far."

Arnold of Bresica ran to join Abelard, and was quickly followed by several other husky scholars, Alan among them, who flanked the sage as he marched out of the cathedral.

Paul of La Rochelle remained in the front row of spectators near the dais. I saw the look on his face as he watched Abelard make his retreat. It was like he had just seen the great library of Cordoba burned anew.

*** *** ***

I found out later from Alan that Abelard made it to Cluny, where he was given refuge by Peter the Venerable, the head of the rich and powerful Cluniac order. The Cluniacs were avid translators of old manuscripts, so presumably Abelard found some use for his talents there. But his days of disputation in the schools of Paris were done, and I am told that confined to the monastery he aged rapidly, and died there a few years later.

Arnold of Bresica continued on to Rome, where he revenged Abelard by causing Pope Innocent a great deal of trouble, going so far as to incite the people of the city to form a commune. This made the Pope so unhappy that he died of frustration, leaving it to his successor, Pope Eugenius, to calm matters by having Arnold executed.

The rest of us returned to Paris. There we received news to lift our spirits, but also to fill my heart with some trepidation. For after studying through the winter, and working through the spring, Papa was prepared to give his great machine a second trial.

Again Eleanor and Alicia accompanied me to Saint Denis to witness the event. This time the crowd gathered to watch was much bigger than the first, for nothing attracts the multitude better than the spectacle of observing others engaged in novel and dangerous enterprises.

I examined Papa's new engine. It was of the same general design as the first, but built much stouter. He had further strengthened it by having thick ropes fastened to the top and affixed at their other end to iron rods hammered deep into the ground. These rods were set off to either side of the engine tower, which had further reinforcing ropes attached in triangular fashion to its cantilevered lifting arm, so that the whole appeared like the mast, spar, and rigging of a ship suited for giants.

A line of posts had been set in the ground, with a rope strung between them to form a kind of fence to keep the crowd out of hazard's way. Town waifs kept ducking under this barrier to get closer, but Abbot Suger had stationed a line of workmen behind the barrier to chase them back. These guards were soon reinforced by burgher women on the other side, who helped by snatching the ears of children they spied advancing too far and pulling them back to safety.

The day was hot and sunny, but not a good one for a test, because there was no wind. So for several hours we sat upon large stone blocks, enduring the heat and passing the time in idle conversation and snacks purchased from vendors who thoughtfully descended upon the crowd with bread rolls and other items left unsold from the morning market.

As the hours wore on, some of the people began to leave, but most stayed, and the assemblage actually grew as idlers from further off arrived, then swelled to great numbers when the afternoon's end released droves of apprentice boys and spinner girls from their daily toils.

It was then, at about five hours after the strike of noon, that a breeze began to blow from the west. This quickly stiffened, and the canvas sails on the wind engine, which had been like drooping sacks for the entire day, turned into wings, and set the arms of the machine whirling about at breakneck speed. The water screw spun like a top, gushing forth a torrent that rapidly filled the basin atop the engine tower.

It was time for the test. At a signal from Abbot Suger, Papa pulled the rope to open the basin. Water poured down the pipe into the first windlass trough, and a moment later, with a tremendous clanking sound, the great wheel began to turn. Then a second trough moved into place, and filling, accelerated the motion of the wheel.

All the workers, the Sisters, the Abbot Suger, and I stood breathless in silence and watched as the rope tightened and strained. As the third trough filled, I said a prayer to the Virgin. The cargo platform began to lift.

Like Elijah's chariot ascending to heaven, the huge load of cut stone soared into the sky to reach the workmen waiting for it atop of the high buttress.

It was amazing. It was a miracle. The workmen cheered. I leaped the rope barrier and ran to hug Papa. Abbot Suger looked up to God in thanks, and the holy Sisters burst into song.

"Hallelujah, Hallelujah," they sang.

Chapter 22

The Fateful Visit of Petronilla

Thus were the first three years of the reign of the great Queen Eleanor spent.

Two more years past, each continuing the work begun before. With Eleanor's support, I continued the instruction of the knights of France in the chivalric code of King Arthur, and gentled them accordingly. We held more tournaments, and the Frankish knights became more skilled therein, displaying many fine stratagems even better than that which had won the day for the clever Lady Anne and the valiant Sir Pierre.

The wondrous cathedral continued to rise. But no matter how tall the walls towered, the mind of my father proved their equal, and was able to devise ever more ingenious lifting engines to build them yet higher.

Then, in the spring of the Year of Our Lord one thousand, one hundred, and forty two, new and portentous events were launched when we were visited unannounced at the palace by none other than Eleanor's younger sister, Petronilla.

Petronilla was seventeen years of age, a girl blooming in her new arrival at full womanhood. Like her sister, she was possessed of extraordinary beauty, but of a more purely feminine type. Her long hair was golden-red, her eyes blue, her features exquisite, her figure tallish yet very slim, her walk soft, graceful, and delicate in its sway. These appearances matched her character, for while Eleanor had taken her molding from Duke William, Paul, Phillipa, and Dangerosa all together, for Petronilla the sole source of education had been the seductive Viscountess, and it was to her arts of flirtation and bewitchment that the girl had entirely devoted herself.

Having come from refined Bordeaux to muddy Paris, Petronilla made her appearance in clothes, jewels, and shoes of the latest style, which caused Eleanor a bit of irk by casting her in the unaccustomed role of a country cousin. But Petronilla, while careful to be perfect in her wardrobe, wasted few words upon the subject. For just as the favorite tales of a fisherman concern not hooks, but fish, so Petronilla chose to deluge us with stories, not of clothes and baubles, but of the game they are purposed to ensnare.

Romance, love, affair, seduction, deception; these were the grist of Petronilla's mill, the font of her inspiration, and the passion of her life. A true lady of Aquitaine, she regarded such games as an expert jouster does the circuit of tournaments, and could spend hours talking about not only her own intrigues and encounters, but those of others, real, rumored, or imagined. About these she had many witty things to say, and much sage advice too, as she could analyze the methods that led to success or failure in any romantic affair with as much precision of intellect as Eleanor might employ to consider the moves that entailed victory or defeat in a game of chess.

Thus, though silly in most ways, Petronilla was wise in one. She was, in fact, a connoisseur of men. Not one walked past her glance but that she instantly sized him up, in most cases with remarkable accuracy. Like a true philosopher, she had developed a system of classification, so that each individual might be assigned to the universal category that represented his proper type, with each such type labeled by an animal of appropriate character.

For example, under this system, a brave, strong man of kingly disposition might be described as a lion. I say "might," because, needless to say, there were no such men to be found at the court of King Louis, so Petronilla had no cause to employ this designation. Instead, all of the knights and functionaries about the place were classified upon proper assessment as either bulls, wolves, pigs, or rats. Abbot Suger was a bear, Bernard of Clairvaux was a goat, and Odo was a snake.

Louis was a hen.

We also journeyed into the city to show Petronilla the sights and curiosities of the place. There we happened upon our scholar friends, who she duly classified as well. Becket was a sly fox; John an owl, wise in external appearance but empty headed inside; and Alan a redoubtable shepherd dog, a verdict which pleased me well, since these companionable creatures are strong, brave, loyal, and clever, yet eminently trainable.

Well, after spending a few days in amusing and instructing us with these fine insights, as well as other sharp and witty observations concerning the comical and crude nature of all things Frankish as seen through the eyes of a civilized foreigner, Petronilla finally found the time right to sit down with us on the terrace and confide to her elder sister the true reason for her visit.

"Dear Sister Eleanor," Petronilla began. "There is something very important that I wish to tell you."

"What is it?" Eleanor asked, clearly intrigued by her sister's sudden change to serious tone.

"It is this," Petronilla replied. "I am in love."

"In love?" Eleanor smiled in amusement. "You mean you have a new affair."

"No," said Petronilla. "I mean that I am deeply, truly, passionately, head over heels, in love with a wonderful man who I simply must have for my husband."

"With who?" Eleanor asked.

"Raoul of Vermandois," Petronilla said.

Eleanor raised a skeptical eyebrow. "Raoul of Vermandois? Count of the Vexin? Isn't he a bit old for you?"

"Oh no, dear sister, you do not understand." Petronilla sighed dreamily. "Raoul is a tiger."

"I see," said Eleanor, evincing instant comprehension. "However, there would appear to be a problem. Your tiger is already married."

"Now what is that supposed to mean?" Petronilla pouted. "You're the Queen. Surely you can arrange matters for your own sister."

"Dear Petronilla," Eleanor said softly. "This isn't Aquitaine. They don't do things that way here."

Petronilla stood up and stamped her foot, and spoke with real distress.

"Don't you 'dear Petronilla' me! I'm your only sister, and aside from Raymond, all that is left of our family. He has Antioch, you have Aquitaine and France, but what do I have? Nothing but a few dozen miserable castles and manors here and there. Now I have a chance to marry a great lover who is also a Count, and attain for myself a station in the world, which if not as exalted as your own, at least would be something. How can you deny me?"

Tears grew in Petronilla's pretty eyes, and she began to cry. "Eleanor, you are not being fair."

Eleanor reached out and hugged her sister, letting the younger girl weep on her shoulder.

Suddenly, the Queen appeared thoughtful. "You know," she said. "It just might be possible."

Instantly, Petronilla stopped weeping and pulled away to smile brilliantly at her sister. "Really?" she said. "How? What's your plan?"

Eleanor started walking about the terrace, talking with her finger in the air like a general thinking through his plan of campaign.

"The Vexin," the Queen began. "Is the county between France and

Flanders. Now Flanders is nominally our vassal, but we have almost no effective control over it, because we are separated by the Vexin. But if the Vexin could be brought into France by marriage to the sister of the Queen, that could change everything. I'm fairly certain Abbot Suger could be made to see things that way."

"Oh Eleanor," said Petronilla. "That's wonderful!"

"But," Alicia said. "What of Raoul's current wife?"

"That's the best part," said Eleanor. "She is the niece of the Count of Champagne, the King's most powerful vassal. By replacing her with Petronilla, we break a dangerous alliance between overmighty nobles, thereby forcing Champagne into proper subjection to France as well. It's perfect! For such a coup, Suger will move heaven and Earth. I suspect he'll find three friendly bishops to perform the required annulment before you can dance half a step."

"Wait here," Eleanor said. "I'll go talk with him now."

She returned less than an hour later, a smile upon her face. "Little sister," she said proudly. "You will soon be a Countess."

Petronilla ran to the Queen and hugged her with delight. "Eleanor," she said. "You are a genius, and the best sister a girl could ever hope for. I can't wait to tell Raoul!"

Her object won, Petronilla left Paris the next day, anxious both to escape the smelly town and to share the joys of victory with her tiger.

***   ***   ***

There was, however, one detail that Eleanor and Abbot Suger did not reckon on when they conceived and executed their plan. This was the unsuspected fact that Count Thibault of Champagne was not only the uncle of Raoul's scorned wife, but also cousin to Bernard of Clairvaux and the chief endower of his order. Thus, in seeking retaliation against France and the Vexin for their insult and betrayal of his interests, Thibault had recourse not only to his secular strength but supernatural allies as well.

So it was, that within weeks of the wedding of Petronilla and Raoul, Count Thibault and Bernard assembled a council of clerics in Champagne who drew up a writ of excommunication. This, being sent on to Rome with Bernard's strong endorsement, received instant approval from Pope Innocent, so that by fall, the ban came back excommunicating not only Raoul, Petronilla, and the three bishops who solemnized their marriage, but Eleanor and Louis as well.

Now Eleanor and Petronilla were from Aquitaine, where excommunication is considered no great affair. Their father, grandfather, and grandmother Dangerosa, had all been excommunicated, to no effect, and so the ban fell upon the two sisters like water on the backs of ducks. Count Raoul was from the north, where excommunication carries more weight, but he was a strong man, and able to bear up under the load. How the ban affected the three bishops, I do not know, as after performing the wedding, they ceased to figure in any account. But for pious Louis, excommunication was the greatest tragedy of his life, and he spent days weeping and wailing about the palace and praying loudly to God to have mercy upon his soul.

Had the matter ended there, this would not have been too bad, as the King was insufferable at all times regardless. However Count Thibault then announced that, as a true Christian, he could not be bound by an oath of fealty to a King who had left the faith, and called upon all the other powers of the realm to join with him in casting off the yoke of the atheist who sat upon the throne. Such a revolution, Eleanor explained to me, must always have been the Count's secret design. With the active support of Rome, which apparently saw advantage to itself in fragmenting the kingdom into a more easily controlled mangle of Dukedoms and counties, Thibault's insurrection threatened to reduce the realm to anarchy.

Chapter 23

The War with Champagne

War was now imminent. For its defense, France could count only upon itself, Aquitaine, Poitiou, and the Vexin. These were more than enough to defeat Champagne. However to the west lay Anjou, Normandy, England and Brittany, and to the north lay Flanders, and were these warlike countries to all join the revolt, the kingdom must surely be doomed. But Eleanor wrote to the Empress Matilda, heir to England and Normandy by her grandfather, William the Conqueror, and wife of Duke Geoffrey of Anjou, and urged her neutrality.

"Dear Matilda," she wrote. "As you and I are both by right Queens, we share a sisterhood and a common interest in the prevention of unlawful revolutions. As we now face the rebel Count of Champagne in France, so you confront the usurper Stephen of Blois, who hopes to steal for himself your own realm in England. Our causes are thus conjoined, for should either aid in insurrection against the other, we would overthrow the principles of justice and order upon which both our thrones depend, and upon which all legal authority must always find its necessary foundation. Rather than be the causes of such catastrophe, dear sister Queen, let us pledge each other our friendship, and as loyal friends agree always to forbear from giving aid of any kind, be it horses, men, gold, or words, to the rebellious enemies of the other."

It was this exceedingly clever letter, written by the great Queen Eleanor with my assistance on matters of style, that saved France. Because of its eloquent statement, carefully uniting in one theme both self-interest and justice, Matilda and Geoffrey rebuffed Thibault's hypocritical rebellion, and chose instead to direct their efforts towards defending their own lawful interests in England. With Anjou, Normandy, and England out of the battle, Brittany was cut off from any involvement too. This was very fortunate, since the Bretons, as is well known, are the bravest and most skillful warriors all in the world, and could have destroyed France in the blink of an eye had they taken it upon themselves to do so. And once the Bretons and the rest had decided to stand aside, Flanders wisely chose neutrality as well, since to join Champagne alone against France, Aquitaine, Poitiou and the Vexin would have been to recklessly enlist with the losing side.

The war was now cast more favorably. But it was clear to both Eleanor and Abbot Suger that, notwithstanding France's current advantage, it was imperative that quick action be taken to thrash Champagne into submission before Matilda finished with Stephen of Blois. Otherwise, despite the presumed sisterhood of Queens, the universal interest of monarchs in lawful order, and all the rest of the high and refined sentiments expressed in our letter, she might change her mind. For principles are to monarchs but elegant clothing for interests, which like all of us, are naked under their clothes. So France needed to invade Champagne.

But when a war is waged to reassert the authority of a monarch to rule over his vassals, the world expects that King to lead the forces who battle on his behalf. For if he will not fight for himself, why should others fight for him? If he cannot play the King, why should he be the King?

Now Louis had gone all to pieces after his excommunication. It was necessary, therefore, for Eleanor and Abbot Suger to find some way to put him back together. This they did by explaining to him, as they might to a child, that it was not any sin of his own that had caused his excommunication, but the miscreance of the Count of Champagne. This rebellious vassal, they made clear, had used his dishonest influence to deceive the good Pope into issuing the ban. Punish Thibault, squeeze him hard enough, and he could be forced to reverse himself. "Do you wish readmission to communion, Louis?" they reasoned. "Then pull yourself together and defeat Champagne."

It may seem strange that two high advisors should need to employ such a convoluted plea to persuade a King to defend his throne. But the fact is that Louis cared more about his personal salvation than he did the safety of his kingdom. Some may call this piety, but I do not. For this very obsession led the King to omit fulfillment of the duties that God truly requires of those He appoints to such office.

Now the intellect of King Louis was not something firm and substantial that could be moved or rotated by a precise sequence of rational arguments. Rather, his mind was more like a pool of mud, upon which a new idea could be placed like a stone which only much pushing and the gradual passage of time might allow to sink in. So there was no single conversation in which Abbot Suger and Eleanor convinced Louis he needed to act.

However, when the King's dim understanding finally grasped their point, he became like a man transformed. Overnight, it seemed, he turned from a headless hen to a second Vercingetorix – not in competence of course, but in militant ardor to come to grips with the enemy. He started tramping about the palace with the gait of a knight, issuing impatient orders for more forces and less delay.

The Kings' transformation aroused considerable enthusiasm among the knights, and indeed many other orders of the people. For it appeared that the peril of the kingdom had caused God to work a miracle, giving the nation a fighting leader in its hour of need. This, together with the fact that our cause was manifestly just, and the odds were sharply in our favor, caused war fever to sweep the whole Isle de France. Victory was now certain, and with victory would come plentiful spoils from the rich lands of Champagne. Droves rushed to enlist, for men love riches, and if they can be won in a just cause, that is a good thing too. A mighty army of knights and mercenaries was thus soon assembled and prepared to march forth.

I was surprised, though, to learn that Alan had also decided to join the expedition, as he was neither so high as to expect a reward of lands as spoil, nor so low as to go to war in the hope of seizing a few cows. He explained it to me, though, over a cup of wine in a tavern the night before he set forth.

"I'm going as the expedition's scribe," he said.

"Not as a warrior?" I asked, wondering, for I knew he had once been trained as a knight.

"No," said Alan. "If I thought the King needed fighting men, I would go in that guise, as the cause is just, and it would be a disaster if France were to lose. But the French have Champagne outnumbered three to one, so there is no fear of defeat. It's not going to be much of a war, more of a few weeks walk in the country I should think. But Abbot Suger came to the school and asked if there were any among us who would be willing to go along as the expedition's chronicler, for victories need to be recorded if they are to be remembered. Much as the history of Herodotus gave a common heritage to the Greeks, the good Abbot wants the tale of Louis' glorious feats of arms written down to inspire all futurity with his vision of a grand France."

I smiled. "I see. So you are to be the Herodotus of France."

"Yes," said Alan proudly. The knights can't write, and the clerics have no understanding of military affairs. So I will be the Herodotus of this war."

"I see," I laughed. "And perhaps compare to the original as closely Louis compares to Leonidas."

This was gentle mockery. Herodotus' hero Leonidas was a fierce warrior king who led the brave three hundred Spartans to fight to the death in defense of the pass at Thermopylae. But sometimes a lass feels it necessary to trifle with a lad, and this was one of those times. Fortunately, my friend did not take it amiss.

Alan blushed charmingly. "Well," he said. "Hopefully I will be able to do better than such a comparison might portend."

I raised my cup. "To a swift campaign, and an immortal history."

Alan touched his cup to mine. Then we drank deep and parted.

***   ***   ***

It did prove to be a swift campaign, and a victorious one too, for the army returned to Paris within three months of leaving, with little loss and few wounded. But as I stood with the other burghers to cheer the returning troops, it seemed to me that there was something amiss. For though the mercenary infantry seemed happy enough with their spoils of geese, cattle, and other petty loot, the knights appeared uneasy in their saddles, and few responded with any enthusiasm to the cheers of the crowd. Then I saw Louis, his face as white as a sheet, his eyes bulging, shivering in his saddle despite the warmth of the day. Odo rode next to him, guiding the King's horse, his mouth set in a grim and determined line. Finally, riding at the very end of the column came Alan, his countenance like stone, staring straight ahead with the expression of one who has seen the apocalypse.

"Alan," I cried, waving to get his attention. "Alan!"

Alan turned, and seeing me, slowly showed some recognition. "Marie," he said softly. Then he dismounted and, taking my hand, silently led me and his mount away from the crowd to a quiet place by the side of the river. He tied the horse to a bush to let it eat, then picked up a stone and threw it in the water

"Alan," I said softly. "What happened? I heard that you won."

"Yes," Alan said bitterly. "We won." Then he tossed another stone, very hard, so it made a loud splash.

"Then what is wrong?"

Alan turned to me, his look verging on anger. "You want to know what is wrong? I'll tell you what is wrong. Your King is a madman."

I noticed that Alan said "your King." Not "our King," or "the King," but "your King." Clearly Louis had done something that made Alan very angry, and even displeased most of the knights. But if the war had been won, what could that be?

"Alan," I pleaded. "Please tell me what happened."

Alan threw another rock. Then he let out a deep breath and faced me again, this time looking more sad than angry. "Very well. I'll tell you."

There was a worn down stone wall nearby, about the right height for a bench, and he gestured to it, indicating that I should have a seat. I sat down and he sat nearby. Then he began.

"Well, as you know, we moved out of Paris in July. Things went well at first. In fact, we advanced into Champagne virtually unopposed until we reached the river Marne in August. There we encountered the army of Count Thibault."

"So then there was a battle?" I said.

"No," said Alan. "His forces were on one side of the river, and we were on the other. We had him well outnumbered, and could have forced the crossing for a direct assault. That's what many of the knights wanted to do, and it's the course I would have chosen as well. But the King's advisor, a cleric named Odo, said this would prove too risky. Instead he argued that we should stay on our own side of the river, and devastate the villages of Champagne. If the Count wanted to stop us, he would have to attempt the crossing in the face of our greater numbers, and all the advantage of the battle would be ours. If he refused to do this, we could wreck the farms of all his peasants, and so ruin his revenue for the year. Either way, our victory would be a certainty. The King agreed with Odo, and this plan became our strategy."

"How infamous," I said.

"Yes," said Alan. "But unfortunately it is a standard tactic recommended by cowards under many similar circumstances.

"So we marched along the Marne, seizing everything of value in our path, daring the Count to cross and give battle. This, of course, he would not do, but simply kept pace on the opposite side to offer defense to the other half of his county. Then we came to the large village of Vitry.

"By this time it was September, and the King was getting anxious lest the campaigning season end without drawing the war to a conclusion. So Odo said that at Vitry, we would force Thibault's hand by not merely seizing the livestock and the crops in their fields, but burn the entire place to the ground. Not a tree in any orchard, not a vine in any vineyard, and not a house, barn, mill, or shop in the village would be left standing. The Count would be made to understand, that should he continue his cowardly patrolling on the opposite bank of the river, he would not only lose the revenues of his villages on our side for this year, but forever. Thus he would have no choice but to come and give battle. Louis agreed, and the knights were drawn up by the river to defeat Thibault when he made his move. Then the mercenaries were ordered to prepare to torch the town."

"But the poor villagers," I said, horrified. "What would happen to them with their houses all aflame?"

"Exactly," said Alan. "So I broke my place and spoke up. 'Sire,' I said. 'Surely you must take some measure to protect the peasants from the fires.'

"To this the King thought for a moment, then turned to Odo. 'Odo,' he said. 'Have the soldiers put the peasants in the church. God will protect them there.'

"'But your majesty,' I said. 'The church is made of wood. It may catch fire too.'

"At this the King looked at me like I had committed heresy. 'God will protect those who gather in his own house,' he insisted. Then he turned to Odo and said, 'And see that the doors to the Church are barred once they are inside. I want none going out to be harmed by the flames.'

Hearing this, I had a sinking feeling that I knew what was to happen next. But I could only listen as the story proceeded towards its horrific conclusion.

Alan continued. "I tried to plead with him, but it was to no avail. Then the houses were set aflame, and sure enough, the wind blew the fire upon the church. Soon it was smoking, then burning, and we could hear the cries of the poor people inside shouting and banging upon the barred doors in an effort to escape.

"'Let them out, Your Majesty!' I cried. 'For God's sake, Sire, quickly, give the order to let them out!'

"The King said, 'They are in God's hands.' Then ignoring me thereafter, knelt and began to pray feverishly to the Almighty to save the people in the burning church. He crossed himself more times than I could count, stretched his arms wide, and begged God to show mercy, to bring rain, or snow, or whatever miracle he might will, but only, please rescue the humble people in the church.

"It was a charnel house. You could not only hear them dying, you could smell them burning. But still he would not give the order to free them.

"After a few more minutes the screaming stopped, and there was no sound from the church but the crackle of the flames. When finally the fire burnt itself out, and the place cooled down, we went inside and found the bodies of over a thousand people, men women,. children, and many little babies, all burned or smoked to death."

"Mother of God!" I cried. Crossing myself, I said a prayer for all those poor souls.

Alan waited until I was done. Then he continued. "Well, Count Thibault did not rise to the bait and kept his forces safely on the other bank, but the next day he sent a messenger across the river to seek peace terms. Odo had to handle these negotiations because the King was too distraught to talk with anyone. However the foul cleric got what we wanted. In exchange for our withdrawal from his County, Thibault agreed to arrange with Bernard of Clairvaux to have the excommunications lifted. Further, with Louis' fellowship in the faith reestablished, the Count assented to renew his own oath of fealty to the King."

I shook my head. "So in consequence of burning a thousand helpless people to death, the King has been readmitted to the communion of the church."

"Yes," said Alan.

I didn't know what to say. I knew what Kate would say, but I am not a Cathar. I believe in our holy faith and the virtue and merit of our church. There are some things, however, that I do not understand.

"But," said Alan. "I cannot remain the subject of such a King. I am leaving France tomorrow."

I was very sad to hear this.

"I wish you would stay," was all I could say.

"Why?" he said.

Why? How could he not know why? His answer completely infuriated me.

"Go then," I shouted. "Go, you traitor! I never want to see you again."

Alan's face darkened with anger. He turned from me, took his horse, and stalked away without saying another word

I ran back to the palace, and told Eleanor and Alicia everything.

I had just stopped weeping, when an hour later, Odo and Louis entered the Queen's private apartments.

Chapter 24

The Purification of Paris

"Eleanor," the King said harshly. "You must repent."

"What?" said Eleanor, startled by this commencement. "What are you talking about?"

Louis was livid. "Have you no shame, woman? Look what you have done!"

Eleanor blinked, slowly divining the King's meaning. "Are you referring to the massacre at Vitry?"

"Of course!" Louis exclaimed. "What else would I be referring to. The whole world is talking about it. So many innocents dead! Their blood is on your hands."

"My hands?" cried Eleanor. "I wasn't even there!"

"No," said Louis. "But you were the cause of this war. Your willingness to overthrow holy writ for the sake of your sister's carnal whims, that's what caused it all!"

Eleanor stood firm. "We all agreed," she said. "You, I, and Abbot Suger, that it would be in the best interests of France to create a closer alliance with the Vexin. Petronilla's fancies were of only incidental importance."

"Oh, you were clever," Louis said bitterly. "I'll grant you that. But see what your clever deception has wrought. Have you no conscience? A county has been half destroyed, a thousand poor people have been burned to death, all because of your impiety."

"Louis," Eleanor said sternly. "It was you who killed those people."

"No," said Louis. "No. I was merely acting a part in a pageant authored by you. This war was your creation, and the guilt for its horrid consequence is yours as well."

"I see," said Eleanor. "So I am also to blame for your cowardly decision to make war on the Count's peasants, but not on his knights?"

Odo interrupted. "So what would you have had the King do, Eleanor?" he said in a mocking voice. "Charge into battle at full tilt? Right across the river at the enemy?"

"Yes," said Eleanor defiantly. "That's what I would have done, had I been there."

Odo smiled. "How easy it is for women, who never need risk themselves in combat, to advise men how they should behave in battle."

Eleanor shook her head. "It's also what my ancestor Charlemagne would have done, and did more than once.

"Charlemagne was my ancestor too, Eleanor," said Louis

"Perhaps," said Eleanor. "But if so, I am sure that he spins in his tomb whenever he thinks upon it."

"That was outrageous," said Odo. "How can you say such things? Have you ever stopped to think, even for a moment, why Charlemagne and other so-called hero kings could act the way they did, while our own King Louis must act the way he does?"

Eleanor regarded Odo in a puzzled manner, then shrugged. "Actually," she said. "I wonder upon it almost every night."

"Well then," said Odo heatedly. "Perhaps you might find the answer to your wondering by looking in the glass! King Louis cannot risk himself in battle because, unlike Charlemagne, he has no heir."

Eleanor shook her head. "Are you claiming that it is my fault that Louis does not have an heir?"

Louis broke in. "Of course it is your fault, Eleanor. It is your duty to provide me with a son, and you have failed to do it. So, would you have me throw France into chaos by charging myself into battle? Your failure forced the pillaging tactic upon me."

Eleanor held both her fingers up in the manner of a holy sister about to tell some children an important lesson. "Let me explain something to you Louis," she began. "In order for a man and woman to conceive a child, they must first…"

"Silence, woman!" Louis shouted. "I know your answer for everything. Sin! Sin, sin, and more sin! I know your deceptions now, daughter of Eve, and you shall not tempt me again."

Eleanor closed her mouth and shuddered in frustration.

Louis continued. "Your sinful ways have devastated my kingdom, and caused me to take actions that have placed my soul in mortal jeopardy. But that is over now. I have been readmitted to the church, and from now on I will be a good soldier for the church. Abbot Bernard has explained to me what I need to do. As my first act, I am going to put an end to these heresies that you have been spreading in my kingdom."

Eleanor seemed thunderstruck. "Are you mad? I am no preacher of heresies."

"Perhaps not," said Louis. "But you have brought in your train people who are."

"What you are talking about?" Eleanor asked.

"Don't act the innocent with us," Odo said. "We know all about these people that you have brought into Paris; lovers of paganism, pretended converts, heretics, all here to cast doubt and ridicule on holy writ. They will be brought to account immediately. We are going to issue our first arrest warrants this very afternoon. France will not be turned into another Aquitaine, a country which laughs at God."

"Yes," said Louis. "And you should help us with this, if you value your salvation. For now you have had a chance to see the destruction which such impiety brings."

Eleanor nodded thoughtfully. "I see what you mean. I have sinned and must make amends. Very well then, let us be united in this effort. So hold off until the morrow so we can act on this together before witnesses in the palace chapel after morning mass. Then all will know where I stand."

Louis smiled beatifically. "Oh, Eleanor, I am so happy to hear you say this." He turned to Odo. "Come Odo, let us go to the chapel now and give thanks. This is indeed a great day."

The King walked out the door. Odo bowed lightly to the Queen, then followed Louis out.

As soon as they were gone, Eleanor turned to us with determined eyes.

"We need to get Paul of La Rochelle out of the city," she said. "Tonight."

"And Kate too," I burst out, having followed the meaning of the previous conversation with dismay. "But how?"

"We could arrange for a horse and wagon easily enough," said Alicia.

"Yes," I said. "But the roads are filled with highwaymen, and there'll be constables after them too before long. They both speak like foreigners, so the villagers won't protect them. An old man and a woman traveling alone will stand no chance."

"That's true," said Eleanor. "We need a man, one who can fight."

They both turned and looked at me. It took a moment for me to grasp their implication.

"You want me to try to recruit Alan?" I said.

"He seems the type," said Eleanor. "And none of the knights around here are of any use."

"Yes," I said. "But you don't understand. He hates me now. He won't

169

help."

"Marie," Eleanor smiled. "He doesn't hate you. He's just angry at you."

I shook my head. "You should have seen his face after I called him a traitor. I don't know how I can talk to him. I don't know what to say."

Alicia held her finger in the air in the manner of one giving a lesson. "Here, I'll show you. This is what you say. Do it just like this."

Then she folded her arms together, tilted her head up at an aristocratic angle, and looked down on me through shaded eyelids. "Alan," she said in a lofty tone. "There is a service that I require of you."

Then she dropped her pose and spoke naturally. "That's how you do it."

Eleanor nodded in agreement. "That's right. Say it just that way and he'll do whatever you ask. It works every time."

I started to open my mouth to reply, but Eleanor cut me off. "Now go."

***   ***   ***

I found Alan in the second hour before midnight, in the fifth tavern that I searched. The place was nearly empty, and he was alone at a table with John of Salisbury sharing farewell drinks. He saw me enter, and greeted me with a frown.

"Oh," he said. "So if it isn't the virtuous maiden, come hither to denounce the traitor to her glorious King Louis."

"Alan," I said. "I'm sorry."

"Sorry?" said Alan. "If you were a man you would pay with your life for what you said to me today." He shook his head and gave me a sour look. "Tell me, Marie, what is it that you admire so much about the King? Is it his burning of churches or the people inside?"

"That's not fair," I cried. "I don't follow Louis, I follow Eleanor."

"His wife," said Alan. "And equally great. After all, the world must salute a woman who starts a war so that her sister can commit adultery."

"The war was about politics," I said. "And if Eleanor had been leading it instead of Louis, there would have been no massacre. She would have charged the enemy."

"Ah yes," said Alan. "I can just see it. The great Duke William's granddaughter leading knights into battle in true chivalrous style. Well, I can tell you that there is just about as much chance of that ever happening as there is of the battle of the Marne being writ down in history as France's greatest victory."

"So," he continued. "If you don't follow Louis, why did you call me a traitor? Do you think it's a term to be used lightly?"

"Alan," I said, tearfully unable to hold back truth. "I didn't call you a traitor for betraying Louis. I called you a traitor for betraying me."

"That's a lie!" Alan bellowed. "Betray you? I've never touched a hair on your head!"

"You see, Alan," John said. "How she rewards all your kindness. You treat her like a younger sister and she bites you like a viper."

So that was how Alan saw me, as a younger sister. I felt a dry taste in my mouth as the last of my girlish illusions concerning this man evaporated. Still, I had a mission to accomplish.

John rambled on. "That's what all women are like, Alan. Use them if you must, but avoid them if you can. Take my advice friend, and join the priesthood. It's the only way to live."

I boxed John about the ears. "John," I said. "Shut your head."

As John whimpered from my rough treatment, Alan just shrugged and took a drink. Despite my feelings of disappointment with him, I had to admire his coolness.

I drew myself up as Alicia had instructed me. "Alan," I said, in a fair imitation of her style. "There is a service that I require of you."

Alan put down his cup. "Really. What is this service that my lady requires of her traitor?"

"Treason," I said.

Alan arched his eyebrow, and a trace of smile curled his lip. He gestured to an empty seat by the side of the table, and set a drink before it.

"So," he said. "Exactly what do you have in mind?"

I sat down, quaffed the cup, and explained the situation. The two scholars heard me out in silence.

"So we need your help," I concluded.

"Don't do it, Alan," John said. "It's not worth ruining yourself for the sake of a pair of heretics."

"Alan," I pleaded. "He was a friend of Abelard's."

"Yes," said John. "And look where such friends got him. You should let the two of them be arrested. They're a danger both to the kingdom and to us – the false convert philosopher even more than the heretic. Men like him go about ridiculing holy writ, undermining respect for established belief, law and custom. Look at the catastrophe that has caused."

The similarity between John's argument and Odo's struck me, and I had

171

a dark thought. Perhaps there was a Judas at Abelard's last supper.

"Is that why you betrayed him?" I said.

John blanched at my accusation, but quickly recovered himself. "Not betrayed, revealed," he said self-righteously. "The lawful authorities have a right to know what is going on in their kingdom. If we scholars are to be allowed to carry on our work, we need to show that we are dutiful, orthodox, and loyal, and not a mob of crazed atheists, skeptics, and heretics. Otherwise we risk our entire enterprise."

"And no doubt you will receive preferment from the church for your tale telling," I commented.

"As well I should," John said proudly. "Someone had to tell the truth about what doctrines are being spread in our schools, and that is what I did. A thousand poor people are dead because of the atheistic teachings of that man. He deserves his punishment."

Alan nodded thoughtfully, taking in all that John had said. I made a final plea.

"Alan," I said. "That man fought by the side of the Cid. Will you desert him?"

A fire blazed forth in Alan's eyes. "No," he said. "By God I will not."

Alan stood up so suddenly that his chair fell over backwards behind him. He balled his fists and glared at John with a face so stern as to command instant confession.

John shook in his chair. "I won't do anything to stop you Alan," he said, fear quivering his voice. "I swear. I've spoken my piece, but I'll say not another word to anyone. I swear it, not another word."

Alan regarded his companion carefully, then nodded. "Very well," he said, apparently satisfied. "See that you don't." Then he turned to me. "Come on Marie. We have treason to do, and the night is wasting."

*** *** ***

It was midnight when we reached the house on the Street of Strangers, but it took only one knock on the door to summon Paul, for he was still awake working upon his translation. Upon hearing the news, he instantly aroused Kate, and despite some bickering and much running up and down the staircase, the two had packed up all they would take in a few boxes and cases in less than half an hour. Apparently this was an occasion they had anticipated, and to some degree rehearsed.

172

Alan hauled the containers to the side of the street, all except for three. One of these was a small heavy chest which Kate insisted on carrying herself. This, I concluded, must be her hard won treasury. The other two were a leathern satchel containing one book and many papers which Paul slung over his shoulder, and a long thin box that he held tightly in both his hands. Thus to the last he clung to the book he rescued from Cordoba, but even more did he hold dear his ancient sword from Valencia.

We heard a clattering sound, and from the end of the street we perceived in the dim moonlight a rider upon a horse, and another driving a light wagon. These were Eleanor and Alicia.

Eleanor dismounted, ran to Paul, and hugged him warmly. Then she kissed him lightly upon the forehead, and as she did so, I could see that there were tears in the corner of her eyes.

"May God protect you, dear teacher," she said.

"Thank you, Eleanor," Paul said. "You don't know how much it means to me that you should remember me at such a time. You have made my life worthwhile."

While they were talking thus, Alan was loading the boxes upon the cart. Eleanor turned to him.

"Alan," she said. "I understand you are from Normandy, and planning to return."

"Yes," said Alan. "My father has been asking me to come home and fight with the rest of our family for Matilda. After Vitry, I decided he was right."

"Good," Eleanor said, drawing forth a letter from her cloak. "Then here is a missive from me to the Empress, commending Paul and Kate to her care. Tell her I would take it as a personal favor, and the act of a true friend, if she would provide for their safety."

"Of course," said Alan, taking the letter.

Eleanor reached into the blanket roll behind her horse's saddle and withdrew something long and thin.

"You'll need a sword if you are to make it through to Normandy," she said. "This was all I could find." She handed the weapon to Alan.

Alan drew the sword from its sheath. As he did so, I could see that it was a fine piece of work, made for two hands, and nearly as long as I am tall. The sharp edged blade glinted in the moonlight, and a dozen red and green jewels shown in its gilded handle. I gasped to look upon it, for it was the most magnificent weapon I had ever seen. Alan more fondled it than held it, and his eyes filled with wonder as he scanned its every aspect and part.

"You must name it Durandel," I urged, for such a sword could have no other name. Durandel was the sword of the matchless knight Roland, who was, by the way, a Breton.

"I would," said Alan, with a sad note in his voice. "But I cannot accept it. Such a sword can only be wielded by a lawfully dubbed knight." He handed it back to Eleanor. "I am unworthy."

The Queen seemed dumbfounded by this unexpected response, but only for a moment. Recovering herself, she spoke with dignity.

"Very well," she said. "Alan of Cherbourg, kneel before me."

Alan quickly knelt before the Queen.

"Alan of Cherbourg," Eleanor said, holding out the sword above him. "With this sword, Durandel, I dub thee knight, and charge thee with thy duty to always be brave and fight for the right, defend the weak and helpless, honor and protect women, be loyal to your liege, and ever faithful to your word and honor." Saying this, she tapped him upon both shoulders.

I stepped forward, and balling my fist, delivered the accolade as hard as I could. "And by this, I hold thee always to remember it!"

The blow knocked him halfway over, and hurt my hand so much I had to shake it, but it made me feel good inside.

Alan righted himself, and rubbed the side of his head where I had struck it. "Not bad, Marie," he said, shaking the stars from around his eyes. "Not bad."

"Rise, Sir Alan," Eleanor said grandly.

Alan rose, and smiling beatifically accepted Durandel from the Queen. "Thank you, Your Majesty," he said. "You may count on me to get them to safety."

Eleanor handed him the lead to the horse, which was not her favorite Andalusian stallion Pegasus, but a good war horse of the Percheron type. "Here," she said. "This is for you as well. Now go, and make some distance from Paris, for by midday there will be constables out after you."

Alan nodded, and seeing Kate and Paul both seated already upon the wagon, turned to me.

"Farewell Marie," he said. Then he walked away, and with the wagon following, disappeared into the dark.

That was it. No goodbye kiss, no holding hands in the moonlight, no pledge to return, nothing. Just "farewell Marie," and he was gone.

As we walked back to the palace, I put him out of my mind. Thinking instead upon Paul and Kate, I wondered about their fate, and about their curious companionship. Would they stay together? Despite his age, Paul was not completely helpless. Why did he choose to put up with such a haughty housekeeper?

I asked Eleanor what she thought about this.

"Isn't it obvious," the Queen replied. "She is his daughter."

How strange, I thought, that those who love prefer to act as they do not, and only risk showing it by subterfuge. How strange, that we should so willfully deny ourselves happiness.

Chapter 25

Birth of the Universitas

Thus ended the year of our Lord one thousand one hundred, and forty three. Some friends were gone, but peace had been restored, the excommunications all lifted, and the work on the cathedral of light had advanced greatly.

Around Christmastime, we received a letter from Raymond, telling of much daring feats valiantly accomplished in defense of his realm of Antioch, and of his many grand dreams and projects to turn it into a country of unparalleled magnificence and happiness. He also told of his love for his young wife Constance, who, although an Armenian, was beautiful, charming, warm of heart, and accomplished in every way that a fine Princess should be.

Things slowed down during the midwinter, as they always do, but with the approach of spring came new life, new joys, and new excitements.

The great day arrived during the month of the Ram. I was practicing my lute when a maid entered and told me the news. Mad for confirmation, I ran to find Eleanor.

I found her upon the terrace, playing chess with Lady Alicia.

"Can it be true?" I asked, more breathless from my feelings than from my run.

Eleanor looked up from her game. "Yes," she said. "The Cathedral is to be consecrated."

It was really so! My eyes went wide with joy. "When?"

"Two months after Easter," Eleanor said, then looked down at the board and moved a pawn.

Two months after Easter was just three months hence. How could that be?

"But it is not done," I said.

"Of course not," Eleanor faced up from her game again. "These things are never done. But the Abbot Suger has decided, and I agree, that the time has come for it to be ornamented and blessed so that it may start its service as a house of worship."

Alicia smiled. "It's going to be a grand occasion. All of France will be there."

"O glorious day!" I said. But then I had a thought. "Have they decided what music will be sung?" I asked.

Eleanor shrugged. "Music? I don't know. Some holy music, I suppose. Monks grunting prayers. The usual."

I looked at her with pleading eyes. "Your Majesty, that must not be."

Now Eleanor seemed puzzled. "I don't understand," she said.

"Surely we can do better!" I said, the fire of the idea rising within me. "This new church is a thing of divine inspiration. It must be consecrated by music that is worthy of it; music that fills the soul with the Holy Spirit, even as does the amazing cathedral of light itself."

Eleanor and Alicia exchanged skeptical glances.

"What would that be?" Eleanor asked doubtfully.

"The music of the Abbess Hildegard von Bingen," I replied, waxing ever more enthusiastic. "I have heard it from some of the nuns in the City. It is a new kind of music, sung with many voices, some together, others apart. It sounds like a chorus of a thousand angels!"

Eleanor raised her eyebrows.

"Your Majesty," I cried fervently. "When you hear it, you can hear heaven!"

Now Eleanor and Alicia looked at each other in wonder.

Eleanor stood up. "Well then," she said. "In that case, let's go pay a visit to Abbot Suger and tell him that such is what we want. A thousand angels are not to be missed."

***   ***   ***

So into the town we went, not in disguise, but in our own persons, dressed for the palace and riding upon fine horses with an escort of mounted knights.

As we traveled, commoners of every type cleared the street and bowed low. As we approached St. Denis, a scholar bowed, but then glanced up. It was Thomas à Becket.

He called out to the Queen. "Your Majesty!"

He straightened up and took a step in her direction, but was instantly called out by one of the knights.

"You there," the knight shouted. "Stay back from the Queen."

177

Eleanor lifted her hand. "It's all right, Sir Jean," she said. Then she looked down at the scholar. "Master Becket, how nice to see you again."

She beckoned him to approach, but kept riding, forcing Becket to scurry along swiftly at her spurs to keep up.

"Praise God we have met this day," Becket said. "Have you heard the news?" His voice was desperate. Clearly he was not referring to the announcement of the Cathedral's consecration.

"What news?" the Queen inquired.

Becket said, "Gilbert of Poiree and William of Conches both have had their work proscribed, and are themselves banished from the City."

Eleanor stopped her horse and looked down at the scholar. "Gilbert and William both banished?" she said. "I had heard an inquiry was underway but..."

Becket's words flew out in a torrent. "The Abbot Bernard of Clairvaux sped the matter. He met him them yesterday to debate before the fathers, but without allowing a word in reply, had all their work condemned."

"Just like he did to Abelard," Eleanor said.

I looked at Eleanor and Alicia, my heart filling with dismay. "How can this be?" I said. "Abbot Bernard is reputed the holiest man in Christendom. Some say he is a saint. How can he do such evil things?"

Eleanor's face darkened. "I can see how," she said, but did not explain herself further. Instead she looked down and asked, "So, Master Becket, what has been the response of the scholars?"

"Most are submitting," Becket answered. "But I am leaving. There's no use schooling where thought is forbidden. Duke Geoffrey of Anjou has offered me a place in his court tutoring his son Henry, who has a fair claim for the English crown through his mother Matilda, the granddaughter of the Conqueror."

Eleanor tilted her head. "Sounds like you've made the most of a bad affair," she said, with an odd little laugh. "Fare thee well, Master Becket. Give my regards to Duke Geoffrey and his fortunate wife."

Becket bowed his farewell. Eleanor snapped her reins, and we rode on.

*** *** ***

When we reached St. Denis, we found Abbot Suger in his office. We allowed him to share some of his good wine with us. Then Eleanor asked him if he was acquainted with the new music.

"Yes," Suger replied. "I have heard the hymns of Hildegard von Bingen. Some of the sisters have been singing them for our workmen, to add joy to their labor. But are you suggesting that such novelties should be sung at so solemn an occasion as the consecration of our glorious cathedral?"

"Why not?" Eleanor said. "I am told that they bring to Earth the sounds of heaven."

Abbot Suger nodded his head. "Yes," he conceded. "In a way they do. But Your Majesty, this will be an affair of the greatest moment. And while I am all for women participating in the work of the Church in their way, to have female voices be the ones heard at…"

"Enough," Eleanor cut him off. "If female silver was good enough to build this cathedral, female voices will be good enough to sing in it."

"Very well," Suger sighed. "Actually, I rather enjoy it myself. But Abbot Bernard will probably have apoplexy.

"Indeed," Eleanor said. "Another good reason to use it."

Abbot Suger grunted a mischievous grunt.

"So," Eleanor said. "I heard he had Gilbert of Poiree and William of Conches both banished."

"Yes," the Abbot sighed. "The proscription was read yesterday."

Eleanor looked hard at the man. "Is there nothing you can do?"

Abbot Suger shook his head. "No. The Cathedral school is an institute of the Church, and the orders to deal with that pair came straight from Rome."

"It's a shame," Eleanor said. "Those men are ornaments to our kingdom."

"Quite," the Abbot replied. "Not that I share their irreverence, of course.

But they had a way of arousing the enthusiasm of the young men for philosophy. I'm afraid that with first Abelard, then now these two gone, and the other bold thinkers under threat, we'll lose all the good scholars."

Eleanor's eyes grew angry. "You said we would have a great school here," she said, as if berating a cobbler for selling her a bad shoe. "A school without scholars is no school at all!"

Abbot Suger lifted his hands helplessly. "What can I do?" he asked. "Rome rules in these things. When the schoolmen step too far, they get crushed."

Eleanor looked out the window at the smoky city. "They need some kind of protection," she mused.

The Abbot's face now showed alarm. "You are thinking dangerous thoughts, Your Majesty," he warned. "You know how the Church will respond to any monarch who contests its power. And in any case, Louis would never…"

Eleanor lifted her hand. "Yes, I know," she said. "But still…"

The prospects seemed hopeless. But suddenly, like one who sees when a flash of lightning illuminates the darkest night, I had an idea.

"The scholars need a guild," I said.

Eleanor turned to me. "What?" she asked, bewildered by my comment.

I explained myself in a rush. "They could protect themselves if they had a guild. That is how the builders do it. They set their own rules for the profession. The builders' guild decides who is a good builder. If the scholars had a guild, it is they who would decide who is a good scholar."

Eleanor pondered my words for a moment. Then she turned back to the Abbot. "An interesting idea," she said. "What say you, Father? Can we charter a guild for the scholars of the new cathedral?"

"Make them self-regulating?" Abbot Suger mused. "That would solve the problem. Of course, we couldn't call it a guild, that's much too vulgar, ringing as it does of craftsmen and such. But a polite word which means the same thing would be 'universitas.' We could call it that."

"Universitas?" Eleanor said, testing out the term. "An odd word, but so be it. We shall name this new school the Universitas of Paris."

Chapter 26

The Consecration of Saint Denis

It was a glorious occasion. The bright June sun shone through the windows of the cathedral of light, illuminating its interior like a meadow in daytime, and making the wonderful colored paintings drawn upon the windows glow like visions.

I stood next to Eleanor and Alicia and looked about. I had never seen so many people in one place. All of France was there, and many foreign notables besides. Nobles, knights, priests, nuns, scholars, and wealthy burghers of every trade filled the new cathedral to capacity, and all were dressed their very best, except for King Louis and Odo, who still costumed themselves as monks. On a stage before the altar stood a chorus of a five score holy Sisters, who were directed in their efforts by a little old Abbess. This woman, however, belying her age, quickly moved her arms about, pointing at this group or that to ring the different voices of her choir like bells, singing now together, now apart. The sound of this was so beautiful as to exceed the power of words to describe.

The nuns sang the mass:
"Credo in unum Deum,
Patrem omnipotentem,
Factorem coeli et terrae,
Visibilium omnium
Et invisibilium.

I was so moved, I sang along quietly under my breath. As I did, though, I was aware of Alicia and Eleanor looking about.

Alicia said, "The woman leading the choir, is that?"

"Yes," said Eleanor. "Abbess Hildegard herself. And do you see the sister third from the right in the second row?"

"Yes," Alicia replied. Then she started, as did I.

"Heloise!" Alicia said. "Here?"

I was thrilled. Hildegard of Bingen! The fabled fair Heloise! Together with me at the consecration of the great cathedral of light!

The holy sisters sang on:

"Deum de Deo
Lumen de lumine,"

Eleanor smiled. "I would not have it otherwise," she said.

"Qui propter nos hominess," sang the holy Sisters.
"Et propter nostrum salutem
Descendit de coelis,
Et incarnates est de spiritu sancto
Et homo factus est."

The nuns concluded. Abbot Suger advanced to the lectern to address the assembly.

He looked about for several moments, his face flushed. Then he began.

"Your majesties, noble lords and ladies, brothers and sisters of the cloth, worthy commons; this is a joyous day. Today we consecrate our new house of worship, one which sings out to the world that the days of darkness are over, that our faith brings forth light, even as our God is light."

There was a murmur in the crowd, but Suger did not hesitate. His eyes glowed with the power of his message.

"For our God is Love, and love is light which scatters the darkness of Hate. And our God is Truth, and Truth is light which scatters the darkness of Ignorance. Our Christ commandeth us, 'Seek and you shall find.' He prophesies that the day will come when all truths will be known, and he promiseth us that the truth shall set us free. Thus the Church of Christ is the Church of Light and the Church of Truth, and so shall it be with this house."

"This Church is new. It is not yet complete. But when it is, there will stand at its entrance a monument to those seven sages who have done most to prepare the mind of man for the light. Pythagoras, Plato, Aristotle, Euclid, Priscian, Cicero, and Boethius – these immortal heroes of truth shall stand by our door to do honor to our holy faith, a faith which loves truth even as our enemies, the evil Mohammedans and heretics hate it and fear it."

"The statues of the sages must wait for the hand of Art to do its work, but with us today to represent the seven sages and the seven arts are our first seven scholars."

Abbot Suger gestured to one side, where seven young men, dressed in academic hats and gowns, and each holding a book with the name of one of the sages inscribed upon it, stood proudly, arms folded like a band of brave knights before setting forth together on a heroic quest.

"These seven men will lead the way," Suger said. "They, and those who will join them and follow them, will form a school here that will explore all mysteries the mind of man can explore. Through their great work, the faith of all will be reinforced by understanding, and the Creator will be made known by the knowing of his creation."

Abbot Suger paused for a second and then pointed, first to the scholars, then to the light streaming in through the windows.

"Let there be light!" he proclaimed.

I gasped. My heart stopped. In that moment I felt I was present at the Creation.

Then Abbot Suger gestured to Hildegard, who signaled to the Sisters to resume their holy chorus.

"Pleni sunt coeli et terra gloria tua,
Osanna in excelsis.
Osanna in excelsis.
Osanna in ex-cel-sis.
In in in excelsis."

***   ***   ***

Tables had been set up outside the cathedral, set with white table cloths. Brothers of Suger's Benedictine order stood by with goblets of good wine for all the guests. Because they had stood furthest back in the church during the consecration, the burghers made it to the tables before the nobles, which was only just.

I saw Papa and the other builders at one of the wine tables, and I ran to join them.

I had barely been there for a minute, however, when the Queen herself approached. She picked up two goblets from the builders' table, and keeping one, passed the other to the Lady Alicia, who had followed her. Then she turned to the builders.

"Master builders, well met," Eleanor said graciously. "I compliment you on your fine work."

The builders all bowed low.

Eleanor then turned to me. "Marie, you must be very proud of your father," she said.

183

I was so happy, I had to blink way tears of joy from my eyes. I looked at the Cathedral, and then at Papa, and then I hugged him like a bear. Finally, I found my voice.

"Indeed, Your Majesty," I said. "This is the proudest day of my life."

Eleanor nodded, then turned back to the men.

"Master builders," she said. "You do honor to your craft, and to our realm. Please, come to the palace tomorrow, during the hour past noon, so I can reward you." She faced me. "Marie, please instruct them the way."

The builders all bowed gratefully, and Eleanor smiled her acknowledgement. A churchman approached. It was the Abbot Bernard of Clairvaux. He did not look happy. This seemed to please Eleanor, and she called out to him.

"So, Abbot Bernard," the Queen said gaily. "How did you enjoy the consecration?"

Bernard shook his head. "I do not blame the Abbess Hildegard," he said, his voice bitter. "She is a pious woman and serves the Lord as best she can. But I should like to have words with whoever planned this ceremony."

"Really?" Eleanor smiled. "Then speak. She stands before you."

Bernard's eyes flashed anger. "You? You arranged this travesty?"

Eleanor shrugged. "I thought it was a great success," she said.

Abbot Bernard exploded. "This is outrageous! You should not be involved in such things. May I remind you yet again of your proper purpose? Your purpose is to give France an heir. Why have you not done that?"

The force of Bernard's rage made Eleanor take a step backward. Then she took a breath, and spoke calmly. "I believe I could explain that, but I doubt you would understand."

"Oh, I understand quite well," Bernard snapped. "It is you who does not understand. You are infertile because God is punishing you for your sinful ways. You interfere in the business of the Church. You interfere in the business of the State. These matters are not for women. You need to humiliate yourself and repent! Then you will be able to do your duty and give France an heir."

Eleanor stared ice at the man, and he returned her glance with fire.

Then, nodding to the Queen, Bernard walked off to share his discontent with others

Eleanor, turned to Alicia, her face red in anger. She said, "He wants me to give Louis an heir, does he? Well then, I'll give him an heir."

The Queen looked around the reception tables and her eyes lit on Duke Geoffrey of Anjou who was standing a distance away talking with some of his nobles. I saw her exchange a glance with Alicia, and some understanding appeared to pass between the two, but as I was not included, I cannot say what it was.

***   ***   ***

The next spring, a miracle occurred. Eleanor gave birth to a child. I say a miracle, because King Louis, while pious in most things, lacked the feelings that encourage most men, whether pious or not, to obey the commandment the good God gave our first parents to fill the Earth and multiply. Thus it can only be that, as occurred in the case of Our Savior, the child of Eleanor was conceived by immaculate means. That is what she told me herself, and the King as well, who accordingly gave thanks that Divine grace might thus provide him with an heir born without sin. How dark was his disappointment then, when the child turned out to be a girl. I could not be prouder, however, as the Queen chose to do me great honor by giving my name to the wondrous babe, christening her Marie.

The child was a lusty one, a fact to which I can attest, as I attended both her birth and her baptism, which was performed by the Abbot Suger himself. This latter was both a holy and a royal event, and although Abbot Bernard saw fit to attend, King Louis did not appear. Clearly the King was lacking not only in the natural feelings of a man, but also that of a father.

Queens do not nurse babies, for their duties lie elsewhere. Eleanor was a good and loving mother, however, and spared no expense in finding the kindest, wisest, and most learned women from Fontevrault to raise the girl for her, so that someday she might be as brilliant a princess as the Queen had been herself.

As we left the church the day of the baptism, Abbot Bernard approached the Queen.

"Your Majesty has taken a first step towards salvation," he said. "Come, give me your confession, and perhaps God will see fit to grant you a son."

Eleanor looked as if she would respond sharply. But before she could do so, a messenger galloped up the street, and leaping from his horse, ran up the church steps to kneel before her, holding out a rolled up parchment.

The messenger looked at the ground, not daring to face the Queen as he spoke.

"Your Majesty, forgive me," he said. "I bear dreadful news."

Eleanor looked down at the messenger, but refused to touch his parchment. "Speak without fear," she said. "What is your message?"

"Edessa has fallen," the messenger said.

In an instant, Bernard's face changed from calm to horror. "What?" he said.

"Yes," the messenger fairly wept. "Fallen to the forces of the Turk Nuradin, the fanatic son of Zengi. The Christian men of the city have all been put to the sword; with those not falling in the fight having their heads chopped off before their wives and daughters, who after being violated, were all murdered the same way. The babes they threw in the fire, and the holy relics too, and all the churches turned into mosques for service to the devil Mohammed."

Eleanor clutched her prayer book tightly. Then she shook her head. "This cannot be," she said. "For if Edessa had fallen, my Uncle Raymond of Antioch, would surely have sent me word, as the loss of that city would expose his to the direst peril."

"But your Majesty," the messenger cried, finally looking at her. "This message is from Raymond!"

Eleanor appeared thunderstruck. She dropped her prayer book and staggered down a step, and might have fallen had not Alicia rushed to steady her. "No!" she said.

"Yes," said the messenger. "He says he can hold for now, but send armies soon, or lose Antioch, which once lost, loses Jerusalem and all the Holy Land as well."

Bernard of Clairvaux fell to his knees and lifted his eyes to heaven. "My God, my God, why hast thou forsaken us?" Then he began to pray.

Eleanor looked at me, then at Alicia, her eyes wide. "Send armies? Halfway around the world? How?"

Abbot Bernard rose to his feet, his faced determined. "God has spoken to me," he said. "We must take the cross and join the Crusade."

"Crusade?" Eleanor asked. "Father, the Crusade was fifty years ago."

Bernard spoke with mystical certainty. "Then there must be a Second Crusade. All Christendom must march to save Jerusalem!"

A Second Crusade! Eleanor looked at us, sharing our astonishment.

"Queen Eleanor," Bernard said, his voice now commanding with authority. "Inform your husband. Tell him to appoint a place and assemble all the knights of France. I would speak with them."

And so it was that the great Queen Eleanor and I, Marie, the builder's daughter, having brought chivalry to France, accomplished the construction of the Cathedral of light, and conceived the formation of the noble Universitas of Paris, the first universitas in all the world, heard the words that were to embark us upon a new adventure, the greatest and most formidable of our lives.

Book the Third

The Great Crusade

Chapter 27

The Field of Vezelay

The King responded to Bernard's urgent plea with all the haste he could muster, and in less than two years, a huge assembly of knights from every corner of the vast realm of the Franks gathered on the field of Vezelay, adjacent to the sacred tomb that holds the mortal remains of the sainted Mary Magdalene.

It was springtime, in the year of Our lord One thousand, one hundred and forty seven. The grass was green, the flowers bloomed, and the colorful tents of the nobles gave the encampment a festive air. But the issue to be decided was one of grim seriousness, and the fate of the Holy Land, and perhaps all of Christendom, hung in the balance. Should the Franks and their vassals commit their all and march east to war?

The leading men of the kingdom were gathered upon a raised stage to speak before the multitude. Louis, Odo, Abbot Suger, Bernard of Clairvaux, and Peter the Venerable, the head of the powerful Cluniac order, were all there, arrayed in their varied religious garb. There were also a few high noblemen in armor, which was fortunate, as such men tend to be more useful in time of war than priests and monks, and their presence upon the stage raised the credibility of the leadership group accordingly.

Eleanor had not been invited to Vezelay, but she was not one to miss such an occasion. Furthermore, since the safety of the kingdom of Antioch, ruled by her father's younger brother Raymond, an uncle as dear to her as an older brother might have been, hung in the balance, both reasons of state and of the heart also compelled her presence. So to Vezelay we had gone, and stationed ourselves under a silken canopy right nearby the speaker's platform to listen to the proceedings.

Bernard of Clairvaux was the Crusade's most passionate advocate. We listened to him as he delivered his speech.

"And so, brave knights and fighting men of France, your holy Father in Rome calls upon you, entreats you, beseeches you, to do as your grandfathers did, and take the cross and march with all your might in true Crusade to save the Holy Land from the enemies of Christ."

Eleanor turned to us. "I never thought I would see this day," she said, with a whisper of wonder upon her voice. "It is like something out of the tales of Arthur or Roland. Think of it! A Crusade in our own time."

"It is something to see," Alicia said. "But I must say, that as boorish as they sometimes are, it will be still more boring in Paris with all the best knights gone."

I had to agree. Scholars are fine in their own way, but a palace without knights would certainly be lacking something. "Yes," I said. "I fear we are in for some tedious years, my lady."

Eleanor nodded. "True. Unless…" Here she stopped, as if pondering a thought.

"Unless what?" Alicia probed.

The Queen looked at us with blazing eyes.

"Unless we go too!" she exclaimed.

Alicia took a step back. "What? Are you mad?"

Eleanor's face was flushed with excitement. "No," she said. "We'd be mad not to go! Think you that we should spend the next three years sitting in the palace sewing quilts, and missing out on the greatest adventure of our time, perhaps of all time? That we should stay behind in Paris, a stupid little dung heap town, when we could be traveling the world, seeing the fabled cities of the east. Think of it! Constantinople! Antioch! Jerusalem!"

I looked at her, then at Alicia. It was the most thrilling idea I had ever heard. I saw Alicia was now excited about it too. I turned back to Eleanor.

"Oh, my lady, that would be so grand," I said.

"But think you they'll let us go?" Alicia asked.

"They'll have to," Eleanor said. "A venture of this kind costs a great deal of money, and when money's needed, she who has the purse, rules." She bit her lower lip and smiled, rubbing the fingers of her hand together like one fondling a silver coin.

They couldn't stop us! We exchanged looks of sheer glee. Constantinople, Antioch, Jerusalem, we'd see them all!

Alicia extended her hand outward in the manner of a knight taking an oath. "To Jerusalem then!" she said.

Eleanor and I reached out our hands, and placed them upon Alicia's.

"To Jerusalem!" we pledged together.

Eleanor held up her hand for silence. "Now let's listen," she said, and turned back to watch Bernard.

The Abbot of Clairvaux was drawing to his conclusion. "And so, brave knights, march for your faith. God wills it, and your holy Father in Rome promises absolution from all sins for all who take the cross and join this sacred cause. Heaven awaits you, and victory is certain, for in this Crusade we shall be led not by mere Counts and Dukes, as were those who went in our grandfather's day, but by a King, the greatest warrior in Christendom, our own King Louis of France!"

Thus called upon, King Louis advanced to speak. The crowd of knights applauded politely, but many exchanged skeptical looks.

Eleanor hit her hand to her forehead. "Oh no," she said.

Louis spoke. "My friends, I have sinned. And while I would never accuse any of you, I believe that if you search your hearts you may discover that you have sinned as well. But together, we can go to Jerusalem, to the holiest shrines in the world, where we may confess all and be absolved. Some of you may be concerned about all it may cost you to make this pilgrimage, but think not of it. For what are the things of this world compared to those of the next?"

The knights started murmuring dubiously one to another.

Eleanor covered both her eyes. "Mother of God," she muttered.

Abbot Suger stepped forward. He spoke to the King. "Your Majesty, if I might have a word?"

Eleanor's face brightened. "Abbot Suger, praise the Lord. Here at least is a man with a brain."

The King, having apparently exhausted his little wit with his little speech, seemed glad to yield to podium to Suger.

"Brave knights," Abbot Suger said, speaking loud and clear in his deep strong voice. "You have been told it could cost you all you possess to journey to the Holy Land, and that is true. You have also been told that such costs are well worth it if they are needed in the fight for the faith, and that is certainly also true. But why endure such costs when they are not needed? For indeed, we do not need to go to Jerusalem to fight the infidels. The entire south of France is riddled with Cathars, purveyors of an evil heresy that would destroy our faith."

Eleanor's eyes went wide. "What?" she cried.

Abbot Suger continued. "Instead of ruining yourselves to travel across half the world to defend cities which can and should defend themselves, you can enrich yourselves by despoiling the heretics who threaten our own homeland."

I turned to Eleanor. "My lady, this is horrible. He is calling for a crusade against the gentle Cathars. They have a strange creed, it is true. But they lead virtuous lives, and some are among the greatest bards in Christendom." "I know," Eleanor nodded, her face dark with fury. "And to get them, he'd have this horde overrun Provence like a cloud of locusts. I'll not have it."

Suger concluded. "Peter the Venerable, the leader of the Cluniac order, has just returned from Toulouse, where he has seen this heresy at work. He will tell you more."

Abbot Suger now stepped back and Peter the Venerable advanced to talk. As befit the leader of the rich Cluniac order, he wore a black robe with a gold crucifix encrusted with diamonds and jewels of every type.

Eleanor did not wait to hear what Peter had to say. She walked rapidly to the side of the stage and called up to Abbot Suger.

"Abbot Suger, a word, if you don't mind."

The Abbot looked down and answered. "Of course, Your Majesty." Then he descended from the stage and faced Eleanor.

The Queen lit into him. "What is this madness, a crusade against the Cathars? It is Jerusalem that must be saved."

Abbot Suger's voice was soft. "My daughter, I ask you; what good can possibly come from Bernard's plan?"

Eleanor appeared confused. "I don't understand," she said.

"I think you do," Suger replied. "I'll put it to you more directly. Do you, Eleanor, really believe that King Louis is a man who can lead the army of Christendom across the world to defeat Nuradin in battle? You know your husband. Can you foresee any end but disaster to such an enterprise?"

Eleanor turned away and bit her lip, thinking furiously. Then she turned back to face Abbot Suger.

"We'll have other men with us," she said, defying his point. "War leaders tested in battle; Conrad of Germany, for example, the Counts of Flanders, and Rancon. They can give Louis all the advice he will need."

Abbot Suger smiled sadly. "But will he listen?"

"I'll make him listen," Eleanor said.

Abbot Suger shook his head. "Eleanor, even you cannot turn a lamb into a lion."

And it would be even more difficult to do so with a hen.

Eleanor glared at Suger, and then stalked past him to climb up onto the stage.

I don't want to miss this, I thought, and followed her up.

When he saw Eleanor arrive upon the platform, Bernard, who already had a cross expression from listening to Peter the Venerable, got even angrier.

He sneered at the Queen. "What are you doing here?"

"Watch," Eleanor said.

Peter the Venerable's clever appeals to the assemblage's most cowardly and base feelings were smashing at our cause like an iron ram at a wooden gate.

"Brave knights," he shouted. "I say our cause is just, and those who fight for it will be rewarded, both in the next world and in this one. For in addition to the Cathars, the south is filled with rich Jews, ripe for the plucking."

Eleanor cut him off. "Enough," she said. "I wish to speak"

There were times when Eleanor would talk like a playful girl, and times like a dignified lady. But when she spoke these words, her tone was that of an absolute monarch. Peter froze in his speech, bowed, and stepped back.

The knights murmured as Eleanor advanced to address them.

She stopped at the lectern and surveyed the crowd, silencing the muttering with her regal eyes. Then she spoke, and it was like one of the great orators of Athens or Rome had come among us.

"Cathars and Jews, minstrels and peddlers!" she exclaimed. "These harmless cranks are no threat to Christendom. Would the great King Arthur have measured his valor by testing his mettle against such as these? No, it is the Turks and Saracens who are the real enemy, and who even now are gathering to attack the Holy City. It is these heathens who every Christian knight wishing the repute of a brave man must be willing to face on the field. A knight's calling is not to despoil minstrels, but to do the great deeds that are remembered in their songs."

It was amazing to watch her. The spirit of the ages sounded in her voice and shone in her eyes. She called out to the knights, stirring their souls like a heroic trumpet. "Our duty is clear. Christ himself is calling us to fight in his name. The Holy City is in danger. We must march to save Jerusalem!"

Eleanor finished, and a ragged cheer erupted from the crowd. Then she stepped back to stand next to Bernard. Enemies one moment, allies the next. That is the way of politics. Eleanor and Bernard; together they were formidable.

But Abbot Suger was quick to counter. "Gallant words," he called out to the warriors. "But what does a woman know of a knight's calling? Is it the duty of a knight to go venturing afield when his own castle is in danger? Of what use would Edessa be to us, if in going to reconquer it, we should lose France?"

Bernard of Clairvaux turned to Eleanor. "Your Majesty," he said. "I stand corrected. You spoke well. But I fear it was not enough. Abbot Suger has a way with words that we cannot match."

Eleanor nodded. "Then we must overmatch him with more than words," she said. "Do what you can. I'll be back."

She gestured for me to follow, and we hurried off the platform. Then, adding Alicia to our number, we ran into the knights' encampment and found the tent of an armorer. Eleanor's purse was quick to do its work, and in less time than it takes a hungry dog to pull the meat off of a bone, we had acquired and attired ourselves in complete suits of chain mail, with white tunics with red crosses to cover them. We also got some swords, shields, and coned steel helmets of the Frankish type. Then snatching the nearest steeds, we mounted up, and galloped through the camp of the knights, waving our swords about.

"Jerusalem! Jerusalem!" we shouted; Eleanor and Alicia riding easily, me hanging onto my horse for dear life.

The effect on the knights was immediate. Hundreds leaped onto their horses and joined us in enthusiasm, all yelling our battle cry, "Jerusalem!"

Soon we had thousands following us. With their hooves thundering, Eleanor led our army in a charge right up into the assembly, who rose to join us as well.

"Jerusalem!" we all shouted, lifting our swords in salute. "Jerusalem!"

Abbot Suger stopped speaking. Then Bernard of Clairvaux looked down from the podium at the shouting assembly, exchanged an incandescent glance with Eleanor, and advanced to the lectern. He held up his hands.

"God wills it!" the holy man proclaimed.

"God wills it!" we all replied.

Chapter 28

The Amazons Go to War

The news of Vezelay caused a sensation all over Christendom, and not just among the men. For when they heard of Eleanor's armed exploit and plans for further adventure, daring young noblewomen from all over Europe flocked to her standard.

First to arrive was Torqueri of Bouillon, a bold dame who cut nearly as fine a figure upon a horse as Alicia. Then came Mamille of Roucy and Florine of Bourgogne, fine riders both, pretty young Candice of Troyes, kind of heart and pious of spirit, and Faydide of Toulouse, who was most welcome, as she was a kinswoman of Eleanor and shared her love for sport and song.

Then more came, daughters and wives of knights and barons, and though not all were so well prepared, Eleanor accepted every one, for to do otherwise was to give offense. Moreover, she had conceived the idea of forming a company of Amazons, to prove to the world the capacity of women, even in war, and it would not do for us to be half a dozen. No, to make a proper company, she said, she needed three score, and these she got, and more besides, so great was the enthusiasm with which the fair daughters of Christendom answered her call.

It was Eleanor's desire that her company cut a fine figure upon the field, so she equipped each alike in matching chain mail, white tunics with red crusader crosses, red capes, stylish red leather riding boots, and conical steel helmets without the ugly nose guards that so defaced the countenance of the knights. These we wore without mail hoods, so as to allow our hair to show nicely behind our necks, although my helm was so oversized as to hang down over my ears and cheeks like that of a German. Eleanor dressed herself just like the rest, except that her boots also had gold buckles and intricate golden trim. This was proper, since as our leader she needed a suitable mark of distinction.

Two of the most remarkable members of our company were among the final enlistees. I remember the occasion well, for it was a fine spring day, and we were gathered upon the palace patio, all decked out in our new Amazon uniform attire. Eleanor and Alicia were playing at chess, I was practicing my lute, and numbers of our fair warriors were improving their swordsmanship by dueling upon each other with ladylike blows that would not have hurt a kitten. The delicate character of their fencing had caused me to previously suggest to Eleanor that perhaps some of these dames might do better if armed with crossbows instead, but the Queen would not entertain such a demeaning suggestion. So now, duly censured, I stuck to my lute and left tactics to those who knew better.

A maidservant entered and spoke to the Queen. "Your Majesty, the Countess Sybille of Flanders is here to see you.

"Very well," Eleanor said. "Show her in."

The maidservant departed, but returned a moment later, leading in a woman of almost forty, but stout and hale. This, I surmised, was the famed Countess Sybille of Flanders. She was also wearing chain mail and a Crusader tunic, but her helmet was of the Norman type, complete with nose guard, and her riding boots were brown leather and had clearly seen much service. Eleanor rose to meet her, and Alicia and I did as well.

"Greetings, Countess," Eleanor said. "I see you are here to join our troop of Amazons."

"Yes," said Sybille in a gruff voice, almost like that of man. "I have fought alongside my husband in several wars, and when I heard you were forming a company of woman warriors for the Crusade, I could not refuse the opportunity."

"Excellent," Eleanor smiled, clearly pleased to add such a renowned fighter to our number. "Then allow me to introduce you to some of the members of our force. This is Alicia of Bordeaux."

Alicia and Sybille nodded their heads in mutual recognition.

"I am honored," Sybille said.

"The honor is mine," Alicia replied.

Eleanor then pointed to several more of our officers, each of who exchanged nods with Sybille and she was introduced. "And this is Mamille of Roucy, Florine of Bourgogne, Torqueri of Bouillon, and Faydide of Toulouse."

Then the Queen pointed to me. "And this is Marie."

Sybille raised her eyebrows in curiosity.

"Of?" she inquired.

"Of France," I replied.

Sybille looked at me askance. "A burgher?" she asked, her suspicion evident.

"I am a descendant of Homer, Virgil, and Ovid," I said proudly.

The Countess was not impressed. "In other words, a burgher," she said.

Eleanor interposed. "She is a brave lass, a fine bard, and a good friend."

Sybille exchanged glances with the Queen, then looked back at me.

"Well, then, Marie of France," the Countess said.. "Since Eleanor of Aquitaine calls you friend, so do I."

She then extended her hand, which I took with gratitude.

"Thank you, Countess," I said.

Sybille turned and pointed to the ineffectively dueling ladies.

"And who are these?" she asked Eleanor.

"Noble ladies all," the Queen replied.

"Yes," Sybille said. "But from the way they swing their swords, I'm not sure they'll be of much use in battle. Are you certain you want them for your troop?"

Eleanor shrugged. "I can hardly refuse them. They come from some of the most illustrious families in the land."

Sybille looked doubtful.

"Don't worry, I am teaching them about war," Eleanor added.

"With some pains, I'll admit," Alicia said "You should see the fuss they put up when we told them they had to limit their baggage to just two wagonloads each."

"They'll have to cut it to a lot less than that," Sybille said.

Alicia looked at the Countess shocked. "Really?"

"Yes," said Sybille. "And can they ride astride, or only sideways?"

"We're working on that one," Eleanor said

Sybille frowned. "I see."

At this moment, another woman entered the patio unannounced. She too was wearing Crusader garb, but her boots were black with wear, her chain mail rusty, and there were some knicks on her sword and on her helm. I marveled at her, for she was a full fathom tall, and her skin was as tanned and her frame as wiry as that of a sailor. About twenty five years of age, she had keen gray eyes and long blond hair which she wore in two thick braids.

"Greetings," the new arrival said. "I am Erika of Jutland. I am here to join the Amazons."

Sybille, Eleanor, and Alicia regarded the recruit and exchanged appreciative glances with each other. Then the Countess walked over and squeezed the muscles on Erika's sword arm.

"She'll do," Sybille said.

*** *** ***

And so it was, that on the 14th of June in the Year of Our Lord One Thousand, One Hundred and Forty Seven, we finally set forth from Paris to begin the great Crusade. Our procession of mounted knights and men at arms left the city after a morning mass at Saint Denis, an unbeatable force numbering thousands upon thousands, and on either side of the road, still vaster multitudes of nobles, burghers, peasants and holy Brothers and Sisters lined up to cheer us and strew flowers upon our path

Our army was composed of many nations, and on that day at least, each marched in its appointed place. After the forces of Flanders and Champagne came our Amazon troop, followed by those of Aquitaine, Poitiers, Brittany, Burgundy, and Normandy, with Louis and his Franks, like good shepherds, following in the rear.

The order of our own company was as follows. First Eleanor, who stood out above all for her beauty, her magnificent horse, and her golden trimmed boots. Then came the Countess Sybille of Flanders, riding side by side with Alicia of Bordeaux, distinct with their fine horse trappings, but like all the rest of us, wearing the red leather boots that were our company's uniform. Afterwards I rode, alongside Erika the Dane, who although born to the estate of but an ordinary knight, was much favored by the Queen. I was glad of this, for she was a merry lass, and told wonderful stories of her people of the north which I hope to rhyme someday as part of my music. Behind us rode many such noble ladies as you may have heard. Behind us, I say, because the great Queen Eleanor prized friendship over blood. Some of these could ride like knights, as Eleanor and Alicia had instructed me to ride, while others insisted on riding sideways. These annoyed the Queen so much she put them last in our column, excepting only the baggage wagons, of which we had very many, and the host of maids, cooks, and washerwomen who helped push them.

So we marched through June, our force growing through many additions. We reached the Rhine River near Metz at month's end, all of Gaul armed and ready in fine array, and no one who could have seen us on that glorious day could have doubted for a moment the certainty of our victory. Pope Eugenius himself came to bless us, and then boats and rafts were brought, allowing us to cross the water.

The crossing took six days, which may seem like overmuch, but you must understand that this was the largest army since the beginning of the world, over a hundred thousand strong, not counting the servants and camp followers, who were many times this number. The current in the mighty river was swift, causing much bumping and crashing among the boats, and the running about of frightened horses caused more than one craft to overtip. Yet despite all this, more than nine in ten of our army made it across the river without drowning. So, in fact, to cross in this time with so much safety was a marvel of fine organization.

We then marched across lower Germany into Hungary, where we expected to meet up with Conrad, the German Emperor, and his army, but they were not there. However, as we went further along the river Danube into the Empire of the Greeks, we found evidence aplenty that the Germans had preceded us.

The first such burnt village we encountered was in the land of the Serbs, who are a subject people of the Greek Empire, and therefore schismatics. Our German allies had apparently taken affront, either at this or the lack of willingness of the local maidens to share their favors, and lacking the patience accruing to such more civilized nations as even the Franks, had accordingly put the place to the torch. This made the surviving villagers unhappy, and failing to discriminate as they should have between us and the incendiaries, they cursed us as we marched by. But, being good Christians, we forgave them this sinful behavior, mercifully limiting punishment to the removal of such spare livestock as we observed the offenders to possess.

For the next few days we met with many more such destroyed places, but then the pattern changed as advance word prepared the locals for our allies' arrival. Many towns were thus discovered intact, or nearly so, with well-guarded gates duly decorated by the bodies of stray Germans swinging upon gallows ingeniously constructed for the purpose.

So we avoided the local inns and taverns, and instead spent each night that we were not on the Danube river in the safety of our own camp. This was not so dreary as might be thought, because the army was filled with gallant knights from Aquitaine, and Poitiou, and even some Bretons, and with these we spent many merry evenings feasting by our tent fires.

But the month was August, and the weather was fine, and so the nights on the water were better still. For the Danube is a friendly river, and a joy to float upon in the warm summertime moonlight. And so, as pole-men guided our rafts through the balmy nights, the Amazons would lean back on mattresses and cushions and look up at the stars, while I softly strummed upon my lute.

Such a time it was! If only it could have lasted longer. Truly, if there was ever a more pleasant way to wage war, I should like to know about it.

We reached the sea, then marched south along the shore for nearly a fortnight.

At last, after a summertime journey of some three months, we reached the glorious capital of the Greek Empire, the greatest city in all the world.

Chapter 29

The Sights of Constantinople

Constantinople was a vast metropolis, more than ten times the size of Paris, and far more grand. Filled with splendid ancient buildings of every type, its high walls towered over a magnificent sapphire harbor blooming with sails. Hundreds of commerce laden sailing ships crowded the wharfs, unloading precious goods from far off lands, while upon the water itself, the slaves of the Greek navy rapidly rowed squadrons of fast dromon galleys this way and that, displaying for all to see the power of the Imperial throne.

The Emperor of the Greeks, Manuel Comnenus Porphyrogenitus, sent emissaries to welcome us as friends, but denied us entrance to the city. They had held this policy for the Germans as well, which was understandable. But it grieved the army greatly to be kept out of the city market, where much necessaries could be bought. In place of this, they said, provisions would be sold to us outside the walls. And so they were, but the prices were higher than fair, and made much worse by the Greeks' insistence that before purchase, our silver coins should be changed for equal weights of theirs cast in bronze.

So we encamped outside the city, and the Greeks set up a market, just for us, but surrounded it by a palisade. Before the gates of this market they emplaced tables, behind which sat the bankers appointed by the court, each with a scale. Those wishing to buy from the market had to stand in lines before these tables, and upon reaching the front, give the bankers a bag of silver pennies, which then would be placed upon the scales and precisely balanced with an equal weight of bronze bezants. Only then, equipped with these coins of much weight and little worth, would our knights be allowed to enter the market. The Greeks said that there was no alternative to this, since as loyal subjects of the Emperor, their merchants could not be expected to accept money that was not properly engraved with his majestic head. The banker's bronze bezants made good this defect in our silver pennies, but be that as it may, the effigies of the Emperor distributed in this way did little to endear him to our men, and even less to the Amazons, many of whom had looked forward with some anticipation to market-going in Constantinople.

We had also hoped to worship in the churches of the city, some of which are very old and possessing of many holy relics. This also was not allowed. Instead we were only given access to two little churches of no great repute that were outside the walls, and even this small boon they turned into an insult by washing them out after every mass, as though our presence had been a defilement. This incensed the Bishop Langres so much that he advised the King to storm the city, as their long separation from Rome had clearly left the Greeks Christian in name only, and a good sack was necessary to return them to the faith.

Accordingly, a council of war was held, and many concurred with this inspired suggestion. King Louis, however, would not agree, as he wished to reach Jerusalem with least delay. The grand proposal thus had to be abandoned to the efforts of future ages, but it remains the truth that we had the idea first.

The Emperor's spies must have reported of it, however, as to lessen our anger he finally consented to allow our leaders to enter the city in small groups, and the King and Queen, with a few chosen companions, were invited to dine at the palace. And thus it was that, in company with Queen Eleanor, Lady Alicia of Bordeaux, the Countess Sybille of Flanders, and Erika the Dane, that I entered the famous and holy city of Constantinople.

To say the city was amazing would be to fail at words. For some of the boulevards were so wide, that not even the best archer in Christendom could have fired an arrow from one side to the other. On every side, there were magnificent buildings of the ancient type, beautiful fountains, and noble statues worked of marble or of bronze.

The thronging crowds were enormous, although I must say that many gave the five of us a wide berth when they saw us advancing down the avenue in our Crusader garb. Indeed, the respectable women of the town, heavily covered in shawls, quickly called their children to them to protect them from the very sight of us, while the whores, nearly naked in their bejeweled bands, watched slyly from their windows.

We visited the great market of the City, where the merchant carts abounded with fine silken gowns of every color, even purple, ready for sale. Eleanor and Alicia had a merry time playing about with these, but in the end the Queen forbade purchase, since we had a far road ahead and such stuff could better be bought during the return journey.

We also went to see the magnificent church of Saint Sophia, built over six hundred years ago by the Emperor Justinian. The roof of this place was a dome barely smaller than that of heaven itself, and the eaves and altars were adorned with many ancient icons and sacred relics. I wanted to worship there, but the schismatic priests looked upon me so angrily after I first crossed myself, that I could not do it, and left without saying a prayer.

There were good taverns, public eating places with excellent spiced fish and sugared desserts, exotic dancers and other entertainers both on the street and indoors, and bathing houses where one could lie in pools of hot water and then be scrubbed clean by slaves.

But best of all was the Hippodrome, where chariots still raced just as they did in the days of the Caesars. Being informed that such an event would be held that very day at the third hour of the afternoon, we traveled to this facility to find ourselves amid a flood of humanity of every social condition, from nobles to slaves, all pushing at each other whilst heading towards the gate. This entrance was barred by soldiers, until suddenly two large brass lions standing on tall marble columns to either side emitted a blast of steam from their nostrils and mouths, and roaring thus, rocked back on their pedestals. The soldiers then stood aside, and the crowd, shouting their thanks to the magic lions, stormed into the stadium.

Once inside we found seats in the middle row, surrounded by thousands upon thousands of people. Some of these waved banners of green upon little sticks, while others carried banners of blue. Looking down from our seats we could see six chariots, each with four horses, standing ready for the race. Three of the teams were decked out in green livery, while three sported blue. The blue horses were Andalusians, while the greens were of a type I did not recognize.

"I like the blue horses better," Eleanor said. This did not surprise me, for her own steed, Pegasus, was of this very kind.

The wall surrounding the stadium was adorned with one hundred more brass lions. Suddenly, all of these roared steam and rocked upon their legs. The chariots took off in a rush.

"Come on blue! Come on blue!" Eleanor yelled.

"Blue! Blue! Blue! Blue!" we all chanted.

A half-grown boy with a green banner struck me with it.

He shouted at me. "Green! Green!" Then he struck me again.

I was having none of this. I grabbed the banner from the lad, and hit him back.

"Blue!" I shouted back.

In an instant all those about us with blue and green banners were engaged with each other in furious struggle. Not only banners, but clothes were rent in the strife. Our chain mail, however, was quite up to this test, and so we came off rather better than our green faction assailants, several of whom we sent flying to the rows below in apparel so wrecked as to likely draw upon its wearer the unwelcome attention of the local magistrates.

In the midst of this riot, a blue chariot crossed the finish line first. We raised our fists and cheered. "Hurrah blue!"

Then buffeted by some green miscreants seeking revenge, we returned to the fray.

Afterwards, we repaired to a tavern, where we spent several joyful hours celebrating the victory of our cause, until finally it was time for dinner at the palace.

Chapter 30

Of Greeks and Gifts

The palace of the Greek Emperor Manuel Comnenus was about the size of the city of Toulouse, so that even once we were admitted, it took some time to make our way past the endless gardens, fountains, and gold covered statues to reach the banquet hall. Here we were welcomed by an escort of twenty four slaves, twelve maidens and twelve eunuchs, who led us through a long hall illuminated by ten thousand candles. The floors of this hall were covered with colored tiles so arranged as to create pictures, some of which were holy and others so profane as to be a cause for action by the magistrates had they been in France, or even Aquitaine. At the end of this hall was the dining area itself, where some three score couches were arranged, with a little table set within arm's reach of each one.

At the furthermost end of the dining area was a raised stage, set with two couches upon which lay the Emperor and Empress who were thus elevated above the rest. Before and below them were placed two rows of couches, with those on the right hand reserved for high Byzantine nobles, while those on the inferior left available for members our party.

Closest to the Emperor within our row lay King Louis, no doubt because of our number he was deemed highest in rank. That said, his position was most awkward, as it placed him almost directly beneath the Emperor where he was forced to look upward to speak to that august personage and vulnerable to such spittle as the divine ruler might choose to emit.

Next after Louis, lay Odo, then the Bishop Langres, and the Counts of Rancon and Flanders. All of these faced off against male Greek aristocrats on the couches opposite. Then there were five vacant couches on our side, faced by five couches containing female Byzantines of high rank. We surmised, therefore, that the five vacant couches in the female section were for us. The rest of the couches were all filled by noble Greeks.

By the etiquette clearly in evidence, Eleanor, being the highest in rank among our number, should have taken the couch within our female group closest to that of the Emperor. However, perhaps unwilling to allow her importance to be defined by her proximity to such a self-proclaimed superior majesty, she chose instead the central place within our five,   with me on her one hand and Alicia on her other. The Countess Sybille was thus allowed to dine next to her husband at what the Byzantines would have conceived as the superior end of our row, while Erika guarded our inferior flank.

The food was excellent, or so I was told, as much of it seemed rather bizarre. There were fish eggs, snails, octopus arms, goose livers, sparrow carcasses, frogs' legs, tree funguses, lake insects, horse tongues, and numerous other grotesque oddities that I am certain will never grace a table in France. The spiced goat was attractive though, and I'm sure it would have tasted good too had not the hall reeked so badly from the heavy perfumes sent forth from the candles.

Queen Eleanor was anxious to show the Greeks, who think us barbarous, that we westerners are as civilized as they. So she had instructed all in our party who were new to such things in her polite method of eating with knife and spoon at table.

Thus, when the Patriarch, which is the schismatics' name for an archbishop, concluded his blessing, Eleanor gave her signal and we all took out our dining knives and spoons from our pouches. In the Queen's style, we then carefully started to cut off little pieces of the unknown foods so we could pick them up to eat in the most delicate manner. This was difficult to do, lying down on a couch instead of sitting upwards as we were accustomed to do at home, but our training had been thorough, our determination was of the first order, and thus we managed.

Observing our success, Eleanor proudly looked up to see what impression we were making on our Byzantine hosts. But, horrors: instead of being impressed, they were all giggling, or barely restraining themselves from giggling, at our efforts. Was this mere effrontery? Unfortunately not. For as we watched, each of the noble Greeks took knives and little tridents from places on the table, and using them started to dine in a fashion that none of us had ever seen before.

Those little tridents! The Greeks used them to hold their food while cutting, and then spear the pieces like fishermen. Employing this remarkable technique, they could eat their entire dinners *without ever touching their food with their hands*!

The looks on their faces as they performed this parlor trick were so superior that Eleanor turned beet red with embarrassment. There was nothing for it, however. To copy them would have been to admit inferiority. So we kept on dining with knife and spoon, as we had begun.   However I saw that, when no one else was looking, the Queen placed her arm over one of the tridents lying on the table, and pushing with her fingers, secretly stuffed it up her sleeve.

Two groups of slave girls in jeweled skimpy clothing came out and assembled in performing areas on either side of the rows of couches, accompanied by two groups of fat pasty faced eunuchs wearing trousers but no shirts. Then as the eunuchs sang in shrill voices, the slave girls wiggled their torsos back and forth. Eleanor watched this show for a few minutes, appraising the seductive movements of the girls with the eye of an expert. But then the players reversed roles, with the girls singing and the eunuchs wiggling, and Eleanor turned back to the table with a shudder.

An elegant Greek lady of at least sixty years lay on the couch opposite Eleanor. She spoke to us in refined Latin. "Allow me to introduce myself. I am Princess Anna Comnena, aunt of Emperor Manuel."

"Greetings," Eleanor replied in the same tongue. "I am Eleanor, Queen of France."

"Or Gaul, as the educated call it," said Princess Anna. "I must say, I find it most curious that after all these years, and your nominal conversion to Christianity, that it is still the custom among you Kelts for female chieftains to lead their tribes into battle."

Eleanor did a double take. "I beg your pardon."

"Yes," Anna Comnena said. "Caesar records female warriors fighting alongside Vercingetorix, and of course, some years later, it was Bodica who led the revolt of the Kelts in Britannia. And now, here you are at the head of your own Keltic tribes."

Eleanor gave the Byzantine Princess a hard look. For while there is nothing wrong with being a Kelt, as I should know, since I am from Brittany myself, in the literature of the ancient Romans, the Kelts were barbarians. So to be referred to as a Kelt by an imperial speaking in literary Latin was to be called a savage.

"I am Queen of the Franks, not of the Kelts," Eleanor said coldly.

Anna Comnena shrugged. "Kelts, Franks, whatever. You do wear armor and a sword."

Eleanor fingered her chain mail. "I prefer a silken gown and dancing shoes," she said. "But there are times for swords, and if a woman cannot wear one, she becomes less than a man."

Anna Comnena regarded Eleanor for a moment. "I see," she said.

"You really consider us barbarians, don't you?" said Eleanor.

Anna Comnena smiled. "Well…"

Eleanor didn't wait for the rest of Anna's answer. "You think that just because you eat with those, those things, what are those called anyway?"

"Forks," Anna said, pronouncing the word carefully so we barbarians would get it right.

"Forks," Eleanor repeated. "That just because you eat with those FORKS, that you are more refined than us? Is that all civilization means to you? Forks?"

Anna Comnena tilted her head. "No. Table manners are just a manifestation of politeness, although in this case I would say probably an accurate one."

Eleanor's eyes flashed anger. "Is that so? Then how do you explain why you, who claim to be so civilized, still practice slavery, just like heathens?"

"In any society," Anna said, "there must be the rulers and those who labor on their behalf. The most perfect such system is that in which these roles are most clearly defined. That is what we have."

"But it is not kind," Eleanor said.

Anna Comnena waved her hand dismissively. "Oh, come now. Are you telling me that the lives of your peasants are in any way more pleasant than that of our slaves?"

"Yes," said Eleanor. "They can have families, and dwellings, and villages of their own. They can go to church, or even enter a holy order. If they have true ability they can sometimes rise."

Anna looked skeptical. "And you think such confusion is good?"

"Yes I do," Eleanor said.

Anna shrugged. "Well, to each their own," she said. "However, to return to your original question, I would rather measure the degree of civilization of a society by its literature."

"We have literature," Eleanor said.

Anna Comnena gave a little laugh. "Oh, I'm sure you have your tribal tales," she said. "But a true civilization must maintain its community with the great literature of the ages, and of that, I am afraid, you have no knowledge."

"Really?" said Eleanor. Then looking Anna in the eyes the Queen began to recite:

"I sing of arms and of a man: his fate
Had made him fugitive; he was the first
To journey from the coasts of Troy as far

As Italy and the Lavinian shores."

Anna Comnena raised her eyebrows. "Virgil. How remarkable. But then, being within the Latin Church's flock, some knowledge of Virgil might be expected. Unfortunately, true knowledge is to be found in the writings of the Greeks, and…"

I had enough of this snob. In truth, I can't really speak Greek well, but a bard is not a bard unless she knows her Homer, and I am a bard. I spoke the immortal words:

"Sing Goddess, of the man of many ways, who was driven
Far journeys, after he sacked Troy's sacred citadel.
Many were they whose cities he saw, whose minds he learned of,
Many the pains he suffered in his spirit on the wide sea,
Struggling for his own life and the homecoming of his companions."

Anna Comnena appeared delighted. "Homer!" she cried. "Now I am impressed. I must apologize, for indeed I have misjudged you. Perhaps you could let me make amends, and join me in my chambers after this dinner, as there is a gift I would like to give you."

Eleanor looked at me and shrugged. Then she turned back to the aged Princess.

"We would be honored," the Queen replied.

*** *** ***

The chamber of Princess Anna was filled with plush furniture inlaid with precious jewels. The walls were lined with icons and shelves filled with ancient books bound in leather. There were books in Latin and books in Greek, so many books, at least five for every one that Abbot Suger had; almost as many as I had seen in the vaults of Toledo. In the light of the three candles set upon the table I stared at them in wonder.

Anna spoke to Eleanor. "You know, I was here when the first Crusaders came through."

"Really?" Eleanor said, her astonishment evident.

"Yes," Anna nodded. "I was a girl, just a few years younger than this lass here." Here she pointed at me.

"I met all the great heroes; Bohemond, Tancred, Godfrey, Roger. My, they were men, men such as we do not see today," she said with a sigh.

"They were barbarians, yes, but you cannot imagine how strong they

211

were, how tall, how well built, how handsome, how manly."

"I don't know," said Eleanor. "I have a pretty good imagination for such things."

Anna Comnena said, "I am afraid that your husband and his companions do not measure up."

"I'm sure they don't," Eleanor replied.

Anna pointed at Eleanor. "But you, you are something new. A woman who refuses to be less than a man. A Kelt who refuses to be less than a civilized person."

Eleanor's expression darkened momentarily, then apparently she decided to ignore the insult. "If you choose to put it that way," she said.

"I do," said Anna. "And I like you for it. In an odd way, you remind me of myself at your age. You know, I was supposed to be Empress, to succeed my father Emperor Alexius on the throne. But Manuel stole everything from me, even as I am sure there are men who seek to steal your inheritance and power."

Eleanor nodded. "Indeed there are."

Anna Comnena continued, "And who, if this crusade of yours is defeated, will place all the blame on you, and use it as proof that women may never rule."

Eleanor shrugged. "I would expect as much."

Anna Comnena's voice became bitter. "And here they'll say, aha! How lucky we are, how fortunate we are, that the great Manuel saved us from having Anna as our Empress." She looked at us, her eyes angry. Then she went on. "So I have decided to help you. Listen. You must move your army to Asia at once, for Manuel has betrayed you."

Eleanor was startled. "What?"

"Yes," Princess Anna said. "He has signed a secret treaty with the Turks. He will not help you. He will not supply you. He is trying to hold you here, wasting your silver, while Conrad and his Germans move ahead to be ambushed alone. Once that is done, you will be encouraged to cross the straits. But Nuradin will have blocked all the passes leading forward, and our navy will cut off your retreat, leaving you trapped in Anatolia in winter, with no food, no funds, and no hope."

There was dead silence in the room for several moments. Then Eleanor spoke, her bewilderment evident. "I don't understand. Manuel is wed to the sister of Conrad's wife. How could he betray him to the slaughter?"

Anna Comnena laughed a wicked laugh. "He killed his own brothers, why not his brother-in-law? Besides, he has it in for you because he hates your uncle Raymond. He wants Antioch back in our empire, and he figures to buy it from Nuradin. Buy it with your lives."

Eleanor shook her head in horror. "I have never heard of such foul treachery."

"You have heard of it now," Anna said firmly. "Be assured, Manuel is a devious man. I am proud of my people, but there is a side to us that gives treachery a bad name. You need to learn of it. Here take this."

Princess Anna turned and pulled a thick volume from her shelf and handed it to Eleanor.

Anna said, "Here is a book that I have written. It is a history of my father's time and reign."

"So a woman has written a book!" I blurted out, excited beyond measure.

"Yes," Anna said. "I believe it is the first. It will tell you of innumerable betrayals that have gone on here. I obtained the leisure to write it after Manuel so graciously relieved me of the concerns of power. It is written in Greek, but you can find scholars to translate it into Latin. It is worth your reading, if you wish to be forewarned."

Eleanor held the book in both hands and looked the aged princess in the eye.

"Thank you," the Queen said.

Chapter 31

Our Rendezvous with the Germans

And so, forewarned by the Princess Anna Comnena, we escaped the trap that the evil Emperor Manuel had planned for us and crossed the army into Asia. The Bosphorus is much wider than the Rhine, but it is narrow for a sea, and there were many ships about, including good Christian ones from Genoa and Venice. The skillful captains of these vessels were willing to accept our silver for their ferrying service, even though it did not have the head of the divinely appointed Emperor Manuel marked upon it. It took a thousand ships to carry us all across, just as it had for the heroic Argive host of Agamemnon. However in our case, the face that caused the fleet to be launched was not Helen's, but Eleanor's.

Helen and Eleanor, two most famous queens, their names in fact are the same. Both were so beautiful as to inspire epic tales and epic deeds, both will live on forever in song and story. The former was foolish, the latter was wise. Both lived to enjoy the world, though Eleanor sought also to remake it. Yet, while both married worthless husbands, Helen at least had one that was good looking.

Be that as it may, our crossing of the Bosporus was made without losing a man. But Alicia replied that she thought it rather the result of the good seamanship of the Italians, who clearly knew their boats much better than our knights had known their Rhinish rafts. I felt sorry that she should take such a mundane view of the matter, for is it not sad when a person cannot perceive a miracle for what it truly is?

So we crossed, camped, and then rode on. Eleanor entrusted me with Anna's book, and I must say, that even though I had great difficulty reading it, I was very happy to have it, as its existence proved that my life's dream might well be possible. Of course, as a mere work of history, Anna's book did not compare with my project, which was to write literature, a genre which requires imagination, poesy, and skill and not just the time and ink to record vile events. Furthermore, while very instructive in its way, telling much about battles, weapons, stratagems, intrigues, and politics, the Byzantine Princess's book lacked style, taste, grace, plot, development of character, comedy, and romance, so that, my difficulties with the Greek aside, it was a boring text and clearly doomed to obscurity. In contrast, my plan was to produce a work that would delight the mind, rather than burden it, and thus be recommended from one reader to another until it was copied thousands of times, translated into many tongues, and known and loved throughout the world. For only this is the mark of a worthy book.

We passed the ruins of Troy, famous in the works of Homer, and then set forth for Nicea, a town of great renown, as it was there that the Emperor Constantine had first gathered all the wise men of his time to put down in writing the true creed of our Savior. As we approached this holy place, a great portent showed in the heavens. For though it was the middle of the day, a round darkness started eating away at the Sun, until the Sun was entirely blotted out, and the day became like night.

We stood transfixed at this terrible apparition, and many a brave knight fell to his knees in fervent prayer, while multitudes of others simply panicked and failed to take any effective action at all. Fortunately, after a while an edge of light started to appear on the side of the Sun where the darkness had first begun, and this grew and spread until finally the glowing orb that brings light to the world was fully restored.

The meaning of this message was much disputed, but it became clear enough when, but two days later, near Dorylaeum, we finally caught up with the army of our ally, Conrad of Germany.

There were thousands upon thousands of them: knights, men at arms, camp followers of both sexes, horses, mules, and hounds – a vast battlefield of corpses. Some were scattered upon the plain, others lying in piles, but all were dead and beginning to reek of corruption. Many of the bodies had been decapitated, and their heads stuck upon lances or missing altogether. Others were riddled with arrows. The only living things upon the field were legions of crows and savage Asian dogs that ripped and tore at the corpses.

Witnessing this apocalypse, I crossed myself and fell to my knees to pray for the souls of the departed. Thousands of our force did likewise, but Eleanor and Alicia did not. Rather they stood in solemn sadness, viewing the field in silence. Some may call this behavior strange, but it was just their way.

But there were so many dead. Their remains gave proof of such massacre as no chronicle has ever recorded. Suffice to say, it took nigh a week for us, as many as we were, to give Christian burials to all those poor souls. Towards the end of that horrid time, Conrad himself appeared, with his noblest companions, giving answer to the mystery of the absence of their bodies from the mountains of the slain.

Conrad was a well-built man with yellow hair. He looked the warrior, as did his dozen remaining men, who approached us on horseback while we were giving final rites to the last of his army. However I noticed that, manly as they were, the Germans all lacked shields or lances, and they and their horses were in a bedraggled condition.

According to his report, the valiant Conrad and his chosen knights had attempted to turn the contest with a wide flanking movement, but were delayed in their return to the field by the cowardly Turks, who thus separating Emperor from men, were able to slaughter his leaderless host in unfair battle. For seven days, brave Conrad and his band had pursued the knaves, seeking revenge, but the wretches had escaped him.

All this he explained at length at the campfire of our leaders that evening. Being of lower rank, Erika and I had to stand at the back, but all the listeners were so quiet that there was nothing Conrad said that we could not hear. At several points in his narrative I had to brush back tears, so impressed was I with the ardent valor with which Conrad had fought to save his doomed force, while Erika, being more stoic than I, only frowned and shook her head.

Such was his tale, which I truly believe, although I would be less than complete in my narration were I to fail to relate that there were many in our company more veteran than I, who were so uncharitable as to think rather that Conrad and his friends, having the fastest horses, had saved themselves by fleeing the field.

And so, reinforced by this bold warrior, we marched south, to Ephesus, the very town where once the Apostle Paul preached the gospel to the followers of the false Goddess Diana. This Goddess may be dethroned, but her temples remain, and as we marched into the seaport city, we were surrounded by their astonishing ruins.

King Louis wanted to stay here a while, for the place also had many notable relics and shrines, but we received word that the Turks were gathering a considerable force nearby on the banks of the River Meaender. It was thus resolved that we should march out and do battle. This decision having been made, Conrad, gentleman that he was, declined to subtract though his presence from the glory of the Franks, and instead took ship for Constantinople, and so serve as the herald of our certain victory to all of Christendom.

I have never seen a man so happy as Conrad was that day, waving gaily from the stern of his departing vessel, as our army, with pennants flying, marched out of Ephesus to do battle with the Turks.

Chapter 32

In the Footsteps of Alexander

On the day before Christmas, we met the enemy.

I have told you some of this day already, as it forced upon me the most terrifying decision of my life up to that moment. And though what was to follow was far more horrid, this was my first such encounter, and thus in its way the most formidable. So, let me now recount the scene that led up to my fateful decision, and then tell you what ensued.

We stood on the banks of the famous Meaender, a wide stream that makes a pleasant valley as it cuts through grassy meadows on its way to the sea. The day was overcast, though, cold and windy, with a grim slow rain that soaked and chilled us all, even as it threatened worse weather to come.

On our side of the river, valiant knights of every nation in Gaul massed in a long front of cavalry on a plain that sloped down through the meadow down towards the stream. Behind the crusading cavalry were our infantry.

Eleanor had gathered the Amazons in a tight company in the space between our horse and foot. Looking down the slope, we could see over the knights to the far side of the river, where the Turks were massed in the meadows. Mounted on ponies, they dashed back and forth in front of their wagons, barking like dogs as they waved about their evil trophies – the bloody heads taken from the Germans massacred at Doryleaum – in open defiance of all that is holy.

We stood mounted in a line abreast upon our horses, all in full armor, the hauberk of each covered by a white tunic carrying the cross of red that proclaimed our holy cause. Eleanor faced us, looking up and down the line without saying word. Unlike the rest of our company, she also had a lance which she carried point upright, as knights do before a battle. A cart drew up to us, driven by one of our camp followers. I could see that it was filled with steel-pointed lances.

Eleanor gestured at the cart. "The time has come," she said. "Take your lances."

The Amazons looked at each other in agitation. None of them had expected this.

Then Mamille de Roucy spoke up. "Take lances? Surely you don't mean for us to charge into the battle?"

"That is what Amazons do," Eleanor said, her voice as harsh as the cold wind.

Again the Amazon ranks buzzed with fearful whispers.

Mamille de Roucy shook her head. "We are not Amazons," she said. "We are ladies."

Eleanor looked at the lady in anger for several seconds. "Then what are you doing here?" she finally asked.

Across the river, the Turks started playing a game with the heads of the slaughtered Germans, cheering loudly as they rode about tossing them one to another. I shuddered.

"My Queen," Mamille pleaded. "You yourself ordained our code. It is not our role to fight, but to encourage valor in the knights who carry our colors before our eyes."

Mamille then pointed to the long row of knights, many of whose lances indeed were adorned with colored favors from the ladies.

Eleanor frowned. "That is well enough for gay days at court. But this," she shook her lance, "is for days such as today."

In the hills beyond the river, lightning flashed, and thunder followed.

"You really intend to ride into the fight?" the lady Torqueri of Bouillon asked, her amazement evident.

"I would not miss it for the world," Eleanor answered, and we could all hear the steel in her voice.

Then she called out. "Who will ride with me?"

Without hesitation, Erika and Sybille spurred their horses and rode up to pull lances from the cart and array themselves besides Eleanor. A moment later Alicia looked at me and smiled, then did the same. But the other Amazon ladies all backed their horses away.

I sat in my saddle, unmoving, stranded between the two groups. I didn't know what to do. The cold rain wetted the clothes beneath my armor, the wind blew, and I felt a chill.

Then I heard Eleanor's voice, harsh and imperative. "Marie? Your choice?"

This was my moment of truth.

I looked about, my entire life flashing before me as I shivered in my saddle.

Then I made up my mind. "My Queen," I said. "I am smallish for a lancer, and was not bred to the sword. But I am no coward. Let me accompany you with this, and I will play my part."

Speaking thus, I pulled a small brass bugle from my saddlebag, and held it up.

Eleanor looked at me and nodded. "Very well," she said. "Come then, my four true Amazons. Since we are too few to form a troop alone, let us join my knights of Aquitaine."

Then, as the rest of the Amazons watched astonished, Eleanor turned her horse and led the four of us away towards the front line.

It took us but a minute to reach that part of the front where the Aquitainian knights and nobles were mounted and lined up in row abreast. I recognized several of them, for my old acquaintance Sir Robert was there, as were the Count Hughes of Lusignian and the Count Geoffrey of Rancon, both high noblemen closely allied to Eleanor.

Sir Robert was the first to see us. "My Queen!" he called out.

"Greetings, Sir Robert," Eleanor said. "Count Rancon, Count Lusignian, my brave and loyal vassals, well met."

The splendidly accoutered Counts both nodded their acknowledgement.

Count Rancon looked the Queen up and down, armed and armored upon her horse. "I see you are ready for battle," he said.

Eleanor grinned. "Would you expect less from a Duchess of Aquitaine?" she said.

Count Lusignian smiled. "You do us proud," he said. "If only the Franks had so bold a leader."

"Ride in our company, Eleanor," Count Rancon said warmly.

Eleanor's eyes lit. "I would choose no other," she said.

The Queen then gestured to us, and in accord with her orders we brought our horses around to line up with the Aquitainian knights. Eleanor then rode in front and addressed the entire troop.

"Valliant gentlemen of Aquitaine, my brave Poitevins!," she called out in a voice like that Scipio must have used when he spoke to the legions on the morn of his battle with Hannibal.

"We are gathered here today on the banks of the River Maeander. It was here, on this very spot, over a thousand years ago, that the great Alexander met and defeated the armies of the Persian King Darius. Today, once again, men of the west, you face the eastern enemy on this field. Today, on the very anniversary of the birth of our Savior, you, once again, have a chance to make history. Your cause is just. The world is watching – not only the world of our time, but all futurity. Let you valor shine, so that a thousand years hence, the feats of arms that you do here today…"

At this point, Count Rancon gestured down the line. Following his hand, I saw that the Franks had begun to advance. Eleanor saw it too and stopped in her oration.

"Oh damnation," she said. "Those boors have to ruin everything." She looked at me. "Very well, Marie, sound the advance."

The moment had come. I picked up my bugle and blew one solid blast. As one, the Aquitainian knights begin to advance at a walk. Across the river, the Turks took notice, and started riding more frenetically back and forth on their ponies, their doglike yelping rising to a higher pitch.

"Advance at trot!" Eleanor said.

I blew my bugle twice, and, not only the Aquitainians, but the entire line of Crusader horse, accelerated into a trot.

"Advance at a canter!" the Queen commanded.

Now thrice I blew, and forty thousand armored horsemen spurred their steeds into a canter. The Turks went into a complete frenzy. But then, as we approached the river, they started shooting arrows, even as they continued to ride every which way upon their ponies. These arrows came at us fast and flat, for the Turks' bows were of horn and very strong. A few hit their mark, an eye or a neck, tumbling riders dead to the ground. One flew so close by my head that when I think of it I can still feel the wind upon my cheeks. But most struck armor or shields, and bounced away without harm.

"Charge!" Eleanor shouted.

Lifting my bugle a fourth time, I blew the charge, and the greatest army in the history of the world lowered its lances and galloped at the enemy at full tilt. Forty thousand knights on forty thousand horses; the meadow thundered to the sound of their hooves. We hit the river, and the icy water splashed up at us, but our blood was so hot we could not even feel it. Mad with the moment, I blew the charge again. Then we reached the further bank, our ranks still packed, a solid phalanx of steel and leveled lances moving forward with the speed of the best chargers in Christendom.

For the Turks, that was enough. They stopped shooting, looked to each other for a moment, then turned their horses and fled. Their retreat however, was blocked in part by their line of wagons, and a few tripped from their horses whilst trying to leap the wagon tongues to get away. These were instantly trampled by our pursuing host. Another few did not fall, but their horses were injured in the leap, so that they could not escape. These turned to fight, and scimitar in hand, charged our men with suicidal zeal, only to be lanced and trampled. One such was lanced by Sir Robert, while Erika accounted for another. But the large bulk of the Turks simply galloped away.

It was clear that further pursuit was pointless, and also dangerous, since if our horses became too winded we would become vulnerable.

Eleanor rode to me. "Sound the recall," she ordered.

I raised my horn and blew the recall, causing the knights to rein in their horses and begin to gather. Eleanor turned her horse, and I followed her back toward the Turkish wagons. These, I saw, were already being looted by our infantry and camp follower rabble, who had followed the knights across the river. As we rode slowly back, I surveyed the battlefield.

It was not a scene of vast carnage like the field at Nicosia. There were only a few score Turkish corpses, less than a dozen of our men fallen, and several dying or lame Turkish ponies bloodying the meadow. I thought to myself: this was not so bad.

Then I glanced down, and saw a Turkish lad. His face was still handsome, but his chest had been crushed by a charger's hooves and his entrails spilled out from his torn stomach like a hideous stew.

"Mother of God," I cried, then muttered a prayer for him, even though he had been a heathen.

Eleanor turned to me. "The cowards," she said. "Well, at least we got their wagons."

Louis came trotting over, accompanied by Odo. It was apparent from the spotless condition of their horse trappings and unwinded state of their mounts, that they had not taken part in the charge.

"A glorious victory," Louis said. "God truly showed himself this Christmas Eve."

Odo nodded. "I think he also showed that his foes face a mighty avenger in you, my Lord. For you have broken them with a rod of iron."

Eleanor frowned at the two of them. "Yes," she said. "Well, perhaps it would be wise for the mighty avenger to stop his rabble from looting all the victuals from the Turkish wagons." She pointed at the wagons, which were rapidly being despoiled by the mob. "We have a long march ahead of us before we reach Antioch."

Louis smiled at her indulgently. "Eleanor, Eleanor," he said. "Consider the lilies of the field. Can you not see that the Lord will provide for his flock? Tomorrow is Christmas, which calls for a feast."

The King gestured at the wagons and the happy rabble making off with the goods, then continued. "And He has made one for his people. So, let us camp here, and celebrate the yuletide."

So we did. It proved to be a mistake.

Chapter 33

A Deadly Baptism

In accordance with the King's order, we encamped and celebrated our Christmas on the banks of the river Meaender.

The drizzle of the previous day had turn to hard rain, but we had good tents, which kept us warm and dry.

After morning mass we gathered within, and with Yuletide logs burning bright, we drank and sang from afternoon to evening. Then, with the fall of night, we began our Christmas feast, made all the merrier by the plentiful vittles our valor of the previous day had won for us from the Turks.

We shared our feasting tent with the knights of Aquitaine, for these were Eleanor's favorites, as many were her kinsmen, and what is more, most accomplished both on the battlefield and in all the courtly ways that are pleasing to ladies. It was in this company then, we found ourselves, drinking, singing, dancing, and joking, two hours before the midnight, while yet another fine thigh of beef roasted upon the spit.

I was tightening my lute for another song, when I saw Erika rise from her seat, and cock her head, then walk over and open the flap that served as the door of our tent. She stood there, just inside, with her hand to her ear, as if listening for something. Curious as to what this might be, I rose to join her.

I listened, and heard the sound too. It was low, and quiet, but grew louder with each moment. It did not sound like horsemen though, for it was too constant. It was more like a steady grinding or growling, like a heavy wind, only much deeper in tone. I wondered what it could be.

The clouds broke a little, and the pale moonlight pierced the rain to dimly illuminate the landscape. In that instant we both saw it. From the upstream direction, a foamy torrent was moving down the valley, making straight for our camp,

I turned to Eleanor, who was still by the fire. "My lady, look!" I cried in alarm.

The Queen and Sir Robert ran to the tent flap. I pointed and they looked, and were instantly aghast. For the torrent now approaching was nothing less than a roaring tidal wave, taller than a horse. As we watched in horror, it struck the upstream edge of the camp, and swept away men, horses and tents like toys. One man, seeing the imminent peril ran to the alarm bell, and pulled the rope to send it ringing before the flood washed him away. But he did not fall in vain, for the great bronze bell stood firm on its tall tripod, and rang out the alert to the entire camp.

Everywhere, people streamed from their tents, with many of the knights gripping swords, as they thought we were under attack by the Turks.

Sir Robert shouted to all in our tent. "Run for the high ground!"

Still holding my lute, I fled up the meadow slope to try to escape the coming flood. Many others were dashing about me, but the cloudy moonlight was so dim in the rain that I could not see who they were.

Then the wave slammed into me. My run had gained me some altitude, so the flood was only waist high when it struck, but still it knocked me over. I was washed down under water, and rolled about to a place where the water only came to my knees. There I was able to stand, still clutching my lute, and hold my ground amidst the torrent. Everywhere about in the darkness I could hear desperate splashing and cries for help. I tried to step further towards higher ground, but I could barely make any progress in the raging water.

Then lightning flashed, and I saw upstream another huge wave, even taller than the first, rushing down the valley. I tried to run, but it was hopeless.

Suddenly, I saw someone on horseback. It was Eleanor riding her magnificent stallion. She charged to me

"Marie! Here!" she shouted.

I grabbed Eleanor's hand, and with her help, hauled myself up on the back of the horse.

Eleanor spurred Pegasus into a gallop for high ground. "Yah!" she cried

***   ***   ***

We struggled to the plain above the valley, and spent the night there, shivering in the cold rain.

In the morning, the storm ceased, and the blessed Sun brought light and some warmth. The flood being spent, we descended from the plain into the valley to meet such others as had survived.

It was a valley of mud and death. Everywhere we went, mud-coated and bewildered people staggered about the soaked remains of our camp. Rows of drowned knights, soldiers, and camp followers of both sexes lay in the waterlogged earth. Knights dug about in the mud, looking for arms or armor to salvage, while the camp women wept over the bodies of the dead. Most of the wagons were overturned, and almost all the tents had been destroyed. It was a scene of utter devastation.

We had some joy at discovering that Alicia, Erika, and Sybille had all survived, as had Sir Robert and many others. But we lost half the army in that flood. Fifty thousand knights perished, with many poorer souls and horses, and most of our supplies swept away.

Among the drowned dead I found the corpse of Eleanor's servant Clara. Nearby her was a young man, in humble clothing, and their hands were touching. With a shock I recognized him. He was the apprentice boy who had brought us Gilbert's message from Poitiers what now seemed like so many years ago. Eleanor had ordered Clara to feed him in the kitchen after his interview. What had happened between them? Had they fallen in love and remained a pair? They must have, for here they were, together in death. How little we know of the humble folk about us, who invisibly lead lives as full of passion and meaning to themselves as ours are to us! And here were thousands of such, and knights and renowned nobles too, all now cut short in the midst of life.

How could the good God could do such a thing, I do not know. I asked one of the holy Fathers, but he did not know either. He said though, that we must not lose faith. For God is good, and this we must believe, or lose all hope of salvation.

Mass burials were held. I cried and prayed. Eleanor did not weep or pray aloud, for that was not her way. But as we walked together among the rows of the dead, I saw that she had tears in the corners of her eyes.

It took us a week to bury our dead, the same as it had for the Germans. For though our deceased were fewer than theirs, so were those who would inter them.

At the end of this time, a council of war was held to decide upon our further course of action. Opinion on this score was quite divided, for with the loss of all of the Germans and half our own army, but one quarter of the force that had set out to succor the Holy Land yet remained.

The Count of Champagne was a bold enough man under most circumstances, but he had seen enough. He was skillful with words in council, and as he laid his argument, won many others to his point of view.

"We must turn back," the Count said. "Our enterprise is cursed. The disappearing Sun should have warned us. Then we were sent a flood. How much more evidence of a curse do we require? Fighting Turks is one thing, fighting supernatural powers is another."

The Count paused, then concluded, raising his finger with careful emphasis. "I say again. We must turn back. We must turn back now. This enterprise is cursed."

He sat down, and as he did, I could see that more than half the assembled nobles agreed with him.

Then Eleanor rose. "We are not cursed!" she said, with anger in her voice. "We were tricked! Can't you see? The Turks knew the valley would flood in winter, so they lured us here. Such cowards, they can't face us in fair battle, so they try stratagem."

The Queen looked around at the assembled nobles, her eyes like embers. "Should we let those they murdered thus go unavenged?" she cried. "We still have men enough, and now we know their game. So let us take the high road through the mountains, and see what the knaves dare when they lack waters to do their fighting for them."

Many knights nodded agreement, but not all.

King Louis spoke. "We are being tested," he pleaded. "We are pledged to Jerusalem, and our faith is being tested."

The Count of Champagne shrugged.

Eleanor regarded the knights. "Not just faith," she said. "Our courage is being tested too. Our courage." There was iron in her voice as she said this.

She then looked the doubtful Count dead in the eye. He frowned and nodded.

Amazingly, King Louis actually caught his cue. He raised his sword.

"To Jerusalem, then!" The King exclaimed.

All present saluted with their swords. "To Jerusalem!"

Chapter 34

The Mount Cadmos Massacre

And so we marched into the mountains, pressing ever further on into the high country. First there was mud, then there was snow, and despite the strength of our mighty horses, we ourselves had to push our wagons hard to make them move through it all.

By mid-January we had reached the high passes of the mountains of Paphlagonia. Here the weather changed sharply, for despite the season, the Sun blazed hot, and so we removed our armor to march in greater comfort.

On the twentieth of the month, we approached the saddle pass that leads the way through Mount Cadmos. Louis could never decide for once and all the order of march, and so it was the custom for the nations to take turns. On this day, we Amazons, myself included, were with the main army of the Franks and Flemings, while further ahead, the Aquitainians had the honor to be the van. Eleanor and Alicia joined them in the forward division so as to travel in the company of their countrymen, as did also the King's uncle, the Count Maurienne, for the sake of maintaining the royal authority. It had been decided that all would stop to camp at the crest of the pass.

However, when they reached the summit about midafternoon, the advance guard discovered it to be a desolate tableland swept by the winds. No forage was to be had. Yet all could clearly see in the valley just ahead, green fields watered with cool streams, making it a fine campground for men and horses all tired and hungry from a long day's journey.

According to Alicia, who was there with Eleanor, Count Rancon, and Count Maurienne, when they first reached crest of the pass, this is what occurred.

At first they were all silent for a while, as they considered the situation looking about from atop their horses. Then finally Eleanor spoke. "An unpleasant place for a camp," she said. "What say you, Count Maurienne?"

Maurienne agreed. "There's no forage for the horses," he said. "We'd do much better in that fair valley beyond."

"There's time enough to reach it," Count Rancon said, "the afternoon being yet young."

Eleanor took some seconds to answer. Then she said, "True. Although our orders are to wait here for the main force."

As the Queen was undecided, Count Maurienne reassured her with a dismissive shrug. "No one has seen a Turk in weeks," he said. "I'm sure my nephew, the King, would agree that we should not be over careful and starve our mounts while we guard ourselves from phantoms."

"Very well," said Count Rancon. "Since you say so, I vote for proceeding to the valley as well. I'm sure the King cannot be far behind."

Eleanor looked backward as if trying to see the main army, although the bend in the road made it impossible for her to determine if it was following close by or far. She did not say anything for a full minute, but just sat there upon her horse with a worried look.

Finally she spoke, "Yes. I suppose. After all, how slow can he be?"

Count Maurienne gestured towards the valley and spurred his horse into a walk. Rancon followed suit. Eleanor looked about and sighed, then set forth, leading the Aquitainian advance guard down from the pass towards the green pastures waiting below.

***   ***   ***

As this was occurring, we in the main army were still some ways back, making our way up the mountain path between a steep boulder-covered slope on the one side, and a set of terrible and sharp cliffs and ravines on the other. I was walking besides Erika, playing my lute, while we led our horses by their reins, letting them carry our armor for us through the hot afternoon. A knight who had taken a fancy to Erika walked next to her, making conversation as he led his horse in the same way. Further to the rear, the King also walked, in monk's garb, the monkish Odo walking by his side. In fact the entire army was afoot, knights leading their steeds, except for some of the Amazon ladies, who foot-tired that they were, remained atop the wagons, while their maids and washerwomen pushed. Despite the manifest absence of the enemy, some of the knights still insisted on carrying their swords and shields, but very few were wearing full armor.

I saw a strange bird fly overhead, and turned to Erika to ask her if she knew what it might be. At that moment, an arrow pierced the neck of the knight walking by her side.

Suddenly, the Turks were everywhere. Hundreds of the heathens appeared, then thousands, as if by magic, leaping out of the hidden ravines, charging down the slopes to our side, yelling at the top of their lungs.

"Allah Akbar!" they shouted. "Allah Akbar!"

The air was filled with arrows. Many struck the horses, which panicked, and breaking free of their owners, ran off, leaving the most us without horse, arms, or armor, facing onrushing hordes of scimitar waving Turks. I saw some men at arms try to run, but they were hit by arrows from behind before they took ten steps. Some others turned to grapple, but without swords they stood no chance and were cut down. Three knights nearby managed to get their swords, and began to make a fight of it, but, beset from all sides they fell quickly. As Erika wrestled unsuccessfully with her leaping horse to try to reach her sword, the Turks attacked the Amazon wagons, and hacking like furies, slaughtered the screaming women.

Candice of Troyes jumped from her wagon and tried to run, chased by two giant screaming Turks right to the edge of the precipice. Trapped, she turned, and seeing the heathens coming straight for her, gentle Candice crossed herself and leapt into the gorge. Beside the Amazon wagons, a group of camp follower women fell to their knees before the Turks, begging for mercy. In seconds they were cut in bloody parts.

Another arrow hit Erika's horse, causing the gelding to rear up and punch at the Dane with his front legs. Erika had to let go of the reins, and the horse dashed off to destroy himself in the ravine.

The Amazons' murderers now came for us. There was nothing for it. We ran. We had been leading the Amazon column, so the Turks being to our rear, we dashed up the path towards a forager's cart which was the rearmost element of the Flanders contingent just ahead.

When we reached the wagon, I was in the lead, with Erika just behind me and two fast Turks closing in hard behind her. Erika toppled a keg from the sideboard, causing the lead Turk to stumble, but only for an instant, gaining us but a fathom's distance from our pursuers. Then, as I reached front of the wagon, another Turk came around the side and appeared directly in front of me.

I stopped in my tracks. The Turk waved his scimitar and screamed. "Allah Akbar!"

I smashed my lute across his face. The wood turned to splinters, the strings cried and snapped, and the Turk fell.

Erika snatched his scimitar before it hit the ground. "Well done!" she shouted. Then she turned, and swinging the scimitar with both hands, cleaved the Turk who had nearly caught us. His companion was but a step behind, and struck at her, but Erika whirled out of his way, then whipped back to slice him through.

I jumped up into the wagon. There was a big wooden box marked with the ax symbol. This was where the forager's tools were kept. Pushing as hard as I could, I shoved this off the back of the wagon. The box hit the ground and shattered, scattering axes upon the road. A group of fleeing men at arms picked them up, and turned to make a fight of it.

As Erika and the axe men fought off more onrushing Turks, I threw the rest of the axe boxes onto the ground. Then with the cart empty, I stood up and used my elevated position to see what was happening elsewhere up and down our column.

The slaughter had turned into something like a battle, but one that was going very badly for us. I saw some knots of resistance, but everywhere terrified camp followers and unarmed soldiers were running this way and that being murdered by the Turks.

On the road just ahead, a brave knight defending a group of camp followers was cut down by two Turks. One of the Turks then beheaded him, and held his head up to the cowering cooks and washerwomen. "Allah Akbar!" the heathen screamed, then tossing the head, swung his sword down on the women.

I looked to the rear, where the Franks had been following the Amazon unit. A group of a dozen knights with swords and shields had formed a protective ring around two monks. It was the King and Odo! As I watched, these two scurried up the hillside and hid themselves in a cleft in the rocks. The knights formed a defensive line, their tall leader brandishing a shield marked with blue and yellow squares. Sir Bertrand! My heart rose in my throat as a wave of Turks charged his courageous band.

I couldn't watch, so I turned the other way. There I saw the Count and Countess of Flanders, standing back to back, swords and shields in hand, fighting off Turks who beset them from both sides. The Count was a huge and muscular man, famous as a warrior, and Sybille was laying about herself with a skill and ferocity almost to match him, but against so many enemies, they could not last long. Then I saw a Turk on a pony bear down on the Count, and assault him from above. This is the end, I thought.

But as the Turk swung his scimitar down, Flanders blocked the blow with his shield, and then thrusting with his sword, spigotted the Turk and tossed him out of his saddle. The Count leapt up upon the pony and waved his bloody sword about.

Through the din of battle, I heard his cry. "Flanders to me! Flanders to me!"

As he shouted, dozens of his men, all bearing his coat of arms, started to gather round, forming a shield wall.

I yelled to Erika and pointed. "We must make for the Count!"

She nodded, and, with the axe men following, the two of us dashed off through the melee to reach the Flemings.

Sybille welcomed us through the line. "Erika, Marie. Thank God."

"He'll get scarce thanks from me today," Erika said.

I looked at her, shocked.

Sybille turned to me. "We need to rally more men," she said. "Marie, do you have your bugle?"

This question bewildered me, for I had not expected it, and I was a more than a little dazed from all that had happened. So it took me a moment to understand her. Then I glanced down and saw that my kit bag was still hanging from my shoulder strap. I patted it and felt the bugle inside.

"Why, yes," I said.

"Then blow, Marie," Sybille urged. "Blow!"

I pulled out my bugle and regarded it for a moment. Then lifting it to my lips, I blew the recall as loud as I could. Then I blew it again, and again, with a fervor such as only pure terror can bring.

Up and down the mountain path the call resounded, and scores of fighting me rallied to our force.

***   ***   ***

At this moment, the Aquitainians in the valley beyond the pass were happily pitching their tents. Eleanor, Count Rancon, and Count Maurienne sat on their horses watching the camp go up, their reins loose, so the beasts could graze the while. Wanting to taste the water of the stream, Alicia had ridden off a short ways, and was almost to her destination when she discerned a faint sound in the distance. Immediately, she turned her steed and galloped hard to Eleanor.

Startled, the Queen turned to her.

"What is it, Alicia?" Eleanor asked. "I hear a bugle," said Alicia. "Listen."

All were quiet. Then faintly, so faintly, the sound of a horn echoed.

Count Rancon said, "It sounds like it is coming from beyond the pass."

Eleanor was alarmed. "Could it be a battle?"

"I doubt it," said Count Maurienne.

"We had best make sure," said Eleanor. She turned to her kinsman. "Count Rancon, gather a force of two thousand knights. We need to head back towards the army. They could be under attack."

"Yes, My Queen," said Count Rancon. Then charging to the camp, he shouted and waved his arms, and a force of armed horsemen started to assemble around him.

*** *** ***

I kept blowing for near half an hour. By that time, we had a solid battalion, of mixed arms and every nation, brave fighters all assembled around the heroic Count of Flanders. Our shield wall was up. But from every side, Turks rained arrows at us, and some made their mark.

Sybille spoke to the Count. "My husband, we can't stay here."

"I know," the Count said. The he raised his voice to address his troops. "Men, we need to take the hill. Are you with me?"

The men banged their swords against their shields, the clamor sounding like thunder.

"Then charge with Flanders!" the Count shouted. "Sound the horn!"

I blew the charge. Then men surged uphill, shouting. "Flanders! Flanders! Flanders!"

The Turks upslope fired arrows and rolled boulders down on us, killing scores, but our knights and men at arms kept advancing. Then the Turks charged down the hill, and met our front rank sword to sword. But despite being in the downhill position, the fury of our men forced them back, step by step, killing and dying for every inch of slope. We reached the crest of the hill, and with a mighty shout, the men flooded over the top, fighting madly. I was terrified, but advanced running along with the rest, blowing the charge as often as I could.

Then Sybille saw something in the distance. "Look there! It is Aquitaine!"

I looked. In the distance I saw a column of mounted knights in full armor, headed by Eleanor and Rancon, emerge from the top of the pass. The Turks saw them too and scattered, disappearing almost as swiftly as they had appeared.

Covered with blood from head to foot, the Count of Flanders

triumphantly held up his sword.

"Flanders! Flanders! Flanders!" the men on the hill all cheered.

"Eleanor," I said softly under my breath.

*** *** ***

It was near sunset when I made it to the bottom of the hill to meet Eleanor.

The Queen, Count Rancon, Sir Robert, and others of their force were moving slowly on horseback down the path of the ruined Frankish column. Everywhere there were corpses. Some of the fallen were Turks, but far more Crusaders of every rank and condition littered the ground. We also had many severe wounded, cut in every place, and nearly all of these were doomed as well. This they knew, and it showed in their eyes.

There were survivors too, more than one might think. These emerged bloody and bedraggled from hiding spots between boulders, under wrecked wagons, or dead horses, or clefts in the side of the ravines.

Eleanor said nothing to me when I approached, so I walked quietly by her horse's side as she surveyed the devastation. We reached the place where I had thought I saw Sir Bertrand and his men take a stand.

He was there, dead upon the ground, along with all the rest of his brave band. Some score of Turks lay lifeless about them.

Eleanor looked at him. "Sir Bertrand," she said with sadness.

I felt like weeping. "He was a brave knight," was all I could say.

Then we saw the King and Odo emerge from their hiding place amidst the rocks. There was no blood upon their clothes or on their swords. They approached us.

Eleanor spoke scornfully. "So, my husband, were you searching yonder cave for Turks?"

Odo took umbrage. "You should not speak so," he said, "for the King slew many heathens this day."

"I'm sure," Eleanor said.

Odo pointed at the spotless battledress of the Aquitainians. "Your men give scant evidence of battle," he said.

"No," said Eleanor. "We only just arrived."

"What?" King Louis cried. "Eleanor, where were you? Your force was supposed to be here."

Count Rancon spoke. "We had moved on to the valley beyond for better

234

pasture."

The King looked at Rancon. "By whose decision?"

"Mine," said the Count.

Louis screamed. "Then you are a traitor!"

Odo put his hand on the King's arm. "Hang him, my lord," Odo said. "If not for his disobedience, the battle would have been ours."

Eleanor down at the two of them from her horse. "You shall not hang him," she said, her voice level.

"I am King here, and not you," seethed Louis. "And though he be your vassal, he will hang."

Eleanor glared at her husband. "Then hang your uncle Count Maurienne too, for he decided equally."

Louis and Odo looked at each other confounded. Then Louis turned back to Eleanor. "Very well," the King said, like a petulant youth. "I'll banish him. I'll not have him in my army."

Eleanor swept her gaze across the shambles of our crusading force. "What's left of it," she said.

Chapter 35

A Nightmare Journey

We pushed onwards into the mountains. Again the weather turned harsh, and snow fell all about us. The horror of this march was unending. With our wagons gone, so was most of our food, and we had few clothes but those we had worn on the summer-like day of the battle. Even Eleanor had little more than a woolen cloak to shield herself from the biting cold. The poorest of our force had no shoes, and most of those of the middle sort broke, so that the better part of our infantry had to walk barefoot upon the freezing ground, leaving red tracks in the snow behind them.

Some of the knights ate their horses, and it was a pitiable thing to see so many noble steeds, who had served their masters loyally, through glorious tournament, fierce and deadly battle, and dreary long journey, stabbed through and butchered for a meal. Those who had brought hounds devoured them as well.

But many had no horses, dogs, or hidden biscuits, and these starved. Others, lacking decent cloaks, froze, and many more expired of pestilence. By the hundreds the weak fell to lie in the snow, and no one had the strength to lift them up. So there they perished, to be covered under the drifts, their bodies thus to be preserved until spring made them food for the ravens.

The few tents we had left were nearly useless against the cold, and the last of these were destroyed one evening when a mighty wind blew through our camp. So we all would have frozen had not Erika shown us the way to build houses out of snow. This craft she had learned as a girl on a voyage with her grandfather to the far north, a place where she said islands of ice float in the ocean, there is no night in summer or day in winter, mountains belch smoke, the sky sometimes catches fire, white bears the size of giants hunt for whales as our bears hunt fishes, and a race of trolls dwell in snow houses, worship demons, and eat nothing but meat.

This grandfather of Erika's was himself a believer in the old false gods of the Norse, for he had refused conversion to the true faith when the priest told him that to do so would be to forgo in the afterlife the company of his ancestors, who being pagans, were all in hell. So now he was there too, and

Erika had come on crusade to earn his redemption and that of the rest. But it was the troll wisdom he had taught Erika that now saved us.

You could build a fire in such a snow house, provided you kept it small and placed it on top of a metal covered shield. Otherwise it would melt right down into the snow and go out if the snow was of any depth. So those without metal shields had to dig all the way to the ground before they could have a fire, and this was very tiresome work after a hard day's march. But not to build a fire was to die frozen in the night.

When the snow was new and deep, we had to put leather bags on the hooves of our horses. Otherwise their legs would sink in beyond their knees, making it impossible to for them to move. Our own Amazon red leather riding boots were sound against the snow, but if it were too soft and deep, we would sink in above their tops, so that the coldness got in around our feet anyway. It was here that my woolen stockings proved of better worth than the silk of my noble friends, and it was fortunate that my dear mother, may God bless her soul in Heaven, had before her untimely departure taught me the art of sewing socks from rags of wool, or Alicia and Eleanor might have lost their feet to the frost.

The new snow was deadly to the eyes when the Sun came out, for it was so bright that some of those who looked too much upon it lost their sight. But if the day were clouded and snowy – and sometimes we marched so high in the mountains that we were in the clouds ourselves – it could be even worse, for at such times it was easy to stray off the path, and those who did so were lost forever.

The Turks also gave us no respite, for they hung about the edge of the army, slaying any who might lag behind. And at night, as Eleanor, Alicia, Erika and I huddled together around our tiny fire in our shelter of packed snow, we could sometimes hear the screams as these devils stole into our camp edge to murder the weak or unawares.

They would sometimes attack by day as well. At first this was only by shooting from a great distance, which caused little loss. But as the march wore on, and our men and horses grew so weak that they could not give chase, the Turks grew bolder, and coming ever closer, claimed more and more victims with each passing hour.

It was during a daytime ambush that Alicia lost her Andalusian to a Turkish arrow, an event that left her stricken with grief, for she had raised him since he was a colt, and she was one who felt deeply about horses. Yet after cradling his head in her lap while he breathed his last, she allowed him to be cut up for food, as there was none other left.

For two weeks thus we journeyed through this hell. Then it ended.

It was on the fifth of February, the Year of Our Lord one thousand, one hundred and forty eight. The mountain pass we trudged through seemed like any other, but, when we reached the crest, we gazed before us. In the sunlight was a snow-free slope leading down through grassy meadows to the sapphire Mediterranean, and a walled city filled with Christian churches.

The knights pointed and shouted like the warriors of Xenophon. "The sea! The sea!"

I fell to me knees in prayer. "Thank you, holy Virgin," I cried. "Thank you for delivering us from the wilderness."

Joy filled our souls, and new strength poured into limbs. We scurried down the hill to the beautiful town. As we ran, I could see the smoke rising from hundreds of kitchens, and smell the spiced meat roasting upon the spit. This city proved to be the Greek port of Satalia, and its citizens welcomed us in their customary fashion. That is, they slammed the gates in our faces, and called out their soldiers to man the walls against our approach. None of us were allowed inside, and none of them came out to help.

So we camped outside the walls. There was some forage there, so our few remaining horses could recover some strength. But we had little food, and the only way the Greeks would sell us more was by lowering baskets from the walls, which we had to fill with silver coins. They would then haul these baskets up, and drop down in exchange a parcel of such food as they might care to give. Most of this was old bread or rotten fish, but whatever its condition, it would all be devoured instantly by our famished men, in the case of fish, head and all, without waiting to put it on a fire. And however horrible this food might be, the worst part was that there would soon be no more, for our silver was almost gone.

Our only hope was to reach Antioch, where Eleanor's uncle Raymond ruled as prince. The Greeks offered to take us there by ship, but at four marks a man, only the rich could go. Kind Eleanor paid my passage for me, and so to sea I went with the nobles, while the brave Count of Flanders volunteered to lead those of the footmen who still remained strong in a landward march to Antioch. Thus we parted, with those too poor to ship or too weak to march left behind to the mercy of the Turks.

Our ship was of the bulky type that Greek merchants use for cargo. It had two tall masts, each with a large triangular sail of the lateen sort, and as these filled to take us out of the harbor, I stood on the deck with Eleanor,

Alicia, Sybille, and Erika, while several other vessels of similar design carried the remains of the flower of Gallic knighthood out with us. All our clothes were gone, except for the dirty ragged Crusader tunics that had made the journey with us from Mount Cadmos to the sea.

I looked back and saw the Count of Flanders on horseback leading a column of infantry along the shore. But in our tent camp outside the city, wounded men on crutches still limped about, glancing hopelessly up the slope from time to time towards the mountains. There the Turks were visible, waiting their moment.

I prayed fervently, then turned away. For I could not watch what was to follow.

The first days of our voyage were fair, and Erika offered some diversion by instructing me in the workings of the ship and its sails, a matter in which she had great expertise, and in which I, as the daughter of an enginator, found considerable interest. The dried fish, stale biscuits, and sour wine offered us as provisions were less than wholesome, yet after the starvation of the mountains, served well enough. But then the storms came, and with them an agony of sickness and nausea that was like the plague itself.

For three weeks we sailed, the cruel winds blowing us this way and that. Then, on the twentieth night of our voyage, the horrible weather turned into such a tempest as to make the gale that wrecked Ulysses seem like a sun shower in comparison.

The waves were like mountains, and they tossed the ship about like a toy. Water crashed over the deck, and washed away men and horses the way a kitchen maid's broom sweeps away insects. We Amazons tried to stay safe in the hold, but when a wave swept away the pumping crew, the Captain called us up.

We ran to the pump, and were barely in time to grab the handles when a massive cold billow crashed over the ship, soaking us through. Then lightning flashed, and I saw Eleanor's hair glowing red like flame.

"Push!" Eleanor shouted.

So we pushed, running like madmen at the pump all through the night, while the lightning flashed, the wind roared, and wave after wave blasted us without pity.

Chapter 36

Antioch the Wonderful

Yet God in his mercy is kind, and on the seventh day after Easter, we safely reached St. Simeon, the port of Antioch.

As we sailed into the harbor on a shining spring day, hundreds of little boats flocked around us. Antioch was a vast and beautiful city, with high walls, white marble houses, ancient temples, Christian churches, and terraced gardens rising on both sides of a magnificent blue bay. I was still shaken and ill from the rocking of the storm, but as I stood at the railing of our battered vessel, the approaching town seemed to me like a vision of heaven, and the gulls circling above, welcoming angels.

We came alongside the wharf, and ropes were thrown to the dockmen, who catching them in the air, wrapped them around posts to secure us well. A gangplank with a rope railing was then lowered, and Eleanor led her few remaining Amazons off the ship. Near a dozen had survived the flood, the battle, and the mountains, yet many of these had thereby taken their fill of war, and rather then proceed further, had shipped out of Satalia back to France. If Eleanor had decided to go with them, I would have been more than happy to follow. But the Queen was resolute, and therefore, being her friend, so was I. Thus, of the original five score Amazon warriors, only Eleanor, Sybille, Erika, Alicia, and I were left.

And what a sight we must have been as we staggered down that gangplank. For our crusader tunics were so worn that what was once white was now the color of dark earth, and rent and torn in more places than it was together. Our hair was twisted like the nests of rats, our countenances were sickly, and our exhausted eyes were shot with blood.

A tall man of middle thirty years came striding towards us down the dock from the shoreward end. He wore fine clothes of the flowing type worn by noble Christians in the Holy Land, and was followed by four others dressed nearly as well. This leader was a handsome man, built like a true warrior, and sported well a trimmed mustache and beard, and hair the same red color as Eleanor's.

The Queen looked and saw him, and despite her exhaustion, light entered her face.

"Uncle Raymond!" she cried

Prince Raymond waved and shouted, "Eleanor!"

Eleanor staggered forward and Raymond ran to meet her. Then they met and he grasped her and hugged her tightly to his breast. Eleanor put her head on his shoulders and closed her eyes.

"Oh, uncle Raymond," she wept. "Uncle Raymond."

Raymond stroked her matted hair and spoke softly to his niece. "All is well. You're safe now, Eleanor. You're safe."

As Raymond held her thus, another ship approached the dock on its far side, with Louis and Odo standing at her bow. I looked at them, but they did not return my glance. Instead they stared at Raymond holding Eleanor, and it was apparent from their frowns that they did not like what they were seeing.

***　　***　　***

In Antioch kind Prince Raymond gave us good food and warm beds, the first we had known since Ephesus. He gave us clothes too, both military and female, for we needed both guises, as what we had left were but rags. Eleanor, however, while appreciating her uncle's gifts, wanted to choose clothes after her own fashion. So on the third day after our arrival, already much recovered, we went to the bazaar.

Antioch, in those days, was a grand city, second only to Constantinople in size, but far more beautiful, and dare I say, more interesting. For amazing as it may sound, in this one town, although ruled by a Christian lord, were not only many true Christians, but also Greek schismatics, Jews, Moslems, and members of other eastern sects. This is not the approved custom in France, and while in Aquitaine, Spain, and other such worldly places, non-believers may be found living among Christians, here there were many more. Thus, within one wall there stood churches, basilicas, synagogues, mosques, flame houses, and even the ancient temple of Apollo, all together, and many prayers were heard in many tongues, and diverse foreign costumes seen everywhere, so that it was as if all the world were gathered into one city.

And though it might be thought that with all these gathered into one town they should be at each other's throats, under the wise government of Prince Raymond, who chose to be kind to each, all were peaceable, and even mixed in festivals and marriages, so that there were many in the city who were by halves and quarters of each and every kind.

All this disturbed King Louis greatly, as he wished to keep company only with those of his own faith, and thought all Christians should do likewise. But Eleanor was delighted, for, as she said, manifold peoples make for manifold amusements, and much improves the shopping. And as for me, it made me wonder; if such a town could be ruled this way, why not the world?

And the bazaar of Antioch was utterly fabulous. It stood in the midst of a great plaza, directly before the marble temple of Apollo, while all about there rose terraced green hills, adorned with fountains and laced with churches, mosques, basilicas, and synagogues. Eleanor and Alicia spent half the afternoon playfully picking up and sporting with exotic flowing silken gowns of every fashion and color, while I wandered among the merchants' booths seeing strange curiosities from far off lands and empires barely known to Christendom.

The Queen found great relief from the pains of our journey by buying all sorts of fancy things, and made me very happy by getting me another lute, a fine one wrought with intricate designs and capable of the sweetest tones.

It was shortly after this purchase was made that an event occurred which has since become the source of many bizarre stories based upon complete ignorance.

I am referring of course to Eleanor's encounter with the famous Saladin.

Foolish minds upon hearing report that such a meeting occurred, have embellished it fabulously, to the point of suggesting that the good Christian Queen Eleanor went so far as to have a romantic entanglement with the notorious heathen. Since I was there, I feel it to be my duty to render a true account of this event.

After Eleanor had purchased the lute, we moved on to examine the stall of a merchant from Persia. This man had many fine and curious wares from faraway lands for sale, which attracted the minute scrutiny of Eleanor for some time. Whilst she was thus engaged, Alicia, who had an extraordinary fondness for horses, held communion with that of the merchant, which, tied up nearby, was a very beautiful mare of the Arabian kind.

I also found amusement at the Persian's stall by conversing with the merchant himself. This man was a follower of the creed of Zoroaster, which he said was the faith of his country prior to the invasion of the Mohammedans. As he described it, the Zoroastrian faith sounded to me to be somewhat like that of the Cathars. They believe there to be two opposing Gods, one good and filled with light, the other evil and dedicated to darkness, and call upon all people to join with the forces of light so that the good may emerge triumphant. For this reason fire, the source of all light, is their sacred symbol, and they keep a torch lit in their temples at all times. That is why many people call them fire-worshippers, but in fact it is the light of goodness that they revere. They do not use the Bible in their worship, but have their own book of holy wisdom, which is called the Avesta.

The Mohammedans hate this religion, and have subjected his people to many horrid and unjust oppressions. For this reason he said he hoped that we would be victorious in our crusade.

As we were conversing thus, a Saracen boy of perhaps ten years came running between the stalls, and snatched Eleanor's purse right off of her belt. So quickly did he do this that, before the Queen could turn to follow, he was already five fathoms away.

"Stop, thief!" Eleanor cried.

Alicia instantly leaped upon the horse, and though it had no saddle or trappings, took off after the lad like a shot. In seconds she had caught up with him, and reaching down, snatched him up by his tunic. Then she returned in triumph, her little captive draped over the horse's back in the place where the saddle pommel might have been, kicking and screaming his rage in an incomprehensible tongue.

Eleanor pried her purse loose from the boy's grip, and tied it back more firmly to her belt. Then taking both his hands in hers, she pulled him forward, so that with Alicia still clutching his ankles upon the back of the horse, the boy lay helplessly suspended between the two. This did not stop him from his infernal yelling, however.

"What a rude little Saracen you are," Eleanor said.

The Persian interjected. "He is not a Saracen, he's a Kurd. It's just as well you can't understand what he's saying. It's not fit for any ears."

"So, you speak his tongue then," said Eleanor. "Tell him to be silent or we'll pull him apart."

The merchant shouted something to the boy, who quieted instantly.

"Good," said Eleanor. "Now ask him his name."

The Persian spoke to the boy, who answered, "Saladin."

That is the truth. The great Saladin, when Eleanor met him, was a mere cutpurse boy prowling the bazaar of Antioch. So, as you can see, the tale of an affair between the two is quite absurd.

"Well, little Saladin," Eleanor said. "You are going to have a lesson in proper behavior today." She turned to the merchant. "Tell him he must swear never to steal from or be rude to women again."

The merchant said something, and Saladin barked out a reply.

"What did he say?" Eleanor asked.

The Persian frowned. "He called you a Christian whore."

Eleanor nodded. "I see that it is time for little Saladin's education to begin. Marie, would you be kind enough to find a stick and thrash him a bit?"

I looked about the stall for an appropriate rod, but, with none apparent, was saved by the merchant, who produced an excellent riding crop for me to use.

I gave Saladin a good swatch across his rump, causing him to yelp momentarily, only to resume his defiant demeanor. So I whacked him again, some dozen times until he burst out with some words that sounded like pleading. Such repetition is the key to any sound pedagogy.

Eleanor spoke to the merchant. "Will he swear now?"

There was another interchange between the Persian and the boy.

"He says he will swear it in the name of Jesus Christ," said the merchant. Eleanor shook her head. "Tell him he must swear it in the name of Allah, and further, affirm that should he break his oath, it should be known everywhere that all Muslims are liars, that Mohammed was a liar, and that his faith and all who follow it are worthless."

The merchant spoke to the boy. In reply, Saladin spat at Eleanor's face.

"That does it," said Eleanor. "Marie, this time give him a proper thrashing."

I thought I had done a fair job before, but this time I lay into him with a will, and did not stop before he was truly bawling and crying out in a genuinely sincere manner.

The merchant said, "He has sworn as you have asked."

Eleanor raised an eyebrow. "In all particulars."

"Yes," said the merchant.

"Very well," said Eleanor. She nodded to Alicia, and as one, the two dropped Saladin, so that he fell upon his underside. The boy struggled to his feet, and hobbled off, as quickly as he could whilst rubbing his well-thrashed posterior.

That was the end of the encounter. However, it may be noted that when, many years later, Saladin took Jerusalem, he spared all the Christian women of the town. This chivalrous behavior was the result of the excellent lesson that the great Queen Eleanor and I gave him that day in Antioch, and strongly illustrates the value of proper and timely education in effecting the improvement of the character of children, with many salutary benefits deriving thereby for the betterment of our world.

After performing this important service for humanity, we spent some more pleasant hours at the bazaar, discovering fabulous things of every sort. But it was not only the goods in the market that astounded.

Indeed, my greatest astonishment occurred at the end of the day, when one of the Jewish merchants was making the sum of Eleanor's purchases. These were so many as to fill a small cart pushed by the two maidservants Raymond had lent us.

The Jew scribbled upon a little slate. "And seven of those, at two dinars each," he said, "three of these, at six dinars each, and four of these at eleven dinars each. If you wait but a moment, I will tell you the sum."

The merchant scratched away some more at his slate. I craned my neck to look behind him.

"Where is your abacus?" I asked, as curiously, none was to be seen.

The Jewish merchant kept scribbling. "I don't have one here," he said

I was mystified. "Then how will you do the sum?"

"On my slate," he said, holding it up. "There, you see, the sum is one hundred and twenty eight dinars."

The slate was marked with columns of designs that looked somewhat like letters, but weren't.

"What are those?" I asked, utterly puzzled.

"Numbers," he answered.

I shook my head doubtfully. "They don't resemble any numbers I have ever seen." Indeed, they certainly did not. There were I's and X's, but no V's, L's, or C's. Instead of these there were many new symbols, which looked more like Norse runes than numbers, and they only were set down in small groups of one or two, or occasionally three, together at a time.

I turned to Eleanor. "My lady," I said. "This is impossible. I learned arithmetic from my father. No one can sum so many numbers without an abacus, at least not in the time we have been here."

Eleanor shrugged. "Well evidently it is possible," she said, seemingly unaware of how truly amazing the merchant's ciphering accomplishment was.

The Queen then gestured to Alicia, who paid the money in silver out of a purse. The two began to move off, but I stood where I was.

Eleanor turned to me. "Marie, are you coming?"

I hesitated, for the two of them had all the money, and a bazaar day without a purse is like a lute without strings. But the merchant had raised my curiosity to fever pitch. What was his trick? I had to know, for if his art could be mastered by others, it could be of great value, most especially to the Builders.

"By your leave, my lady," I said. "If you would permit it, I would stay here a while and discover more of this."

"As you wish," Eleanor said, and led Alicia off to look at more gowns. I spent the rest of the afternoon with the Jew, and by the end of the day had made such good acquaintance with the man that he let me copy down his numbers on a sheet of new kind of parchment they use in Antioch. This stuff is made from crushed sawdust, and because of the common nature of its source, can be produced so cheaply that the Jew allowed me to keep the whole page without asking any money for it all. He also gave me a piece of solid sugar half the size of my thumb, asking nothing more than a song in exchange.

Think of it! Parchment for free! Sugar for a song!

I returned to the palace at sunset, amazed by all I had seen.

Chapter 37

Constance of Antioch

The next morning our spirits were raised further, when the Count of Flanders arrived, leading our seven thousand surviving men at arms, by the grace of God marched safely hence from Satalia. These, together with our remaining four thousand mounted knights, made us a force to be reckoned with again.

We assembled on the palace steps to greet them. What a sight they were, the brave and manly Count upon his horse, the column of veteran infantry behind him marching, drums banging, pennants flying, like they had never known defeat and never could.

Flanders! Now there was a man! I was standing next to Sybille when he arrived, and I can tell you that the woman was transported, for she had never expected to see her husband again. He dismounted, and she rushed into his arms.

The rest of the day was spent in joyous reunion, for as you may imagine, the Count of Flanders and those who had shared his epic march had many stories to tell. They had even won the better of the Turks in some encounters, and while these were but skirmishes, it was remarkable to observe how such a small force with but a Count to lead it should fare so much better in war than had our grand army led by a King with many high and holy advisors besides.

Later that afternoon, Eleanor, Alicia, Erika and I retired to a private terrace Raymond had set aside for us for some light refreshment. A woman we had not met before emerged from the palace door to join us.

She was a slim raven-haired beauty of medium height, perhaps just past a score years old, her flowing eastern-style clothes were of the finest quality, and she walked with the grace of a princess.

"Greetings," she said in a soft and sweet voice, her slight Armenian accent making her Frankish all the more charming. "I am Constance of Antioch. I apologize for my late appearance, but I was in the country visiting one of my estates when you arrived."

So this was the bride of Raymond! We had heard so much about her, now her she was, and her appearance and manner justified her husband's every praise. Eleanor stepped forward to warmly greet her kinswoman.

"Dear Constance," Eleanor said. "At last! I am so glad to finally meet you. I am Eleanor, and these are my good friends, Alicia, Erika, and Marie."

Constance nodded to each of us as we were introduced.

Eleanor smiled. "I can see that Raymond did not lie about your beauty."

"Nor about yours," Constance replied, returning a compliment that was justified in both cases.

"So," Eleanor said. "Am I to call you 'Aunt Constance?'"

Constance laughed, for she was at least seven years Eleanor's junior. "That seems rather awkward. Perhaps 'cousin' would be better. Or, if you would have it, 'sister'?"

"Sister," said Eleanor. "For Raymond has always been like a brother to me, and now we should be sisters."

She took both of Constance's hands lightly in her own, and the two locked warm eyes on each other for some moments, sealing the bond.

Eleanor stepped back and took a goblet of wine and passed it to Constance. "So, dear sister," the Queen said. "Tell us. How did my clumsy uncle Raymond manage to win a prize such as you?"

Constance laughed. "Well, actually, he arranged with the Patriarch to have us wed when I was nine. That's how he took over the city."

I started. For while such things sometimes are done, they are not the usual beginning to a happy romance. I could see that Eleanor was startled by the report as well.

"Yes, I know how it sounds," Constance said. 'But let me tell you the whole story."

"By all means," said Eleanor, gesturing to the benches. We all sat down and listened as Constance told her tale.

"It was eleven years ago. My mother was widowed, and everyone agreed that she needed to marry again, for this is a dangerous part of the world, and the city needed a man at the helm. Raymond had proven himself both valiant and clever in war against the Turk, and being of excellent family as well, the invitation was given to him. However, when he arrived here, he decided to set my mother aside and marry me instead. You see, he wanted to be Prince and ruler, and not royal consort and captain of the guard."

Eleanor's eyes were wide. "Yes, but didn't this upset your mother?"

Constance smiled. "Oh, mother was livid, but there was nothing she could do. Raymond quickly showed that he was a wise, efficient, and generous ruler, and won the hearts of all the diverse peoples of the city, whereas she had been at best an indifferent governor. So, excepting her, nearly everyone agreed that his takeover was a Godsend."

"And what did you think?" Eleanor asked. "A child, suddenly wed to a grown man, and a mighty one at that; were you not frightened?"

"Yes indeed," Constance said. "At first I was terrified. But Raymond did not touch me. Instead he appointed tutors, to instruct me in languages, music, poetry, chess, and dancing, so that I should grow up to be a proper princess. Then, when I became sixteen, possessing the full body of a woman, he still did not take me, though he might have done so with the full approval of the world, since I was of age and we were lawfully wed. Instead he courted me, as he might have done to a noble heiress who had the full freedom to bestow her love as she might choose. He sent me flowers, composed poems for me, and sang them outside my window at night. He took me riding, and hawking, and boating, and joked with me and danced with me, and so won my heart, that one night, here in the garden, it was I who pulled him close to me to begin our first kiss."

Constance smiled. "It was a very long kiss."

"What a wonderful story," Eleanor said, and I could see how proud and happy she was to hear how nobly her uncle Raymond had conducted the affair. How many other men, if given such power over a woman, would have chosen to act so well?

"Yes," said Constance. "I love him. I love him, I love him, I love him! He is the most wonderful man in the world. And not just to me, but to everyone. Do you see how he governs this city, so that everyone lives together in harmony? Why even the Muslims are loyal to him. He is so strong, so brave, so wise, and has so many ideas for projects! What a world this could be if all kings were like him."

"I am so happy for you," Eleanor said, but though her voice was warm there was a slight note of wistfulness in it.

"I'm sorry," Constance said softly. "I did not mean to brag at your expense."

Eleanor immediately understood. "So then, you have met Louis."

"Yes," said Constance sympathetically. "Raymond had told me about him, of course, but the reality was still unexpected."

"One could put it that way," said Eleanor, shaking her head.

"So then," said Constance. "You truly have to lead the army yourself?"

"Someone must do it," said Eleanor.

"Well, I am so glad I don't need to," said Constance proudly. "I am married to a real man. I just need to stand behind him and love him, as a woman should. He can do the fighting, and whatever else that a throne requires of a man." Then the princess caught herself. "Forgive me. I meant to give no insult."

"Nor was any taken," Eleanor replied. "I would be the last to dispute Louis' merit against Raymond's. However, as you do love Raymond, you may wish to reconsider the role you have assigned yourself."

"How so?" said Constance.

"Well," said Eleanor. "Even a man as strong as Raymond needs a wife who can guard his back. Statecraft is a dangerous occupation."

"Yes, but to charge into battle like a knight," Constance shuddered. "What good could I possibly do?"

"I understand," said Eleanor. "That is hard for anyone, and for a woman to do it, she needs to be trained to it from youth. Moreover, as you point out, in your case, it is not necessary. You have married a real man. But when he goes out to do battle, someone needs to hold the city for him. The best person for that is the one he trusts most."

"Meaning me," said Constance thoughtfully. "So you are saying I need to learn about politics."

"And war," said Eleanor. "They are two horses pulling the same wagon. To hold a city, you need to be able to lead its defense."

"I wouldn't even know where to begin," Constance said doubtfully.

I stepped forward. "Princess Constance, here is something that may help. This is a book written by Anna, Princess of Constantinople. It teaches much about politics and war."

Constance took the book. "Why, thank you," she said gratefully, unaware of the fact that I had grown weary of the boring, if instructive, text. She opened it, and scanned a page, apparently having no trouble with its over-stylized formal Greek. "Thank you so much. I shall read every page. But even with such knowledge – to defend a city myself? I don't even know how to hold a sword, let alone swing one."

"You don't need to swing it," said Eleanor. "All you need to know is how to lift it aloft to inspire your troops, and that I can show you how to do. Here, stand next to me and do what I do."

Eleanor gestured to Alicia who brought over two swords. Handing one to Constance, Alicia adjusted her grip upon the hilt to the proper form, then stepped back. The Queen adopted a bold stance, her right foot before her left, and waited whilst Constance copied her.

Eleanor raised her weapon aloft. "For Antioch!" she shouted.

"For Antioch!" cried Constance, lifting her sword like a veritable Goddess of war.

I lifted a wine goblet. "For Antioch!" I said, and took a drink.

Chapter 38

Our Departure from Antioch

And so that night, refreshed in body and spirit, restored in hope, and suitably attired from our purchases at the bazaar, we betook ourselves to the pleasures of the table and the joys of the dance.

Raymond's palace had an elegant banquet hall, which he lit brightly with hundreds of candles, of a kind that burned nearly without smoke. All about were the finest decorations, beautiful tapestries, Byzantine mosaics, paintings both secular and holy, and ancient pagan statues. These latter were somewhat profane in their subject matter, depicting youths and maidens not only naked, but sharing their embraces in such condition. Yet, with all that, they were of a craftsmanship so refined as to be wondrous.

Prince Raymond, being a man of culture, had not one bard in his palace, but four. These were fine musicians, troubadours from Toulouse, and I had a merry time playing my lute with them to entertain the nobles. Of these there were many that evening, for they included not only those of rank of our party, but Raymond and the Aquitainian aristocrats of Antioch, all dressed in the flowing garments of the east.

As we concluded a song about two maidens, each of who found happiness with the betrothed of the other (for the Aquitainian troubadours make much of such themes), Prince Raymond called out to us. "Well sung, bards," he said. "But now for the dance."

So we hit our strings, and gave them a melody suitable for frolicsome feet. Raymond rose, bowed to Eleanor, and taking her hand, walked her out onto the floor. Another Antiocene noble asked Constance, several others took the hands of Alicia and the ladies of Antioch, and soon all were dancing. I was happy to play for them, for they were all expert in their movements, and a joy to watch.

Then I heard a voice. "Fair Miss, would you care to dance?"

I looked up. Sir Robert was standing before me, his hand beckoning. My heart soared. Sir Robert, a worthy knight of Aquitaine, had called me "fair Miss," and was asking me to dance with him in the palace of the Prince of Antioch!

We should not refuse God's gifts. I smiled at the knight, set down my lute, rose, and gave him my hand. We joined the dance. I was not so skillful a dancer as Eleanor or Alicia, but I had learned from them, and if Sir Robert and I did not cut the finest figure on the floor, we were more than passable. I enjoyed myself immensely. For a moment as we whirled and stepped about, war, massacre, and flood were all forgot. There was just the music and the dance, the palace and the candles, the knight and me.

But then my eyes strayed to the group remaining at the table. King Louis and Odo were there, staring at Eleanor and Raymond dancing together.

Prince Raymond was not just an expert dancer, he was superb. If ever there was a man worthy to dance with Eleanor, it was him. When these two moved together, they were like magic.

Apparently, however, this was not at all pleasing to Odo and King Louis. Raymond left Eleanor to partner with Constance on the second dance, but this did not change their mood. Indeed, they only seemed to grow more aggravated as the evening drew on, and the Prince periodically returned to dance joyously with his niece.

*** *** ***

There were many other amusements in the town. For in Antioch they have a glass as transparent as air, and placing some of this on the bottom of boats, make it possible to see beneath the ocean.

So we went to the harbor with Prince Raymond and Sir Robert and set out upon the bay. Raymond, our helmsman, sat in the stern with the tiller, we sat amidships over the glass, while forward of us, Sir Robert rendered fine service as a galley slave with a pair of strong oars. At first there was not much to view, but then we traveled over some rocks of a kind I have never seen before, and soon we discovered a hidden world of such beauty and so many colors and such diverse and curious fishes and other creatures as I can hardly describe. There were eels and lobsters and crabs and turtles, and a giant flat fish with wings that flew underwater in the same manner as birds do when they fly in the air. There were fishes that swam together in crowded multitudes, all moving as one, and a mighty shark which traveled in company with tiny colored fish who feared him so little as to swim within his mouth to pick his teeth, and emerge again, their trust never betrayed by their benefactor.

How many more such wonders has God put in the world? What a joy it is to seek them out!

But our time of joy was not to last. The end came that very night. Prince Raymond was such a kind man, and he cared so much for
Eleanor, that he had provided her with a private sleeping chamber in his palace. Eleanor though, was much too generous to keep such a boon for herself only, and so she had invited Alicia and me to share this room with her as well.

Thus it was that on our tenth night in Antioch, at the midnight hour, that we three were sleeping in this chamber, when suddenly we were awakened by a pounding at the door. Before we could even rise to answer it, the door was thrown open. Louis, Odo, and some knights entered with much stomping of their boots.

Startled, Eleanor leapt out of her bed and faced them. We rose and stood by her.

Louis spoke. "Come Eleanor, it is time to go."

"What?" said Eleanor. "What is the meaning of this?"

"We are leaving for Jerusalem," Louis said. "At once."

Eleanor shook her head as if trying to rid herself of a bad dream. "What are you talking about? That's madness. We need to stay here and join with Raymond to retake Edessa."

"I think you've done quite enough joining with Raymond," Louis said, smirking like a half-grown boy with evil thoughts.

Taken aback, Eleanor glared at Louis in shock, then slapped his   face. The sound of the slap echoed in the room.

"How dare you!" The Queen said, her face dark with fury. "That is the final straw. Our marriage is over."

Louis seemed shaken for a second, but then his smirk returned. "You can't divorce me Eleanor," he said. "The Church will never allow it."

Eleanor, though, had seen the King's moment of fear, and observing this, regained her composure. "Divorce, no," she said, coldly. "But nullify it they must."

The Queen then smiled as she would to a chess opponent whose confident victory she was just about to dismay with a surprise move. "I've discovered that we are fourth cousins," she said, almost as if genuinely surprised.

Odo frowned. "That discovery is hardly new."

"It doesn't have to be new to suffice for nullification," Eleanor said. "It just has to be true. And it is. So we are done." She waved her hand as if shooing away a begging dog. "Go on to Jerusalem then. Go! I'm staying here."

"So you can live in sin with Raymond," Odo leered.

Eleanor spat in his face. It was good heavy spit, worthy of a true Amazon.

Odo wiped his face with his hand. "I'm afraid that hardly suffices for legal refutation," he said. "You are a traitor to your husband, your King, and your God. Your duchy is forfeit."

Eleanor tilted her head and looked at the King's advisor sharply. "So that is what this slander is about then, Aquitaine?" she said, as if seeing some hidden humor in the matter. "How very clever of you, Odo. Except you forget one thing."

Odo drew himself up and faced her back. "Oh, and what is that?"

Eleanor spoke with deadly softness. "If you make this charge, not a single one of my vassals will march a step further in your company. I swear it. Not one man."

Odo and Louis looked at each other uneasily.

Then Odo spoke to the King, the fear evident in his voice. "They are near half the army we have left, Your Majesty. Without them we could be slaughtered."

The two regarded each other in confounded silence for a full minute. Fain to interrupt this reflection, Eleanor folded her arms and waited.

Finally, Louis turned to the Queen. "So, Eleanor," he sighed. "What are your terms?"

Eleanor was ready. "Just this," she said. "I will go with you, and my forces will stay on for the rest of the campaign. But afterwards, the marriage is annulled."

Louis and Odo looked at each other helplessly.

Odo shook his head. "There's no choice," he said to the King. "We dare not go further without them."

Louis gritted his teeth. "Very well," he muttered.

Eleanor raised her finger, indicating that she was not yet through. "And one more thing," she said. "As terms of our separation, I keep the lands and title I was born with."

The King's face turned red, then he nodded.

"You've won this round," Louis said bitterly. "But mark my words, Eleanor, God has a way of punishing the wicked."

Eleanor stared at him defiantly.

Chapter 39

Jerusalem

And so, the following dawn, we set forth on the final stage of our journey to Jerusalem. The travel was easy, for the road was Roman, and its complete route was through the land of Christian kingdoms, so we were safe enough. The credit of the houses of Aquitaine, France, and Flanders was good in Antioch, so our entire remaining army of eleven thousand had been resupplied; the knights with horses, the infantry with good shoes, both with adequate arms and armor, and plenty of carts and food for the journey. What's more, it was spring and the weather was fine.

So the trip should have been a holiday. But the feelings of cold hatred between the King and Queen so rent our ranks that, in some ways, this march seemed even more unhappy than the one through the mountains. Indeed, for nearly the entire way, Eleanor rode in silence upon her horse, her face as grim as famine in winter.

But then, in June, we finally reached Jerusalem! We entered the city, drums beating, banners flying, the crowds cheering us from the side of the road. How long I had waited for this day! Yet it was not as glorious an occasion as I might have hoped.

In the first instance, nearly nine parts in ten of our army was gone, not counting the camp followers and Germans, who were practically all dead. In the second instance, the coldness between the King and Queen as they rode at the head of our column into the city was so apparent as to chill all hope for a favorable outcome to the war, which after all, still lay ahead of us now that we had reached the theater of action.

But what damped my spirits most was the sight of Jerusalem itself. For the city was smallish, filthy, and dusty, with run down brick buildings much less impressive than the marble temples, fine houses, and terraced gardens of Antioch. Jerusalem was so famous, so important to history and to our Faith. I had really expected more.

Trying to rouse myself to enthusiasm, I turned to Alicia, who was riding beside me. "Jerusalem at last," I cried. "The holy city!"

Alicia looked about and shrugged, her aristocratic eyes evidently being even more unimpressed than mine by the place.

She shook her head and frowned. "So much shouting for such a wretched little town."

I noticed that nearly all of the throng that was cheering us appeared to be of European stock. There were some Jews and Arabs among the shops behind the crowd, but not many, and these looked upon us with sullen faces.

"Mostly Franks," I mused, looking at the crowd. "Where are all the Jews and Saracens?"

"Our grandfathers killed most of them when they sacked the place," Alicia said.

I looked at her, shocked.

"Even the children?" I asked.

Alicia frowned and nodded.

I rode the rest of the way to the palace in silence.

***   ***   ***

Jerusalem was ruled by Queen Melisende, who was the cousin of Sybille of Flanders. This Queen, who was about forty years in age, greeted us all at her palace steps. Her clothes were rich and regal, with much silk and jewels. But she was not beautiful. Rather she had the look of a crafty one, as surely she had to be to keep her throne amidst so many men who would gladly have snatched it from her. She introduced us to her little boy, Baldwin, in whose name she ruled, then sent him away and invited our leaders to come inside to meet. Eleanor gestured for Alicia and me to follow her in to the council, and so we did.

The meeting room was nearly barren except for a large table at its center, upon which laid a map of the Holy Land, with all the cities, roads, castles, rivers, springs, wells, and mountains duly marked. Around this table the leaders arranged themselves, with the notables in attendance being Louis, Odo, Eleanor, Bishop Langres, the Count and Countess of Flanders, Queen Melisende, and Everard De Barres, the Commander of the Knights Templar. This last person was particularly noteworthy, as he was even taller and more muscular in build than the Count of Flanders, but so utterly filthy as to create a horrid smell wherever he walked. Such is the nature of the Templars, who in addition to being great warriors, hold two holy vows. These are, firstly, never to wash, and secondly, to avoid any intimate companionship with women. Without question, the former vow must greatly assist them in the performance of the latter.

Queen Melisende spoke first. "I thank the Lord you have come. Join your forces to mine, and together we can take Damascus."

Eleanor looked at Melisende strangely. "Damascus? But strategy ordains that we should return north and retake Edessa." Eleanor picked up a stick that lay on the table and pointed to Edessa and all the roads that led from it. "That is the key to the security of all of overseas Christendom."

"That is what your uncle Raymond told you, is it not?" Odo said, his voice sardonic.

Eleanor did not yield an inch. "Yes," she said firmly. "And it is true, as we all knew when we left France."

"I think, Eleanor," Sybille said with a knowing smile, "that your desire to add Edessa to the realm of your dear kinsman blinds you to other opportunities."

Eleanor returned Sybille's look. "As does your relation to our noble hostess, Queen Melisende."

Odo broke in rudely. "At least she does not seek to sleep with her relations."

Eleanor looked at him, and raised the map-stick. Odo backed away.

"You sir, have a foul mind," Eleanor said. Then turning away from him, she faced the others. "Come then, let us ask the Templar Commander. He knows the war here best. Sir Everard De Barres, what do you think of this plan to assault Damascus."

Everard De Barres stood silent for a moment, then spoke. "I think it unwise. The Emir of Damascus is a worldly man, and fears the fanatic Nuradin even more than he fears us. Should we attack him, we would turn an ally into an enemy."

Louis shook his head. "I don't see how any Moslem can be our ally," he said, incredulous.

"You don't see," Eleanor said, her voice aggravated. "What's so hard to see? The Emir hates Nuradin. So do we. Therefore we should be allies."

"Eleanor," said Louis with pious superiority. "Your placement of strategy above faith is sinful."

"Sinful is as sinful does," Odo mocked.

Eleanor's eyes blazed. "I am as good a Christian as any of you! But we have marched so far. We have lost so many friends. Is their sacrifice to be for nothing? If we are to accomplish anything, we must use strategy!"

"Well," said Louis. "We are not returning to Antioch, so you can forget about joining with Raymond to take Edessa."

Melisende jumped in. "And if not Edessa," she said, "then Damascus is the only Saracen city of note within reach."

Sybille faced her former comrade. "So Eleanor, it is Damascus or nothing. Would you have it all be for nothing?"

Eleanor shook her head, then threw up her hands.

"Oh, very well," she said, with a fatalistic shudder. "Let's march on Damascus."

We followed Eleanor out of the meeting room into the great hall of the palace.

Her hands were shaking. "Madness," she kept muttering. "Utter madness."

***   ***   ***

And so it was that the great Queen Eleanor was defeated in council, not by dim- brained men such as her husband, but by two women, Sybille and Melisende, both nearly remarkable in their own way as she. One had been her comrade, and the other might have been, were it the case that women of wit and courage all were of a common band. But in truth, women are no more united in their aims than are men. This is unfortunate, for were we of one cause, we could readily take over the world's affairs, with many salutary benefits accruing thereby to peace, civilization, and ourselves.

Many good Christians may wonder why Eleanor was so wroth with the decision to attack Damascus, which city, after all, was ruled by a heathen. Was she, as her opponents alleged, so caught up in the interests of the house of Aquitaine that she could not see the merit of crusading combat when it did not serve such ends? It is true that the plan to attack Nuradin in Edessa would have helped her uncle Raymond best, since Antioch, being the closest Christian kingdom, would have gained the city had the victory been ours. Damascus, on the other hand, stood to be the prize of Jerusalem, and thus Melisende and the house of Flanders.

But these considerations, as important as they were, did not weigh on Eleanor as the matter of first importance. I know, because in our many nights together sitting at campfires upon the trail, she had explained to me her remarkable views of the affairs of the east.

To an untrained mind, all stones may look alike. But a keen-eyed master Builder sees many types when he looks, and knows that this kind may be used this purpose, and that kind only for that. So it was with Eleanor. For while many in Christendom look upon Islam and see it as all of one piece, her expert examination revealed manifold particularities and divergencies, and these of no inconsiderable importance for the success of our enterprise. Thus, for example, she saw Nuradin and the Emir of Damascus as being creatures not of like, but unlike natures. For while they were both blaspheming Moslems, and thus doomed to hell for all eternity, Nuradin's primary preoccupation whilst he remained in this world was to destroy Christendom, whereas the Emir was chiefly devoted to the enjoyment of his harem. This, said Eleanor, was an important distinction. So, while divine justice might in the end deal with them in similar fashion, considerations of strategy dictated a different approach while they persisted among the living. In this, she pointed out, her ideas agreed with no less a Christian hero than the Cid himself, who in his own situation, found basis for alliance with the worldly Moors of Valencia against the fanatical Almoravids. Indeed, the fact that the Emir chose to use his great wealth in the pursuit of pleasure rather than jihad made him an object of scorn and hatred by Nuradin, and that hatred made the Emir despise and fear the Turk in return.

Prince Raymond, being a wise ruler, employed many spies, and from these he had obtained report that the Emir and Nuradin were at such odds, that each had sent assassins to visit upon the other. This Raymond had told Eleanor, and further, that should the Christians resolve upon a united and resolute attack on Nuradin, the Emir had let him know by secret messenger that not only would he offer prayers to Allah on our behalf, but would assist with intelligence and money as well. However, should we instead march upon Damascus, the Saracen ruler would have little choice but to seek alliance with the Turk.

All this being the case, it was Eleanor's true conviction that attacking Nuradin, but not the Emir, was our wisest strategy. By himself, the Emir was no threat, and once Nuradin was gone, he could be left alone or be disposed of as desired.

Unfortunately this argument was too complex for the fogged and feeble mind of her husband to grasp. Odo must surely have understood it, for he was a devious one, but his primary ambition as an advisor consisted of saying that which was pleasing to Louis.

The consequences of this folly would soon be apparent.

Chapter 40

The Secret of the Templars

As we entered the great hall of the palace, Everard De Barres and another equally filthy Templar knight approached Eleanor

Everard De Barres bowed. "Queen Eleanor," he said. "I regret that your strategy was not the one chosen. Still, a war with the Saracens anywhere is a war for the faith, and should we succeed at Damascus, it will be a great victory for Christendom. So, as we are to soon march together into battle, we Templars would like to honor you, as well as your husband, by showing you our most holy relic. It is kept in a very special place." He gestured towards the door. "Can you come with us now?"

Eleanor exchanged curious glances with Alicia, then turned back to the Templar.

"Lead on," the Queen said, and accompanied the Templar commander and his man towards the palace door.

I turned to Alicia in wonder. "The most holy relic of the Knights Templars!" I said. "What could it be?"

Alicia shrugged. "Probably just some goat's bones," she said.

I shook my head. "No. It must be extraordinary. I must see it too."

Eleanor was still within sight, but I had not been invited to accompany her. So I looked about to make sure that I was not being observed, and then, as secretly as I could, followed the Queen and the two Templars out of the hall.

When I reached the palace door, I looked down the steps to see Eleanor with her two Templars meet King Louis who was accompanied by two more. Then the six of them set forth through the street. I waited a bit to give them some lead, and then followed at a distance.

Through the narrow streets of the city they went, walking swiftly past the poor shops that lined the way. Sometimes they would stop, and I had to quickly hide behind some merchants' stall or passing camel to avoid being observed.

I trailed them through
the streets and alleys and up a hill. There we came to a glorious church at the summit, built in the style of an immense domed mosque. As I hid behind

a barrel watching, Eleanor, Louis, and the Templars went inside.

At that moment a Jewish merchant came by, wheeling a cart with some small wine barrels in it past the place where I was hiding.

I spoke to him. "Sir," I said, for I believe it is good to be polite to everyone. "What is this place?"

The Jew looked at me, frowning at my Crusader tunic with its red cross. Then he shrugged and answered. "It is the Temple Mount."

My mouth opened in astonishment. I knew then where I was, and had a fair idea of what might lie inside. And having come this far, I had to see it. After a moment's hesitation, I dashed across the street to slip inside the church.

I stepped quietly through the church, following the sounds of the footsteps of the royal party ahead of me. I slipped through a door, and was suddenly stopped by a large and filthy Templar knight who placed his hand upon my chest.

"Hold!" he commanded in a deep voice. "What business have you here?"

I was frightened, but I did not want to give up. "Please sir," I pleaded. "I must see the holy relic."

The Templar looked at me with a forbidding face. "It is not permitted for the unchosen," he said, breathing fetid air upon me. Then he pushed a little at my chest to make it clear that I had to turn back at once.

I glanced down at the Templar's grimy hand. Then I blinked and looked at the hand again. I was so surprised I gasped. For upon his hand was a ring marked with the sign of the free builders! I reached beneath my tunic, and pulled out the amulet still hanging from my neck after all my travails, embossed with the same sign.

Now it was the Templar's turn to be shocked. "Where did you get that?" he asked, his voice filled with suspicion.

In answer, I made a secret sign with my hands. The Templar recognized it, and responded properly with the hand sign of the second interrogatory. I then showed him the sign of the sacred three. He extended his hand, palm up, as did I, and we touched by edges in the approved manner.

This satisfied him. In a different tone, he now spoke.

"Very well. Sister, you may pass. The shrine can be found off the last door to the right."

I nodded my thanks and stepped swiftly down the dark corridor.

It was thus, through the secret fraternity of the free builders' guild and

262

the Knights Templar, that I was admitted to the holy shrine. But though rumor had caused me to suspect, I was not prepared for the reality of what I encountered.

I reached the shrine room and peeked inside. The chamber was dim, lit only by the orange light of two smoking torches. As I looked in from the doorway, I saw Everard De Barres standing before a large wooden cross, blackened with age. Three other Templars stood behind him. There were half-inch holes in the cross, stained with rust, and around the holes further dark stains on the wood. Eleanor and Louis stood facing Everard.

Everard De Barres spoke. "It is the One True Cross."

I gasped and crossed myself, and fell to my knees. As I did so, I could see Louis drop to the ground and pray feverishly. Eleanor, however, remained on her feet, although I could see that even she was amazed.

The Queen looked at Everard curiously. "In truth?" she asked

"Yes," said Everard, in a tone that left no room for doubt. "The very one upon which Our Savior died."

The King's praying became more frenetic.

Eleanor pointed to the stains around the holes on The Cross. "And that stain, is it…?"

"Yes," said Everard. "It is the blood of Christ."

I nearly swooned, but somehow I retained the presence of mind to silently whisper a prayer. Louis collapsed into praying hysterics.

Yet still, Eleanor remained standing, though now breathing hard. She bit her lip and after a moment, spoke.

"May I touch it?" she said.

Everard De Barres opened his mouth in shock but could say nothing. Apparently taking that for a yes, Eleanor advanced a step, crossed herself, and swiftly walked forward to touch the holy bloodstains on The Cross. Then she quickly stepped back and took a few deep breaths.

"We should take it with us," Eleanor said.

Everard De Barres spoke as one startled. "To Damascus? Into battle?"

"It will assure us of victory, will it not?" asked Eleanor.

"Certainly," said Everard. "Of that there can be no doubt."

Eleanor nodded.

"Then we should take it," she said. "We haven't come this far to lose."

Chapter 41

Damascus and Destiny

And so, in the heat of the summer of the year of Our Lord one thousand one hundred and forty eight, our army set forth on the road to Damascus, trodding upon the very same path that the Apostle Paul had when he met God. The road was Roman, and the boots of our men thundered when they marched upon it in unison. For we were all hardened veterans now, and notwithstanding the heat, all marched with full arms, shield, and armor.

Our army had been reinforced by the sacred band of the famed Knights Templars, the greatest warriors in Christendom, excepting only the Bretons. These fierce fighters were most welcome, despite the stench which accrued to them in consequence of their holy vow never to wash. While their filth affronted the nose, it did add to their formidable aspect, and we consoled ourselves with the thought that they were certain to provide the Turks with an annoyance far greater than any way in which they afflicted us. The Knights of the Temple wore their red crosses upon brown cassocks, but whether the brown was chosen to hide the dirt, or an artifact of its presence I cannot say.

The Templars carried with them the One True Cross which was to be our sure talisman of victory. This they mounted upright on the back of a horse drawn cart, so that it traveled with us like a battle standard for all to see.

We also had with us the forces of Queen Melisende, who were of good use, as they included in their numbers Christian men at arms, called turkopoles, who had learned the art of fighting on horseback with bows and light armor in the manner of the Turks. In thus manner they were able to ride fast along the flanks of our column and keep the devils from annoying us excessively during our march. Of the Amazons, only Eleanor, Alicia, Erika, and I were left, as all others surviving had sailed for home. Even Sybille had departed, as she was needed in Flanders to defend the lands of her Count, although since having triumphed for her cousin Melisende over Eleanor in council, she was no longer welcome in our number anyway.

So we rode, Eleanor, Alicia, Erika, and I, in full armor, with the Aquitainians, the Queen grim and determined all the way, while Louis and

Odo, in their monks garb, rode at the head of the Franks singing psalms.

The march took three weeks, starting from the first of July.

Then finally we reached Damascus, and our rendezvous with destiny.

***   ***   ***

On the twenty fourth of July, we massed for the assault.

I sat on my horse alongside Alicia and Erika, while nearby, Eleanor discoursed with Everard De Barres, Sir Robert, and the Count of Flanders about plans for the coming battle. From our hilltop position, I could view the entire theater of action, and all the forces arrayed upon it.

On the plain below us, I could see Damascus, a walled city filled with mosques. Green banners of two different types hung from the parapets. In front of the city there was a large orchard, and in front of the orchard a field, upon which a large army of Turks and Saracens was lined up in full battle array. Looking to my left, I could see our own army assembled on a gentle rise above the plain facing the Turks.

Sitting together upon their battle steeds, Eleanor and the other leaders were surveying all these dispositions with great interest.

"So," said Everard. "The forces of Nuradin and the Emir have banded together."

Sir Robert held his hand up to shade his eyes so as to get a better view. "It looks like they are going to take a stand," he said.

The Count of Flanders grunted. "At last." He fingered his sword hilt. "I've been waiting for this," he said, then ran his tongue along the edge of his teeth.

Eleanor nodded grimly. "Very well gentlemen," she said. "We have a score to settle, and, by God, today is the day we shall do it. Assemble the troops. Tell the men to press them hard. If they break, we'll follow them through the gate."

She pointed at the tallest minaret in the city. "A thousand marks to the man who first plants one of our banners on yonder mosque."

The leaders nodded to each other, then each spurred their mounts to rejoin their battalions. Eleanor and Sir Robert headed for the Aquitainians, and the three of us followed.

An hour later, all was ready.

The Christian knights were lined up across the plain, armored on horseback, lances to the vertical, facing the forces of the Turks less than a mile away. Behind our horse stood our infantry, massed and armed for battle as well. The Turks were similarly disposed, with their horsemen to the front, and infantry to the rear.

Our army was separated by national contingents, with the Templar group at the center, along with the chariot holding the One True Cross. To their right were the Flemings, led by their heroic Count, and then further right were the Franks. On the left of the Templars were the forces of Aquitaine, then the Normans and Bretons, while the light cavalry of the Kingdom of Jerusalem guarded both flanks.

In the moment before the battle, Eleanor rode before the Aquitainian contingent, to which Alicia, Erika, and I were also attached. She looked at each knight, and each of us, saluting us with her eyes. Then she turned her steed to face us, and began to speak in a voice such as that the great Alexander must have used on the morn of his decisive battle with the Persian emperor Darius.

"Brave knights of Aquitaine," she called out, "valiant Poitevins. This is your moment! Four hundred years ago, your grandfathers' grandfathers, bold men whose blood runs in your veins, saved Christendom by defeating the Saracens at the battle of Poitiers. Now they are smiling down from heaven at you. For, conquering many travails, you have brought the war to the home of they who once came to try to enslave us. But though it is their home, it is not their land. The city before you is Damascus, sacred in the Bible as the city of Paul. It was once a Christian city, until the enemy enslaved it to their heresy. Today we shall liberate it, and by so doing, accomplish a feat of arms that will be remembered through all the ages.

"Remember the mountain pass, when those men, those men right there across the plain, attacked us when our armor was off, and then, having run to ground many washerwomen and other poor helpless folk who followed our camp, scorned their pleas for mercy, and chopped off their heads. And then, while bathing in the blood of their victims, they screamed 'Allah Akbar,' which means 'God is great.'

"What kind of God is that, who orders such foul deeds? And they would have it that all men, everywhere, worship this god of murder."

"Never!" the knights shouted, making clear their derision for any such surrender to evil.

Eleanor waited for the clamor to subside. Then she continued.

"We Christians believe that God has given us conscience, to know right from wrong, and free will to choose to do the right. They say no, there is no conscience, and no freedom, there is only submission; submit to Allah, submit to fate, and murder all those who refuse to do likewise.

"What is this war about? We fight an enemy whose God tells his worshippers that they should sin for him, and die for him. We fight for a God who was willing to die to free us from sin, a God who died for us. And if you have ever doubted that, then doubt no longer, for look there!"

She reached out her arm, fast as an arrow, and pointed at The Cross.

"There is the very cross upon which He died, there the holes of the spikes which rent His hands, there are the stains of the blood He shed for you. He is with us today! And by that sign we shall conquer!"

Eleanor waved her lance about, then reared her stallion up high on its hind legs. In that instant she appeared like a vision of Victory. All the knights cheered madly.

Then she looked at me. "Bugler," she said. "Sound the advance!"

I lifted the bugle to my lips and blew one long note. The Aquitainian horse began to move forward at a walk, and seeing them advance, the neighboring contingents did likewise. For so it had been arranged by Eleanor, who not wishing her speech to be ruined by the Franks as it had been at the Meaender, had made our advance the chosen signal for all the rest.

So we advanced, the combined forces of our crusade, the Templars, and those of Jerusalem; six thousand horse and ten thousand infantry all told. Facing us was an enemy near double our number. But they could not match our armor, our valor, or the truth of our faith.

At the Meaender, the Turks had reacted to our advance by riding about madly and yelping like dogs. But now they sat silent and motionless on their horses in front of their line of infantry, row upon row, their scimitars all drawn and held at the ready. This, we could see, would be no mock battle. This day, the Turks meant to fight.

"Advance at trot," Eleanor said.

I blew the bugle twice, and our entire line of knights accelerated into a trot. Behind us, our infantry marched forward at the double, trying to keep up.

The Turks still remained motionless.

Now we were but two hundred fathoms distant from the enemy.

"Advance at canter," Eleanor commanded.

I blew thrice, and we started our canter. Our horses hooves pounded upon the plain, and the gap between us and the foe closed swiftly.

One hundred fathoms, fifty fathoms; as one, the Turkish foot behind their horsemen loosed a huge volley of arrows. I saw it arc upwards, a cloud of death.

"Charge!" Eleanor shouted.

I sounded the charge. In an instant, six thousand lances dropped from vertical to level, and with hooves thundering like doom, our entire line galloped direct at the enemy at full tilt.

Now the arrows came flying down. But the Turks had not reckoned on our sudden charge, and most of their volley fell behind us.

I saw the commander of the Turkish horse snarl in rage, then raise his scimitar.

"Allah Akbar!" he cried, and all the other Turks did the same. Then they spurred their horses and galloped right at us.

The two forces collided at immense speed. It only took an instant, but for me that instant was like an hour, so many things did I see in that one moment. Along a front of more than a mile, thousands of lancers struck at thousands of Turks, running them through, or unhorsing them to be trampled in a trice. But not all of our knights were so fortunate, for many lances were splintered or thrown wide by Turkish shields, allowing the heathen warriors to close and kill with their swords.

Erika and Sir Robert both speared their opponents, and Alicia managed to knock hers from his saddle But Eleanor's lance hit her enemy's shield at an angle, and splayed outwards uselessly to her right and his left. I watched in horror as the Turk then galloped along the side of the lance, straight at Eleanor, who now held no effective weapon.

The Turk struck at the Queen with his scimitar. Reacting fast, Eleanor blocked the blow with her shield, then dropped her useless lance to try to reach for her sword. But she could not do it. For the Turk struck again and again, and Eleanor could only fumble about with her right hand as she desperately warded off scimitar blows with the shield held in her left. She could not last long.

I called out in alarm. "Sir Robert! The Queen!"

Sir Robert turned and saw Eleanor's peril. Instantly he drew his sword and charged forward to rescue her.

But before he could get there, Eleanor reared her horse upward, so that its hooves rose to the level of the Turk's head.

"Strike Pegasus!" Eleanor yelled. "Yah!"

Upon command, Eleanor's magnificent stallion punched out his front hooves and kicked the Turk full in the face. The heathen rolled out his saddle to escape the full impact, but before he could rise from the ground, Eleanor reared up her stallion again and brought his hooves down on the man with a crushing blow. Then she did it once more, turning what was left of the Turk into a bloody pulp. She spat on the body.

At that moment, Sir Robert reached her, reining in his horse sharply to halt his mad dash to her succor. She looked up at him.

"You wish to inspect my work, Sir Robert?" she said, a touch of pride evident in her voice.

Sir Robert shook his head, astonished but pleased. "An interesting technique my Queen," he said with a grin. "I've never seen lance and hoof so well used in combination."

Eleanor glanced down at the Turk with contempt. "The coward would not let me draw my sword," she said.

Then she looked around, as did we all. The Turkish horsemen had been annihilated, and their footmen had turned and were rapidly retreating into the orchard to their rear.

Sir Robert pointed. "They're running already!"

"They won't get far on foot," Eleanor shouted. "After them! Charge!"

The day was ours! I blew the charge again, and our entire cavalry took off in hot pursuit of the fleeing Turks. We had no formation, for there was no need for one once the enemy had broken, and regardless, no power on Earth could have held us back once those fiends had shown us their backs. Swords drawn, we raced madly to run them down.

The Turks had the start on us, and they made it into the orchard before we could reach them, but no matter, on our horses we were closing fast.

With her terrific stallion to ride, Eleanor was among the first to follow the Turks into the trees. I galloped after her, riding faster than I ever thought I could.

Suddenly fire arrows started landing in the trees, which I now saw were covered with some mysterious black substance that took flame instantly. In seconds, several trees were ablaze, and then the wind gusted, turning the entire orchard into a fiery inferno.

My horse spooked, and raced forward past everyone, even Eleanor. With the beneficence of luck and sheer force of will, I just managed to stay in my saddle by grasping my horse's mane with all my might. But then a flaming branch dropped in front of her. She reared in terror and threw me, then sped off into the smoke.

As I scrambled to my feet, Eleanor galloped past by in full battle madness, pointing her sword after the fleeing Turks. But suddenly, the horse's hooves went right though the ground, and Pegasus crashed down into a concealed pit. Eleanor's sword went flying, and a stake ripped up through the horse's stomach, showering the Queen with blood.

Eleanor tried to get out of her saddle, but the horse's right side was wedged in the pit, pinning her leg. A huge muscular Turk with shield and scimitar emerged from the burning trees and ran straight at her. Seeing him, the Queen struggled desperately to get free.

"Mother of God," I gasped.

There was nothing for it. Screaming at the top of my lungs, I charged the Turk.

Chapter 42

A Battle in Hell

Only a few strides separated the Turk from Eleanor. As he loped towards her, the broad flat side of his scimitar reflected the red firelight like glowing blood. His eyes fixed on Eleanor, like the eyes of a hungry wolf as it leaps to kill a lamb. The Queen's appearance marked her out, and Nuradin had put a prize on her head. The heathen's greed shone upon his face like pure evil.

I ran so hard my heart nearly burst, but I was too late. The savage reached the side of the pit and smiled at the Queen, lifting his scimitar and swinging it sideways to sever her head. But Eleanor ducked swiftly, and the blow went wide.

Then the huge beast of a man saw me, running full tilt at him, not three strides away. He turned, with just enough time to present his shield, before I hit him at a full force run.

I didn't hit him with my sword, although I had one waving about in my right hand. I just ran right into him and collided, shield upon shield. His weight must have been thrice mine, but he had not time to gain his best balance. I was wearing helmet and chain mail, and running fast. The force of the blow knocked him over, but I tumbled to the ground as well.

We both scrambled to our feet at the same time. I faced him, shield in one hand, sword in the other, shaking like a leaf in a stiff wind. For the warlike spirit that had wiped away all fear during my mad charge had fled, leaving me terrified as I realized that I, a mere bard, small and unskilled in arms, had now to duel to the death with this fierce, evil, hulking madman.

The brute looked at me for a moment, and assessing my sex, smallness, and manifest panic, he laughed. Then he sauntered towards me, swinging his scimitar down with a mighty blow. I thrust my shield in the way with nary a moment to spare, and though shaken by the jolt, managed to strike in return. But the sword was heavy for me, and I couldn't swing it fast enough. The giant parried my blow powerfully with his shield, knocking my sword arm wide. Then he stepped in and delivered another blow, which somehow I blocked, although I felt as if I had been struck by a runaway cart. Reeling backwards from the force of it, I flailed at him uselessly, and once again barely survived the counterstroke.

"Marie, look out!" Eleanor shouted, still struggling madly to get loose.

From off to my side, two more Turks were sprinting out of the burning trees directly towards me. I was drowned in horror. If the odds had been hopeless before, now they were beyond hopeless.

"Virgin save me!" I cried in a final desperate prayer.

Suddenly Erika was by my side, and Sir Robert and Alicia appeared in the clearing to take on the other two.

"Enough, little one," Erika said. "This one is mine."

She beat the Turk back with several furious blows, smashed his shield right through, and then cleaved him, just in time to do the same to two more Turks who charged into the clearing. Sir Robert cut down his opponent and took on successors, while Alicia thrust and parried like a dancer, keeping her enemy at bay.

In the next moments, as I stood there dazed, dozens of knights, infantry, and Turks on foot swarmed the clearing, and the fight became general.

I heard an urgent shout. "Marie, assist me!"

It was Eleanor. I turned, and taking hold of her arms, pulled her off her horse and out of the pit.

I stood before her, and gazed up at her bloodstained countenance. "I'm sorry, my lady," I said, close to weeping. "I almost lost you. I'm afraid I'm not much of a knight."

Eleanor put her hands on my shoulders.

"Marie," she said warmly, looking me in the eyes. "You were magnificent."

I felt so proud. For courage is the true virtue of any soul. And who displays more courage, she who dares combat though utterly lacking in prowess, or he whose might and skill gives him little to fear upon the field?

I smiled weakly, then looked around. The grove was in flames, and all about men were battling, dying from sword wounds and arrows that flew into the clearing from Turkish archers and Christian crossbowmen.

Eleanor looked down at her horse and blinked away tears. "Poor Pegasus," she said.

A knight fell backward next to us, a Turkish arrow protruding from his eye.

"My lady, I think we are in hell," I said, shivering with the horror of it all.

Eleanor nodded. Then through the flaming orchard we saw the Templars advancing. Their front rank hacked and slew Turks like farmers scything wheat, while from behind, others pushed forward the cart carrying The One True Cross.

Eleanor pointed at the holy relic. "Then let Christ lead us out," she said. "Forward men!" the Queen shouted. "The Cross is with us! Come on! Let them have it! Vengeance for the murdered! Onward! Christ and Victory!"

With a mad cheer our knights surged forward, slashing furiously. The Turks battled hard, hand to hand, but the weight of our armor and the depth of our fury were too much. Though our losses were nearly as appalling as theirs, step by step we slowly forced the heathens back.

I stood next to Eleanor in the rear ranks as she shouted her exhortations urging our men on. It seemed like we might yet win. Then suddenly a group of Turkish archers let fly a volley of fire arrows at The Cross. In an instant, The One True Cross, the holiest relic in Christendom and the key to our victory, was all ablaze.

"My lady," I cried out. "The Cross is aflame!"

Many of our Crusaders saw it as well, and looked at it horrified. Some began to waver, and our advance halted.

"Someone has to save The Cross!" I cried, as I realized with a jolt that this could be the reason why the Virgin had answered my prayer and saved me from the Turk.

I dashed through the burning orchard towards The Cross.

"Marie, no!" Eleanor called after me. "It's not really…"

What did she mean "it's not really…?" I think she might have meant to protect me from danger by telling me The Cross was not genuine. But I knew that it was. For unknown to her, I had observed her and Everard with the One True Cross in the secret shrine of Templars, and this *was* that cross. It had to be saved.

I grabbed the blood-soaked cape off a fallen knight, and leaped up on to the cart of the Templars. I desperately swung the cape against the flames on the cross, but even flinging myself up could only reach its lowermost part.

"Lift me up!" I called to a nearby knight. He nodded and scrambled on to the cart, then jointed his hands together to make a stirrup for my foot. I stepped into it, and he boosted me up, as high on The Cross as Our Savior had been in his last hour.

I swung the cape at the left arm of The Cross, dousing part of the flame.

The Turks saw what I was doing, and started shooting arrows at me, and propelling yet more fire at The Cross. Miraculously, their first volley missed me, but many hit The Cross, starting fires in more places. I swung the cape manically, but I could not keep up with so many new fires, and more arrows would hurtling my way any moment.

"Crossbowmen!" I heard Eleanor scream. "Crossbowmen!"

I looked down, as at the Queen's command, a group of Poitevin crossbowmen assembled in a line and let fly at my assailants. Some they killed, and the rest were distracted to return the volley.

This gave me my moment. I furiously swung the cape again and again, beating at the flames until they expired. Then steadying myself by wrapping one arm around The Cross, I used the other to wave the cape in triumph.

"The Cross is saved!" I yelled.

"Forward with the Cross!" shouted Eleanor.

With a mighty cheer, our men rushed upon the enemy, driving them hard. The Turks could not hold, and we forced them back ever faster.

Suddenly we broke out of the burning orchard, and there in front of us were the walls of Damascus. At the sight of it, our men cheered again, and redoubled their efforts. From my perch atop the Templar cart, I could see the Turks begin to panic. For even as their front line continued to resist in their ever more rapid retreat, the bulk to their rear had turned, and were jamming the gate as they tried frantically to flee into the city. I could see Erika and Sir Robert at our very front alongside some Templars, hacking furiously, pushing towards the gate.

"Forward!" Eleanor shouted. "Press them hard. Follow them through the gate! Take the town!"

Our men pressed on, the combination of their holy faith, their battle ardor, and their pent up anger making them unstoppable. The Turks still fighting tried desperately to slow them, as their comrades to the rear crushed each other pushing through the gate in a panicked mob.

At our very front, Sir Robert, Erika, and several mighty Templars drove ahead like the heroes of Homer, cleaving all before them and vaulting over the dead as they approached the gate.

Now they were on the drawbridge, now they were under the gate itself, then they were though the gate, breaking into the courtyard with a cheer.

"Damascus is ours!" Sir Robert shouted. "Victory!"

Dozens of knights poured through the gate, cheering madly.

Suddenly, the godless Turks above the gates poured molten

lead down on the drawbridge and its environs, killing several knights instantly and causing the rest to either run forward intro the town or retreat. An instant later, a pair of iron grated gates swung together behind the Crusaders in the courtyard, and a massive iron bar dropped down to latch them in place.

The clang of the falling post resounded like the crack of doom. I could see right through the holes in the iron grate, as our knights in the courtyard suddenly realized that they were cut off. I watched powerless as they turned and faced the thousands of Turks around them in the courtyard. Against such an imbalance of force, they stood no chance.

I saw Sir Robert and Erika look at each other. Then, with all the other Crusaders in the courtyard, they yelled their battle cry and charged forward against impossible odds.

In the chaos of the fight, I could not see much more, but the sounds of their desperate battle could be heard readily through the grate.

Eleanor looked every which way, searching for some recourse. Seeing the Count of Flanders approach, she ran up to him.

"Flanders, quick!" she said. "Bring up some rams and burst the gate. Our men are trapped inside."

The Count of Flanders shook his head. "There's no time," he said.

Even as he said this, the sounds of battle from inside the gate began to diminish as fewer and fewer swords were left to clash with the enemy. Then from within the gate, I heard Erika's voice in a death scream. I gazed to heaven and said a prayer for her soul.

For a moment, silence reigned. Then the cheers of the Turks thundered from inside the walls. The cheering rose louder and louder as thousands of jeering, cheering, Turks and Saracens crowded the tops of the walls to hurl insults and abuse down at us.

As we watched, the Turks then raised several dozen severed heads and waved them at us in mockery. I stared at the display aghast. Among the heads were those of Sir Robert and Erika.

Eleanor covered her eyes in horror. "Oh God," she said.

Then she looked up and faced the Count of Flanders with resolution. "Flanders," she said. "I want this town taken, do you hear? I want it took, and every devil that helped in that put to the sword."

Count of Flanders glanced up at the desecration on the walls, and curled his lip like an angry dog ready to bite. Then he nodded to Eleanor. "Consider it done, my lady," he said. "For we have them trapped like rats in a cage. We'll starve them out."

At this moment, Louis and Odo rode up on fresh horses, their monkish garb spotless from non-participation in battle.

Louis smiled genially. "Count Flanders, Eleanor. Good day to you both. We have had a wonderful victory here today. I hope you will both thank God for it."

Eleanor looked up. "My husband," she said with force. "We need to send to Queen Melisende to arrange some caravans of supplies for the army, so we can camp here and siege the Turks till hunger takes them."

Louis shook his head. "That won't be necessary."

"What do you mean?" Eleanor asked, puzzled.

"I mean," said Louis, "that we have accomplished our purpose. We have traveled to Jerusalem and confessed at the holy shrines, and we have defeated the Turks in open battle, thereby satisfying honor. There's nothing more to do. It's time we went home."

The Count of Flanders was utterly confounded. "But my lord," he pleaded. "We have Nuradin and the Emir and all their forces trapped in the town. We control the field. By laying siege now, we can take them all and win the war. If we don't, this battle will count for naught."

"Less than naught," Eleanor added. "Our attack has united the Emir and Nuradin. We either take them now, or the entire Holy Land will be lost for certain."

"Such worldly concerns are not my affair," Louis said firmly.

Eleanor was livid. "You!" she screamed, pointing at the King. "You are not worth a rotten pear!"

Louis shrugged. "We start back for Jerusalem in the morning. Then on to France. It is done."

Chapter 43

The Consequences of Folly

And so, having won the battle, we instantly abandoned the siege, and by so doing, lost the war. All Islam rejoiced, and all Christendom grieved, and many on both sides said it was the will of God, punishing us for our sins, that caused our catastrophe. But I say this, I who was there, and whose faith is as strong and pure as any who have ever followed Our Savior; that God had nothing to do with it. No, our loss was caused solely and completely by one man, if he can be called that, since to call him a man fatally insults all men, however vile, and that man was Louis, King of France. For that over pious wretch, that Pharisee who cried so much for his own salvation, cared not a whit for Christendom. That coward, that worm, that crowned ass, that dung heap in the clothes of a monk, chose willfully to ignore all sense and reason, and snatching defeat from the jaws of victory, single handedly transformed the triumph that should have rewarded all our toils and travails into a pile of foul ashes.

***   ***   ***

We marched back to Jerusalem on the same road by which we came, but not with the same spirit. In place of the warlike resolution with which we come, we returned in a state of utter dejection. The army did not look like one that had been routed, for it had not been. But I would wager my hopes for salvation that no victorious force ever marched away from its battle in so foul and sullen a mood.

Nearly the entire army traveled on foot, the horses nearly all being lost in the orchard. Even Eleanor walked, though as Queen she could have gotten herself another steed. For Louis and Odo had kept their mounts, and she would rather be one with the soldiers than as one with them. Indeed, had Louis any sense in his head, he might have reconsidered his mode of travel, for the muttered curses he received from the knights and footmen as he rode by would have sufficed to send a legion of kings to perdition.

There were no cheers when we reached Jerusalem. Some Christians did turn out to watch our entrance, but their faces were disdainful. Among the stalls of the Arab traders though, I saw some smiles and knowing glances.

While Louis led the entire column into town on horseback, bowing to acknowledge cheers he did not receive, Eleanor stayed back a ways to make her entrance on foot at the head Aquitainian contingent. Walking in her bloody crusader tunic and chain mail, the Queen ignored the sneers of the crowd and stared straight ahead with a visage of absolute fury that I shall never forget.

Such was our triumphal return to the Holy City.

We wasted some months in Jerusalem, at whose shrines the King prayed while the army deserted. But then, with the coming of spring, we proceeded onward to the port of Acre. There Eleanor received further news that nearly broke her heart. For a messenger arrived bearing tidings that Nuradin, now united with the Emir and rid of us, had marched north to besiege Antioch.

Prince Raymond, bravely attempting to defend the city, had been slain with all his knights and sergeants. The marvelous town was surrounded, and with but frail Constance and the town militia to defend it, its once happy people soon doomed to be raped, slaughtered, or made into slaves.

These grave tidings reached us even as we stood upon the dock on the afternoon of our intended departure. When she heard them, Eleanor closed her eyes and shook like one possessed for several seconds, and staggered so wildly that if Alicia had not caught her, she would surely have fallen into the water. Then hugging her oldest friend, Eleanor breathed deeply for some moments, until she recovered herself enough to wipe away her tears and turn to face Louis.

"My lord husband," she said. "We must take what forces we have left and sail north to relieve Antioch."

"My dear," Louis said with irritating sympathy. "You know that is impossible."

"Impossible, why?" the Queen demanded. "We have ships, we have men. Antioch is not far. We could be there in a week."

"Eleanor, you need to be reasonable," said Louis. "We have only a few hundred men left. What good could they possibly do against the united armies of Nuradin and the Emir?"

"They could stiffen the town militia," Eleanor insisted. "You heard what the messenger said. Constance's burghers still hold the walls. Our knights could officer them. At least then they might stand a chance."

"I'm sorry," said Louis. "They're all in God's hands now."

"God's hands!" Eleanor exploded. "Why you sniveling hypocrite!" she shouted and launched herself to claw at him with her bare hands.

It was fortunate for the King he had several knights nearby to pull her away, for the Queen was stronger than he and so enraged that she might have torn him to pieces in seconds. As it was, his face was so rent by her nails that we had to postpone sailing whilst he could be properly bandaged by a surgeon of the town.

Thus the day of our intended departure from Acre became a day of mourning. For the Queen was so stricken with grief that she stood on the dock for hours, crying, praying, screaming, covering her eyes with one hand while pounding a wooden post of the dock with the other.

Missing the tide, we were forced to pass the night in the town. At my suggestion, we spent the time in a church, praying for Raymond's soul and Constance's safety. This was not the sort of thing Eleanor was wont to do, but on this occasion, she agreed, provided that Louis, who was pretending to grieve for Raymond as well, did his mourning in a different church.

In the morning, when we returned to the dock, Eleanor approached the Captain of her own vessel, and asked him if, despite the King, he might sail her and her own picked knights to Antioch to rescue Constance. She offered him a goodly sum to do this, but he refused, saying that word had come during the night that the city had fallen and all within put to the sword.

And so we set sail with heavy hearts. Of the hundred thousand who had left France, of the eleven thousand who had reached Antioch, we returned with but three hundred, as these alone of those who survived had fare to pay their passage. The Queen insisted on traveling in a separate ship from the King, since by now, as you may understand, she found his company past endurance. She took with her Alicia and I, and the twelve remaining knights of Aquitaine. The rest she let travel with Louis, for she refused to have about her those she feared were not her friends.

Our ships were of the Mediterranean merchant design, with high bow and stern castles and large triangular lateen sails held up on two masts. The two vessels traveled in convoy. For the first week of the trip, Eleanor, dressed in black, spent most of her time at the rail staring at the ship carrying Louis, shaking her head and mumbling under her breath. But gradually she returned to something like her old self.

We sailed near a month in mostly fair weather, stopping at Cyprus, Rhodes, and Crete for fresh water, the pleasant nature of the voyage serving to raise our spirits at least a little. But then, as we approached Cape Malea, which tips the southernmost point of Greece, a new menace appeared which was to subject our fortitude to its ultimate trial.

Chapter 44

Treachery at Sea

The day was bright, the waves were mild, and the wind was fair. I stood with Eleanor and Alicia at the rail of the windward side of the ship, taking in the Sun and the sea breeze. Suddenly, a lookout sailor standing in the crows' nest at the top of the main mast called out.

"Ships ho!"

Alerted, the Captain, who had been standing on the sterncastle next to the helmsman looked up.

"What ships?" the Captain shouted. "How many, what sort, and what direction?"

"Galley warships of Constantinople," the sailor shouted back, "at least twelve, bearing down on us hard."

Eleanor rapidly crossed the deck and scrambled up a ladder to the sterncastle. Alicia and I followed.

"Captain," Eleanor said, what's happening?"

The Captain looked in the direction of the approaching warships, then turned to face the Queen. "It would appear," he said, "that we are about to have a meeting with the navy of Emperor Manuel Comnenus."

"Can we escape them?" Eleanor asked.

The Captain shook his head. "In this tub, not a prayer. Your husband has some three hundred knights aboard. Do you think he will choose to make a fight of it?"

Eleanor rolled her eyes. "That monk. Not a prayer"

The Captain nodded and grinned ironically.

A minute later the Byzantine warships were in plain sight. I could see they were dromons, long, thin, low, deadly galleys with two banks of fifty oars each on a side, and mounting a sharp above-water ram in the prow.

Even from a mile away, I could hear the drum beat of taskmasters commanding the efforts of the galley slaves, whose synchronized rowing scooted the ships across the waves. The squadron altered course slightly, and rapidly bore down on our ship at the breakneck speed of ten knots.

Surprisingly, despite the fact that there were twelve of them, the galleys all headed for our vessel, allowing that of Louis to sail off into the distance without interference.

Observing this, Eleanor frowned. "It would seem he has no need to fight, either."

The helmsman, who was standing by the tiller next to the Captain, now spoke. "They're signaling us to heave to."

The Captain nodded. "Very well, helmsman," he said. "Bring her into the wind."

Eleanor was taken aback. "What?" she cried. "You are giving up, just like that?"

The Captain shrugged. "There is no choice," he said.

Eleanor looked at him with dark suspicion. "Really," she said.

As our ship turned up into the wind, a Byzantine dromon approached alongside.

Led by Sir Guy, the dozen knights of Aquitaine we had aboard came running to the end of the deck near the stern castle, all armed and ready with swords and shields to give battle for their liege lady, whatever the hazard.

Sir Guy called up to Eleanor. "You orders, my Queen? Our swords are yours."

Eleanor shook her head sadly.

"Put down your swords, brave men," she said. "I'll not have you die needlessly."

"Lower starboard boarding nets," the Captain said.

Responding to this order, some sailors threw thick cord nets with large webbing over the side of the ship facing the dromon. Immediately, the Byzantines grabbed it, and a score of their marines climbed up the net and clambered aboard our ship. These were followed by a dignitary wearing a purple silk robe girded by a belt that held a gold-hilted sword in its scabbard and a jewel-handled dagger in its sheathe.

Eleanor looked disdainfully at the Captain "You certainly made that easy enough," she said scornfully.

"No point in being discourteous," the Captain said.

The Byzantine dignitary and his marines crossed the deck to confront the knights. Sir Guy looked up to Eleanor, for he was still prepared to fight. But the Queen gestured to him to put his sword down, and obeying reluctantly, he threw his weapon on the deck, and the other knights did likewise. Emboldened by this development, the Greeks then quickly surrounded the knights closely, and stripping them of their daggers and remaining armament, placed them under guard.

Seeing the ship thus secured, the silk-robed dignitary gave a few orders to his men, then climbed up to the sterncastle. He looked at Eleanor and bowed politely.

"Greetings, Queen Eleanor," the Greek said. "I am Commodore Nicholas Andronicus, brother to Michael Andronicus, who is Admiral of this fleet."

Eleanor was in no mood for pleasantries. "What is the meaning of this?" she snapped.

"The meaning, fair Kelt," Andronicus explained with mock politeness, "is that you are being brought to Constantinople to be held for ransom."

"Are you mad?" Eleanor scoffed. "Do you suppose for a minute Louis would ransom me?"

Andronicus and the Captain looked at each other and smiled. Then the Greek turned back to the Queen.

"No," he said, shaking his head doubtfully. "I would hardly imagine he would choose to do so. After all…"

"After all, with me out of the way he keeps the Aquitaine," Eleanor said, her voice sour.

Andronicus raised his eyebrows like a teacher acknowledging the correct response from a young scholar. "Astutely concluded," he said.

Eleanor's eyes flashed anger. "He put you up to this, didn't he?"

Andronicus struck a dignified pose. "Now, now," he said. "Please don't pry. That would be telling."

"My sainted husband," Eleanor muttered sullenly. "That blackguard."

Andronicus seemed amused. "Really," he said. "Don't pout. If you were half as clever as you make yourself out to be, you would have expected as much."

Eleanor nodded ruefully, and was silent for a moment as she watched her husband's ship disappear in the distance. Then she turned back to the Commodore.

"So," she said. "What then is to become of me?"

Andronicus had apparently been waiting for this question, for a look of some satisfaction lit his face. "As I said," he replied, "you are to be held for ransom. Louis won't be bidding, but I understand that both the Emir and Nuradin have offered goodly sums. If I were you, I'd hope the Emir wins the auction, as a place in his harem is far to be preferred to the fate the Nuradin has in mind for you."

Eleanor's eyes went wide with horror. "You would sell me to the

Turks!" she cried.

Andronicus shrugged. "And your ladies too," he said. "Business is business."

Eleanor, Alicia, and I looked at each other in total dismay.

The Captain then turned to Andronicus. "Speaking of business..." he said.

Andronicus cut the Captain off. "Right," he said, and with a sarcastic bow to Eleanor, continued. "Queen Eleanor, if you would be good enough to leave the sterncastle, the Captain and I need to have a few words together."

Glaring first at Andronicus, and then at the Captain, Eleanor turned and stalked off, followed by Alicia. I was the last to go. As I lowered myself down the ladder, I turned while my head was still just above the sterncastle deck. In that brief moment I saw Andronicus hand a leather purse heavy with coins to the Captain, and toss a smaller one to the helmsman.

I joined Eleanor and Alicia on the deck just in time to see the Byzantine marines herd our unarmed knights down into the cargo hold. Then they locked the hatch in place using a wooden pole as a bar.

Eleanor beckoned, and we followed her across the deck away from the Greeks.

I whispered to Eleanor. "The Captain and helmsman are in Andronicus' pay."

Eleanor nodded. "So I surmised."

I looked about. Our predicament seemed so hopeless. We were just three women alone, friendless, and doomed to the mercies of the Turks. What could we do, what could we even try, against the score of Byzantine marines holding us prisoner, let alone the fleet of warships backing them up.

"My lady," I said, trying to hide my terror. "What do we do now?"

Chapter 45

The Secret Weapon

"Do not despair," Eleanor said, her voice now calm and resolute. "There's always hope. Alicia, did you not say you heard several of the sailors speaking our mother tongue?" By mother tongue she meant the langue d'oc dialect of the peoples of Provence, Aquitaine included, which even the nobles there learn from their nurses before they learn French.

"Yes," Alicia said. "That one there, by the rail, and those two further up the deck."

"Then let's have some words with them," said Eleanor

We walked up the deck to where a sailor dressed in rags was leaning against windward railing. He was about thirty years of age, and his skin displayed the deep tan and wrinkles of a man who has spent many years amidst sun, wind, and salt water.

Eleanor took a position on the rail close by his left, and Alicia and I close in on his right. He looked about, startled but not unpleased, to find himself so suddenly surrounded by three fair women.

Eleanor smiled. "Greetings, countryman!" she called out merrily in the southern dialect.

The sailor reacted with surprise and delight. "You speak the langue d'oc!"

"Of course," said Eleanor. "I am from Aquitaine. Where is your home?"

"I was born in Marseille," the sailor said.

"Marseille!" Eleanor exclaimed. "Oh, I have been there, what a beautiful town!"

"Yes," Alicia chimed in. "I used to go there in the winter. Ah, the gardens, the wine, the beach in the moonlight! It is such a lovely place." She sighed.

The sailor smiled. "Aye, that it is."

Eleanor spoke. "So, tell me, sir, I'm sorry, I didn't catch your name."

"Jean," the sailor said. "I am called Jean."

Eleanor nodded. "So tell me, Jean," she said. "Don't you ever wish you could go back to Marseille and buy a vineyard, find a nice girl, have a family?"

Jean hesitated. "Well..." he began, uncertainly.

Alicia interjected. "Or maybe have a tavern of your own near the dock, a lively place, filled with wine, women, and song?"

Jean smiled. "That might be more my style," he said. "But no, the sea is my home now."

Eleanor looked out on the water for a long moment. "Yes, the sea is a beautiful place too," she said, then turned back to Jean. "So how long have you been a sailor?"

"Since I was a boy," Jean replied, "almost twenty years."

"Twenty years! Such a long time," Eleanor said, her voice touched with sympathy. "Don't you ever get tired of taking orders all the time?"

Alicia adopted the gruff voice of the Captain. "Heave ho! Haul in! You're luffing!"

Jean gave a short laugh at her mocking impersonation. "Yes," he said. "It would be better to be an officer."

"Or a captain?" Eleanor suggested. "One who owns his own ship, so you can sail where you like, with no master at all?"

"Now that is every sailor's dream," said Jean with a rueful smile. "But a poor man like me will never have enough to buy a ship."

Eleanor leaned in very close so that her body touched Jean, and looked him in the face from less than a foot away.

"Really?" she said, her eyes peering into his. "How much would a ship like this cost?"

Jean froze in silence for several seconds. Then he turned and faced Alicia, his eyes wide, as if seeking confirmation of his dawning understanding of the bargain being offered. Alicia and I nodded and smiled our reassurances. He turned back to Eleanor.

"You have the wealth to deliver on such a promise?" he asked, looking about.

"I am Queen of France and Duchess of Aquitaine," Eleanor said.

Jean exhaled sharply. "I would risk anything for my own ship," he said. "But I am just one man."

"Then get more," Eleanor urged. "Speak to your friends among the sailors, those you trust, but no officers. If they'll but be my sailors for a day, I'll make them ship owners ever after."

Jean tilted his head, and laughed a short knowing laugh. "On that bargain, you'll get them all," he said. "But still...." He pointed at the Byzantine marines crowding the deck, and the Byzantine warships all about.

"Ask no more questions," Eleanor said, her voice as level as that of a knight giving the watch assignments to his men at arms. "Speak to your fellows, and stand ready."

Jean gave the Queen a look of acknowledgement, and then departed up the deck to speak with some more sailors. We watched them converse, the other men's expressions changing suddenly. They looked back at Eleanor, who responded to their silent inquiry with a nod. For the merest second, Jean displayed his thumb to us in an upward position, and then moved on.

Alicia turned to Eleanor. "So we've got ourselves some sailors," she said. "But I still don't see how…"

At that moment the lookout on top of the main mast called out. "Ships ho!"

"What ships?" the Captain shouted back from the sterncastle, a tinge of alarm evident in his voice. "How many? What bearing?"

"Normans from Sicily," the lookout cried. "King Roger's warships, nigh a dozen, bearing directly towards us."

Eleanor looked smugly at Alicia. "Consider the lilies of the field," she said.

Alicia gazed at her friend in astonishment.

Eleanor turned to me. "Marie, why don't you go and fetch your lute."

"My lute?" I said, utterly puzzled.

"Yes," said Eleanor. "It could come in handy."

The lute being nearby, it took just a minute to fetch it.

"I have brought the lute as ordered, my lady," I reported upon my return.

Eleanor nodded. "Very well," she said. "Let's go have a visit with Commodore Andronicus."

Saying this, she led us up the ladder to the sterncastle, which was manned by Commodore Andronicus, the Captain, and the helmsman.

The Captain barely had time to acknowledge our return when he received a call from above.

"The Admiral's flagship is signaling us," the lookout shouted.

"What are they saying?" the Captain called back, holding his hands around his mouth to make his voice louder.

"I'm not sure," the lookout cried. "They're ordering some kind of maneuver."

Captain turned to the helmsman. "These idiots," he said. "They spend their whole lives at sea and still can't read maneuver flags."

"I can, sir," the helmsman said.

The Captain nodded his approval. "Very well," he said. "Go aloft. I'll take the helm."

Handing the tiller to the Captain, the helmsman hurried off the sterncastle and began climbing the mast. As he did this, Eleanor looked down the deck to where Jean was standing by a railing. He met her eyes and nodded. Eleanor turned and approached Andronicus.

"So, Commodore Andronicus," she began breezily. "It would seem that you are going to have some lively company today."

Andronicus looked at her sharply. "You arranged this?" he asked, a touch of hysteria evident in his voice.

Eleanor was nonchalant. "Now, now, that would be telling," she said. Then, observing his angry countenance, she continued. "Oh please Commodore, there's no reason to be so upset. After all, if you were half as clever as you make yourself out to be, you might have anticipated it."

Andronicus shook his head. "You Kelts," he said bitterly. "You believe you can do everything. You charge into a part of the world of which you know nothing, and think that your youth and courage will allow you to overthrow powers that were ancient when you were still eating raw fish and painting your faces blue. Now you challenge the navy of Constantinople, heir to the Empire of invincible Rome. Well, you are in for a surprise."

I looked across the waves. The Norman squadron was now clearly visible from the sterncastle. There were twelve of them, a force to match the Byzantines, perhaps more than match, because the Norman rowers were free warriors, not galley slaves like those of Constantinople. Their banners showed large black crosses atop the traditional red and white stripes of the sea fighters of the north. Once such ships had been the terror of Christendom. Now they were its strong right arm. My heart rose at the sight of them.

"I don't know," Eleanor said. "I'll wager on the youth and courage of those Normans against your slavish Greeks in a fair fight any day."

Andronicus frowned. "But war isn't a fair fight," he said. "I'm surprised you haven't learned that yet."

The helmsman now reached the lookout post. He called out to us.

"The flagship wants us to fall in battle line directly to her flank."

"Very well," the Captain shouted in return, and moved the tiller a bit to adjust course.

As we held this new course, the wind shifted and strengthened. When it settled, I observed that our vessel was now heading almost directly downwind.

The Captain noticed it too. He called out to some sailors. "You there, ease off on those lines. Trim for running with the wind."

The maneuvers completed, the two squadrons of warships now lined up abreast and approached each other rapidly.

Suddenly, a huge fountain of flame shot out of the prow of the Greek flagship. It was the most startling thing I have ever seen, for it shot as far forward as an arrow could fly, and the fire continued to burn upon the water where it landed.

"What was that?" Eleanor said in alarm

Andronicus smiled in condescension. "That, my fair Kelt, is our secret weapon, kept on every flagship of our fleet. And that is why, a few hours from now, all your brave young Norman friends will be so much roast meat served to the fishes."

The flagship shot out another stream of flame, and the Norman galley that was rowing aggressively towards her started to hastily back water.

Eleanor shook nervously, then looked at me.

"Marie," she said, her voice tense. "Why don't you show the Captain your lute?"

"My lute?" I said. Then I realized what she had in mind. "Ah yes, of course."

So I took the lute from off my shoulder, and started walking towards the Captain strumming it as I went.

"Spin wheel, Wind Mill," I sang.

At that moment, several ships of the battle lines towards the flanks came together with a mighty crash, and Normans and Byzantine marines leapt onto the prows of their ships to fight hand to hand. But then, in the battle's very center, the flagship shot out its flame again and engulfed its Norman adversary in a blazing inferno.

I froze in my tracks and watched in horror as dozens of brave men who would have been our rescuers were covered in a flame that would not leave them, and screaming piteously, jumped into the sea.

The flagship turned to pursue another victim, and the other nearby Norman ships all started backing water rapidly to try to escape. In seconds, the entire center of Norman squadron collapsed into disarray.

"You see," Andronicus said to Eleanor. "You have already lost."

Eleanor stared at the unfolding debacle in disbelief, then turned to me.

I was standing equally dazed but half a fathom from the Captain.

"Marie," she shouted. "Now!"

Her call reawakened me to my purpose. Grasping my lute with both hands, I smashed it across the face of the Captain. The fine instrument broke into splinters and the big man fell to the deck like a sack of grain dropped from the back of a cart.

In the next moment, as I turned to grab the tiller, I saw Alicia, who had been inconspicuously sidling up to Andronicus, reach down by his waist, pull his jewel-handled dagger from his waistband, and hold it to his throat. The Commodore, who had just started to move in response to my assault on the Captain, now froze in terror. Then Eleanor stepped over and pulled his gold-hilted sword from its scabbard.

Alicia pressed the knife against the Greek's neck. "Put your hands in your back belt!" she ordered. Receiving instant compliance, she then reached down with her left hand, and twisted the front of his belt tight, effectively binding his hands behind his back.

It was time. Using all my strength, I pushed the tiller hard over, turning our ship across the wind.

There was a menacing luff in the main and fore sails. All the sailors saw it and ducked. But the Byzantine marines took no note, and an instant later, the sails swept across the deck with tremendous force, throwing half a dozen of them overboard. Many of the rest were knocked down, and their swords clattered across the deck.

I completed my song. "The breath of God sets us free."

Eleanor shouted to the sailors. "Take the ship!"

From their perches in the rigging, sailors took hold of ropes and swung down to crash feet first into the disoriented marines, knocking them down and scattering more of their weapons. Jean snatched an ax from its mounting on the sterncastle wall, and with one blow shattered the pole barring the hold imprisoning our knights. In a trice, the hatchway was thrown open, and Sir Guy and the other knights came leaping out. Taking in the situation instantly, they grabbed weapons from the deck and charged into the fight. In moments, combat was general all over the ship as the sailors and knights did battle with the remaining marines.

Eleanor pointed her sword at the flagship. "Set course that way," she said.

I pushed the tiller harder and the ship started heading across the wind. We had no one to manage the sails for us, but the lines controlling the sails were still tied to the side of the deck where they had been before our wild jibe, so the sails remained close-hauled enough to stay full. In seconds we were sailing on a fast beam reach straight at the side of the flame-shooting flagship.

"What are you doing?" Andronicus cried in alarm. "You're going to collide with the flagship!"

"Astutely concluded," Eleanor said evenly.

We had only fifty fathoms to go to reach the flagship, and the stiff wind sped us over the water at a good six knots, so all it took was half a minute. The Admiral on the flagship saw us coming and waved for us to pass astern. In the last instant, he must have realized that we were under unfriendly command, for he turned and shouted to his helmsman. But he was too late.

Our massive vessel struck the flagship's starboard oars and they cracked like toothpicks. The galley slaves screamed and pulled at their chains in a useless effort to escape, and some of the Greek crossbowmen fired a desperate volley. Then we crashed through the low beam of the flagship, breaking her in two with a massive crunch. As we sailed right on through, the two halves of the flagship turned up on end and started to sink. Men were thrown into the water, some drowning instantly in their armor, others managing to swim or clutch onto fragments of wood that were floating about. Then, with a sound like the crack of doom, steam exploded in the bow half, and burning pitch spread all over the water, engulfing the survivors in flame and smoke.

On the Norman ships facing the Byzantine center, men began to cheer madly, and their Captains raised their swords to order their ships to advance at ramming speed. Seeing the destruction of their flagship, the other Byzantine vessels tried to turn and flee, but many were rammed amidships as they made the attempt, while others were snagged and boarded.

Eleanor turned to face her prisoner.

"So, Commodore Andronicus," she began with a wicked smile. "It would seem that you are about to be a guest of King Roger of Sicily."

Andronicus' eyes bulged in alarm. "You would turn me over to Roger? My squadron just fired a ship full of his men. Do you have any idea what he'll do to me?"

"Not really," Eleanor sidled up next to the captive Commodore. "However I seem to owe him a favor and you are the only present I have to give right now."

"You wouldn't want me to seem like an ungrateful guest, would you?"

she said dryly.

"But he'll have me racked, flayed, and burnt alive!" Andronicus cried.

"I'm sorry," Eleanor said in a sympathetic voice. "But business is business."

She patted him on the head as a woman might do to reassure a distressed child. "Don't worry," she said. "I'm sure that no matter what he does the torment can't be made to last more than a fortnight."

Andronicus turned white as a sheet and fainted. Observing his unconscious form, Alicia pulled forward, then released her hold, allowing the Greek's limp body to crash to the deck.

Eleanor shrugged and turned to look around at the battle. Our men were in full control of our own ship, and the Byzantine squadron was in the last stages of defeat.

The Queen leaned back against the rail and smiled.

"That worked out well," she said.

Chapter 46

In Which Women Fly

And thus it was, that Eleanor, who through her foresight had sent word ahead to the brave Norman King Roger of Sicily to arrange her protection, escaped the evil conspiracy of her husband and Emperor Manuel Comnenus.

Roger took us to Sicily, where we received joyous news. For there we learned that our Captain, being in league with King Louis and Emperor Manuel in the plan for our capture, had lied to us about the fall of Antioch. In fact, Constance had rallied the people of the town so well that they beat back Nuradin's assault, and afterwards the clever Princess had broken his siege by inviting knights and nobles from everywhere to come and fight for her, with her hand, and thus the princedom, offered as prize to he who should prove the most valiant. So many had come in response to this summons, that not only had Nuradin been forced to withdraw, but wily Constance, like a second Penelope, had been able to play her suitors against each other and keep the power of the city for herself.

We also heard other good tidings. For, taking advantage of the distraction our crusade had imposed upon Islam, a fleet of Bretons, Normans, and English had descended upon Lisbon, and liberated that city from the Almoravids.

Lisbon! The town takes its name from the great Ulysses, who founded it during his final voyage into the unknown western ocean. What did that brave explorer find on that last journey of no return? Was it the Hesperides, or the secret land of the Carthaginians? What will we discover, now that this bold port of far adventure has been joined to Christendom?

This was grand enough. But what excited me all the more was to learn that the first knight to storm the walls was none other than Sir Alan of Cherbourg, and that it was this man, laying about like a second Roland with his unmatchable sword Durandel, who had made the glorious victory possible.

Our lives in this lower sphere are filled with much pain, but we are also granted our share of miracles, which though they come in strange and unexpected forms, must never be forgot. Observe the truth of this in these two events. For if Eleanor and I had not journeyed to Antioch, Constance would never have been prepared for the role which fate was to require of her, and Raymond's noble city would surely have been destroyed. And if Eleanor and I had not brought Alan back to his true calling, the wayward lad would yet be an indifferent scholar in Paris, and Lisbon still enslaved by the enemy. So it is that we, with our most obscure acts, providing only that they be good, may sometimes become the instruments of divine grace, and for this we should give thanks.

From Sicily we traveled to Rome, where Eleanor had words with the Pope. I was not admitted to this audience, but while waiting outside in Saint Peter's, I had the leisure to make the acquaintance of a number of the scholars that hung about the place. I tried to interest these men with the curious new numbers I had found in the east, but most thought them of little note. One, however, a bright young boy named Bonacci, was amused, and made a copy of my tablet for his further inquiry and entertainment. He invited Alicia and me to spend the afternoon drinking with he and his fellows, and I am certain that we had a better time with them than Eleanor did with Pope Eugenius.

When we returned to the Vatican, that evening, I was surprised to encounter my old acquaintance, John of Salisbury. This aspiring young man had made good on his betrayal of less orthodox scholarly colleagues to become the Pope's secretary. He greeted me with great enthusiasm, and told me how much he was now doing to assist the advance of scholarship since gaining a position of high influence. Such is the way of the world.

Thus our time in Rome was spent. Moving on, we returned safely to France in November. Here Eleanor rejoined Louis, if sitting on two thrones in the same room without ever exchanging a word or a look may be considered rejoining. Indeed, anyone who saw Eleanor's face of ice when she sat near Louis could feel the chill palpably in the air, and know with certainty without hearing a word, that this woman and this man were enemies unto each other.

This situation was not helped when, in the spring of the following year, Eleanor gave birth to another immaculate daughter, just nine months after leaving the court of the handsome King Roger. She named the girl Alicia, after her second best friend, and as in the case of my namesake, arranged for the child to be raised and instructed by wise sisters from Fontevrault.

There thus remained the matter of having the marriage nulled. Notwithstanding the fourth cousin relationship of consanguinity that

Eleanor had discovered between herself and Louis, Pope Eugenius and the Abbot Suger both urged that the marriage should continue, for they wanted Aquitaine to remain with Frankdom. But Eleanor would have none of it, and though it took two years, finally achieved the nullification. It was during this time that old Suger finally died, and it was perhaps a kindness that the Lord chose to take him before the nulling was done, as it portended the ruination of his life's dream of a great and powerful France.

However, when they saw the separation could not be stopped, Louis and Odo conceived of a new plan, which was to put Eleanor in a nunnery, and then take her Aquitaine. Of this plan, as you may understand, Eleanor did not approve. But what could she do? After the nullification, she who had been Queen was kept virtually a prisoner in the palace until she should agree to take vows. And if she could escape, what refuge could she find? Who that might wish to help her could be so mighty as to refuse, when the King of the Franks demanded her return, or so incorruptible that he would not do so for money? And of those so ruthless and spiteful of the throne that they might not obey Louis, who, upon gaining Eleanor in his power, might not choose to force her to be his bride whether she would or not, under rules and conditions of his own making, and by so doing, seize the Aquitaine for his own barbarous self?

As a mere bard, I was free to leave the palace anytime. But what could I do?

Thus was the Queen's dismal predicament, when, on the first of April, in the year of Our lord one thousand, one hundred, and fifty two, I reencountered Thomas à Becket.

It was a fine spring day, and I was walking near the Cathedral of Notre Dame to take in the morning and perhaps encounter some interesting scholars, when I bumped into him coming around the corner. I recognized him instantly, although he was older, plumper, and much better dressed than he had been in his student days. Indeed, I had grown much since that time too, in many ways, but in hard earned wisdom most of all.

"Master Becket!" I cried, happy to meet an old friend. "How now! I see fortune has been kind to you."

Becket gazed at me and nodded. "Yes," he said. "I have done well in the service of Duke Geoffrey of Anjou. And you, do you still keep company with Eleanor?"

"Indeed I do," I replied

"Then it is good that we have met," he said. "I understand that she has need of a husband."

"That depends," I said, with an ironic laugh. "I think she would rather be a nun than have another husband like Louis."

Becket looked me in the eyes. Then he said, "How about a husband from the house of Anjou?"

I raised my eyebrows in surprise and stared at the man.

We went into a tavern and discussed the matter further.

***　　***　　***

That evening at the palace, Eleanor, Alicia and I gathered around a table, and I showed them the little painting that Becket had given me. It depicted a very handsome young man, with red hair and a powerful build, clean shaven and dressed in fine clothes.

Eleanor looked at it with admiring eyes. "So this is his miniature?" she asked.

"Yes," I replied. "That is Henry of Anjou, the son of Geoffrey. Becket says that through his mother, Matilda, the Conqueror's Granddaughter, he bids fair to become King of England."

Eleanor nodded thoughtfully. "And with the silver of my Aquitaine to support his claim, would be certain to make it good."

Alicia spoke. "He seems very young, Eleanor, barely nineteen, a good eleven years your junior."

Eleanor smiled. "That is a sin I can forgive," she said, flashing Alicia a look filled with mischief. Then she turned back to me. "But I would know more about him. Is he a courtly man, educated, clean, fashionable, intelligent, liberal, considerate of women, not over pious; is he a dancer, a poet, a singer, a joker, a philosopher, a drinker, a chess player, a hawker, a hunter, a warrior, and withal, a natural man, for I would not marry another Louis."

"Becket says he is all these things," I said.

Alicia was suspicious. "Becket says," she repeated.

"He seemed truly in earnest," I told Eleanor.

Eleanor searched my eyes, as if by doing thus, she could see into Becket's. Then she gazed down at the miniature fondly, and shrugged. "Well," she said, "since the choice is to chance it with Henry, or take the veil, I'll chance it."

She looked at me. "So Marie, what is your plan?"

***   ***   ***

It took more than a month to come to final agreement of marriage terms with Henry and make all the arrangements for our escape. This job was mine, for only I could pass back and forth, taking messages from those within the palace to those without. But by the second week of May, all was ready.

The night was dark and moonless as I snuck through the palace garden, just outside Eleanor's tower. Looking up, I saw the candlelight glow from her window. I whistled the call of a lark, twice, as agreed, and waited. A moment later, I heard a gentle thud as a rope was thrown out the tower window. Then I saw the silhouette of a woman appear at the window, and climb out to descend the rope. This proved to be Eleanor. When she reached the bottom of the rope, I hissed to her, and she scrambled over to join me in the bushes. A moment later, Alicia followed.

"Which way?" Eleanor whispered.

I pointed, and we ran across the garden to reach the three fathom high wall that surrounded the palace grounds. Resting on the grass was a wooden platform affixed to a rope that led upward into the darkness above. I stepped on to the platform, and beckoned the other two to join me. As soon as they were aboard, I pulled twice on the rope.

There was a muffled cranking sound, the rope stiffened, and the platform lifted us from ground. High and higher we went, until we were well above the wall. We could look down and see the palace on one side of the wall, and the City of Paris, torches glowing in the windows of a hundred taverns, on the other. Then we looked up, and all about us were stars, myriads of them, bespeaking the glorious majesty of heaven.

"So we learn to fly," Eleanor said softly, the starlight shining in her eyes.

The platform began to move sideways, and as it did, we could hear the sound of a cart moving with muffled axels and hooves. Slowly we flew over the wall, and then gently descended on the other side.

Papa stood by the crane cart with Patrick and Michael. Nearby stood three good riding horses, saddled and ready. I gave Papa and my brothers warm goodbye hugs, then the three of us leapt on the horses and galloped off into the night.

***   ***   ***

And so riding through the darkness, we escaped Paris for Chartres, there to meet Henry.

It was dawn when we arrived, and a pleasant spring mist was rising from the ground. As we rode into the town at a walk, the cocks were crowing and peasant boys and girls were just setting forth for their errands.

"So this is Chartres," Eleanor said, her horses' steps echoing among the quiet houses.

Then I saw it. "Look, a cathedral!" I cried.

We spurred our horses and cantered up to the magnificent structure. It was an almost-finished cathedral of light like the one at Saint Denis, but grander and more excellent in every way. At the front portal there was a beautifully executed frieze depicting the greatest philosophers of all the ages, assembled together in a group. Boethius was there, and Pythagoras, Plato, Aristotle, Priscian, Euclid, and the immortal Cicero, greatest of orators.

I pointed to them. "See, the seven sages. There will be a great school here too."

Some scholars carrying books started to walk past us into the Cathedral. As we watched, one young scholar stopped beneath the window of a wealthy house and gently threw a pebble to arouse the occupant. In response, a pretty burgher girl leaned out the window, and the lad passed a flower up to her. As the girl smiled upon him, the scholar got down on one knee and gesticulated to her in true courtly fashion. Then a bell in the Cathedral rang, and the scholar rose and threw his love a kiss, which she returned in kind before he hurried off.

"Yes," Eleanor said softly to Alicia. "That is how it should be." Then she turned to me. "Where were we to meet them?"

I pointed down the street. "At the west end of town," I said.

Eleanor nodded, and we rode forward to the western edge of the city. There on the dirt road leading out into the country, we saw a small cavalcade of horsemen a half mile out, but coming towards us. Spurring our horses into a trot, we rode out to meet them.

Soon they were clearly visible, and I saw a man who could only be Duke Henry of Anjou, accompanied by Becket and a group of well-trimmed knights. Henry was indeed a tall strapping handsome youth, with fire-red hair and eyes blue as the sea, clean shaven, and dressed in handsome breeches, a clean tunic, and a beautiful purple cape. His expression brimmed with vitality, and he carried a colorful bouquet of spring flowers on his pommel.

Our two parties came to a stop facing each from two fathoms distance. "Queen Eleanor?" Henry inquired.

"Just Duchess Eleanor now," Eleanor said.

"No, Queen," Henry replied. "For you are Queen of my heart already, and will be Queen of England soon. And never did any woman deserve better to be Queen of both and more besides."

Eleanor smiled at this, and Henry rode slowly forward.

He held out his bouquet. "I have flowers for you," he said. "They are but poor things, all I could gather during our fast ride here, but if you will accept them from me you will make me the happiest man in Christendom, for my highest prayer is to please you."

Eleanor took the bouquet. "I will accept your flowers, Henry of Anjou," she said, looking in his eyes with some warmth.

Henry bowed gently in his saddle. "I thank you, fair Queen. Then, with your permission, these young men have begged to come with me to be squires to your beautiful companions, at least until such time as they might choose others who please them more."

Two handsome knights rode forward, each with a bouquet of flowers. Both were fine men. The taller was a complete stranger, but the other I thought I recognized.

Alicia and I regarded them, then exchanged glances with each other. "For the Lady Alicia of Bordeaux," Henry said, pointed at the taller knight, "this is Sir William of Rouen. And for the famous bard, Marie of France, our own brave Sir Alan of Cherbourg."

It was Alan, the same lad who I had known so long ago as a young scholar in Paris. He had changed much, but it was he.

"Alan," I said with some warmth. "You certainly have become a knight."

"Yes," he said. "Although as I recall, you seemed to have something to do with it." He smiled and kneaded the side of his head where I had given him his accolade. "It seems to suit me better than scholarship, although the letters I learned have served me well."

Henry broke in. "Yes, but now that he has proven himself a knight, he also fancies himself a troubadour. Perhaps you can help him, and all of us, by teaching him to sing."

Alan blushed red, and all his friends laughed with good spirits.

Alan looked at me somberly. "Marie, there is something you must know. When we took Lisbon, and freed the Christian slaves, there was an old

Breton woman among them who gave her name as Morgan of Nantes, wife of Peter the Builder."

"My mother!" I gasped.

"Yes," he replied.

I quaked with the news. "Does she yet live?" I asked, dreading the answer.

Alan shook his head. "No, she died during our journey north. But not before she reached the tomb of St. James of Compostella, and confessed her sins there. It was there that she took ill, and while dying, heard the glad tidings of your safe arrival in Sicily. She asked me to tell you that she was very proud of you, and requested that I give you this."

He reached out and handed me a silver emblem on a chain. I recognized it at once. It was my mother's crucifix, a cross not such as are made today, but of the kind used by the Bretons during the time of King Arthur. It had been in our family since ancient days, and my mother had kept it for me, even as she kept to her faith during all her years of captivity. Tears formed in my eyes.

"She was buried in holy ground," Alan said. "And the monks of the shrine said a mass for her soul."

I dismounted from my horse, knelt on the ground, and offered a prayer of thanks to the Virgin for this mercy.

When I was done I felt Alan's hands, gently pulling me to my feet beside him.

"Marie," he began. "I want you to know that all these years since we parted I have thought oftentimes about you. I erred grievously then, for I did not see you for the magnificent creature you truly are until it was too late. Please let me make amends."

"Alan," I said, grasping Mama's crucifix. "For the service you've rendered here any wrong you might have done me in the past is amended a thousand times over."

"Yet I would do more," Alan said, "much more, would you but let me. I want to serve you, and protect you, and stand by you now, and all the years ahead. I want to be your knight. Marie, will you be my lady?"

Warmth filled my heart, and a smile filled my face, even as I blinked away my tears. "Yes," I said, meeting his eyes directly with mine.

Alan stood there, stupefied. "I don't know what to say now," he muttered.

"Kiss her, you fool," Eleanor called out.

So he did, and I must say that it was a proper kiss, in fact a grand one, better, I think than any Helen got from Paris, or Dido from Aeneas, Guinevere from Arthur, or even, dare I say it, Heloise from Abelard. Perhaps Ulysses and Penelope, finally reunited after their long separation, might have exchanged such a kiss, although Homer's description is inadequate for me to state such for certain. Be that as it may, ours was a kiss deep enough to write a ballad about, and long enough to waste the morning. Such heavenly nectar is rarely tasted in this world.

But then we heard the Duke coughing, and had to leave off. I accepted Alan's courteous help in remounting my horse, even though I did not need it, then watched with pride as he nimbly leaped upon his own.

"Well then," Henry said, facing Eleanor. "We must be off. The French are about, and we have some miles to go before we reach safety. Besides, I'd like to reach Anjou by nightfall. There is a crazy old Spaniard there who is raving that he needs to show you this famous book he has finally translated, and I want to put your reported skill as a dancer to the test."

He tilted his head gently back and forth so that his eyes danced.

Eleanor smiled. "I have little fear that Louis will ever catch us, Henry," she said.

Henry laughed. "Indeed, my lady, you're right there. But we still need to dance. So, shall we ride?"

Eleanor turned and looked about, and I looked with her. In the direction of the town, scholars could be seen trooping up the path to the cathedral, whose bells were ringing music. All around us the countryside was dotted with windmills, and groups of peasant girls were dancing the windmill dance before them as the mills whirled busily away.

Eleanor whispered softly. "No, it wasn't all a waste."

"What did you say?" Henry asked.

Eleanor bit her lower lip. "I said, let's ride!" she shouted. "Yah!"

Then she spurred her horse into a gallop, and we all followed her down the road, into a future unknown, exciting, and filled with hope.

Epilogue

That Which Ensued

And so it was that Eleanor, escaping that abominable, cretinous, pathetic, witless, unnatural snail Louis, married Henry of Anjou, who indeed, with her help, did become Henry II Plantagenet, King of England. In this way, Aquitaine, transferred from France to England, made the latter mighty and the former small, a development that so crushed Louis, that Eleanor, remembering it, had a song in her heart forever after.

Together with Henry she created the most brilliant court in all Christendom, grew London, and had eight children, for Henry, as you may have heard, did not have Louis' problem. They spent some thirty years together, many happy, and many not, but through it all, they drank in full the cup of life. Together they ordained the glorious Common Law, a code of justice better, wiser, and more fair and merciful than was ever laid down by any monarchs before them since the beginning of the world. And then, after Henry died, Eleanor reigned, as her son Richard the Lionhearted was too busy crusading to rule. She pardoned all the poachers, helped all the bards and artists, and did many other fine things, including building great cathedrals at Canterbury, Rochester, Glastonbury, Chichester, Winchester, Wells, and Lincoln; and starting a second universitas, at Oxford, which promises to produce many excellent discoveries. She also taught the English the use of the fork, which she brought back from Constantinople, and taught it so well that most of them continue to use it to this day. And when, at the age of eighty, she wearied of the concerns of the world, she retired to Fontevrault, there to be buried by the side of Henry, in a place where she might enjoy precedence.

As for me, I traveled with her to England, and there became ennobled through marriage to my old friend Alan, the bravest of King Henry's knights, who, though he never became a good troubadour, nevertheless proved to be a very good man. I am old now, and have seen much greatness and even more folly in my time, but I still have hope. For I have seen Antioch, and know that a better world is to come.

Oh, and did I mention? I have published my book, and it has been well received and translated into Frankish, English, German, Latin, Spanish, and Norse. No, it is not this tale I have just related to you, for what instruction could anyone gain from such a miserable chronicle of sordid events? No, such books are for the likes of Anna Comnena and others who wish to glorify treachery and massacre by calling them history. I would not sink to that. Rather I have chosen to make my book a work of fancy, which is the noblest sort of book. For in such works truth may appear more clearly than it does on this, our lower sphere, and through it men can be taught that virtue will be rewarded, vice punished, and good will triumph over evil in the end. Because in this, and this alone, all may and must have faith.

The End.

Eleanor's Crusades

Translator's Notes

Eleanor's Crusade is the story of an extraordinary woman living at an extraordinary time, told to us first hand by an almost equally remarkable associate.

Eleanor of Aquitaine was beautiful, intelligent, well educated, forceful, imaginative, inquisitive, innovative, courageous, indomitable, and incredibly rich. The untraditional and wildly romantic granddaughter of the first troubadour, and heir to a duchy comprising a third of modern France, she was in love with life, in love with love, and unwilling to accept any limits on what she might see, do, or accomplish.

Born in the year 1122, Eleanor lived for 82 years, during which time she was Queen to two kings (Louis VII of France, and Henry II of England) and mother of two more (Richard the Lionhearted and King John). Her life thus virtually spans the Twelfth Century, a key formative period of western civilization.

For five hundred years after the fall of the Roman Empire, Western Europe had been relegated to barbarism. But in the 11th Century, with the threatened catastrophe of the Millennium safely past, political entities finally gelled in Europe capable of beating off the Viking, Saracen, and Magyar raiders that had been destroying Christendom from without, and imposing some degree of internal order over the local robber barons that had been creating chaos from within. Freed of these terrors, Europeans finally had a chance to open up their eyes to the world of the mind, and begin to create a civilization for themselves. What followed has rightly been called the "Renaissance of the Twelfth Century."

It was during the Twelfth Century that most of the great cities of Western Europe were truly born. It was during this period that the first Gothic cathedrals were built, and the first universities founded. It was a period of intense intellectual controversy, with the birth of rationalist and scholastic schools of thought, the rediscovery of much of Greek philosophy, the spread of diverse heresies, and a clerical counter with the start of the first Inquisition. It was the time of the troubadours, and their creation and dissemination of the King Arthur myth, which became the basis for   the spread of the new code of Chivalry that reshaped European manners and ethics and greatly elevated the status of women. It was a time of commercial and technological revolution, which saw the first great market fairs and the invention and exponential proliferation of windmills and improved watermills that freed huge numbers of people from lives of brutal drudgery. It was a time of play, with Europeans enjoying news games ranging from jousts to chess, dancing, romantic literature, and hearing for the first time the new sound of polyphonic music. It was a time of conflict, between rival monarchs, between Church and State, and above all, between Christendom and its archenemy Islam, with Europeans finally on the offensive in their epic adventures known as the Crusades.

During her life, Eleanor was in middle of all of this, and the cause of much of it. She patronized the troubadours, and forced the introduction of the code of Chivalry into both the French and English courts. She knew Abbot Suger, who designed the first great Gothic church at St. Denis, and she was there the day its opening was celebrated. She knew the famous rationalist intellectual Abelard, and the clerical giant St. Bernard of Clairvaux, and saw the two of them square off in debate. She knew Thomas Becket, and almost certainly knew and patronized such Arthurian creators as Geoffrey of Monmouth, Chretien de Troyes, and, especially, Marie de France, the first western European woman to write a book. She also met Anna Comnena, the Byzantine princess who was the first woman to write a serious work of history, and according to legend, now confirmed by Marie, even encountered the boy Saladin, who later became her son Richard the Lionhearted's arch opponent during the Third Crusade. An ardent feminist, she established "courts of love" where women debated and set rules for proper male behavior during courtship. She was there when the Second Crusade was declared, and not only joined it, but, at the age of 25, recruited a troop of similarly minded self-styled "Amazons" to accompany her. During the crusade she journeyed to the fabled cities of Constantinople, Antioch, Jerusalem, and Damascus, took part in battles on horseback, climbed mountain passes riddled with ambushers, endured long marches through heat and snow and freezing rain and every other kind of privation, saw the reputed One True Cross in the headquarters of the Knights Templar, and was captured and liberated in shipboard battles at sea.

Hardly what one would term a cloistered life.

The Times of Eleanor

The view of the high Middle Ages presented in Marie's account differs considerably from that popularized by Walter Scott and Hollywood. It shows a world that was simultaneously far more crude *and* more advanced and intellectually alive than that depicted in the stereotypical canon.

Two prominent examples representing each side of this are the cases of sleeping arrangements and the use of machinery.

Sleeping arrangements:

In Chapter 3, Eleanor asks Alicia to lead Marie to "her quarters," and Alicia leads Marie into the great hall of the Palace where the two bed down on the floor amid dozens of other sleepers. Marie's account reveals how things actually were. In the Twelfth Century, feudal retainers, even nobles of high rank, slept together in the hall of their lord's house, just as their (not so distant) barbarian forbears had slept together in the halls of their chiefs' lodges. Except for the King and Queen, no one in palace of Louis VII had any privacy.

Machinery:

While a consideration of the social habits of Twelfth Century western Europeans might lead one to the conclusion that they were just out of the forest, examination of their use of machinery presents the exact opposite picture. Twelfth Century Europe was heavily mechanized, and was in the process of becoming radically more so. Already, in the late Eleventh Century, the Norman Domesday Book records over 10,000 water mills in England. By the mid Twelfth Century, water powered mills were everywhere; with the undersides of bridges in Paris filled with them, from one bank of the river to the other, as engineers (variously called "enginators," "ingenators," or "machinators") strove to exploit every drop of available water power. Legal records are filled with disputes with various parties suing others who had built water mills upstream or downstream of theirs, thereby robbing them of power. Water mills had originally been invented in the Roman Empire of the First Century A.D., to the great delight of girls, who were freed from the drudgery of grinding grain (Verse survives from a First Century Roman poet who comments that, now that there are water mills, all the girls sleep in late.) But such mills remained rare in the slave-labor-dominated Roman economy. However with the transition from slavery to serfdom in post-Roman Christian Europe, water mills proliferated (peasants can pay to have their grain ground, slaves can't.) By the Twelfth Century, water mills, greatly improved in efficiency from earlier Roman models, were also being used to drive forges, sawmills, and perform numerous other industrial tasks.

It was in the Twelfth Century, somewhere in northern France, that a new source of energy was discovered – the wind – to augment the Europeans' nearly tapped-out water power resources. The thing that makes wind power so much more difficult to master than water power is the fact that the wind changes direction. Islamic enginators in earlier centuries attempted to deal with this by placing an obstacle to one side of a vertical axis paddle wheel, but such systems are very inefficient and only work when the wind is coming from certain directions. It was a northwest European enginator who hit on the idea of the post windmill, which mounts the blades of the windmill on a horizontal axis, which in turn is allowed to swing with the wind to always maintain correct facing for the machine. This is the basis for nearly all windmills since. With this invention, the power available to medieval Europeans became unlimited, and the European economy and population began to grow very rapidly as a result.

Applying such forms of mechanical power, Europeans created all kinds of complex machinery, which was essential to the building of the great cathedrals.

To me, the contrast between the medieval Europeans' primitive mode of life and their technological wizardry is extremely striking, and makes their positive accomplishments, such as building of cathedrals, all the more impressive.

The post windmill could turn to face the wind. Invented in northern France during the mid-Twelfth Century, it radically expanded Europe's mechanical energy resources and contributed to rapid economic growth.

Until the discovery of *Eleanor's Crusades*, there was no evidence of Eleanor having been a sponsor of windmills, but they originated in France during her reign, and she was probably among the first to see one. No doubt she would have welcomed their effect on her tax base, and as an ardent feminist (see below), valued the boon they offered to women of the middle and lower classes. For Twelfth Century women, the advent of windmills had the same significance as the coming of washing machines did for those of the Twentieth Century

Depiction of women using a water mill to grind grain, taken from the Twelfth Century manuscript of Herrade de Landsberg. Note the complex gearing. Powered mills had the same significance for women of the Twelfth Century as washing machines did for those of the Twentieth.

The Grand Pont in Paris. To exploit all available water power, the spaces under bridges were filled with water wheels.

Construction was done using complex machinery

Feminism:

Modern day feminists, who think that their cause originated in the 1960's, or perhaps with the Nineteenth Century suffragettes, need to take a back seat to Eleanor and her crowd. In the early Twelfth Century, a Breton religious teacher named Robert d'Abrissel developed a doctrine, which, based upon veneration of the Virgin Mary, held that woman were morally superior to men, and therefore should have a leading role in society. Eleanor's grandmother, Phillipa of Toulouse, thought that this was an excellent idea, and so she sponsored the building of the Abbey of Fontevrault, as a community of monks, nuns and lay brothers and sisters, all governed by an Abbess and her sisterhood. She also founded the Order of Fontevrault to spread this concept further. All this was a bit much for Eleanor's grandfather William IX of Aquitaine, so he dumped her and married his mistress Dangerosa, the Viscountess of Chatellrault. (Neither William nor Dangerosa were deterred in this affair by the fact that both of them were already married. Dangerosa kept custody of her daughter Aenor, and since she wanted her blood to have some place in the Aquitainian line, suggested that Aenor marry William's son (William X) by Phillipa. This was done, and Eleanor was born.)

However, while Phillipa went off to run Fontevrault full time, William, known as the "First of the troubadours" proceeded to create a body of poetic literature based around a concept of courtly romantic love, wherein the worshipping suitor must render his love homage and prove his devotion and loyalty to her. Only once this was done would the woman, if not wed, consent to do so, or if already wed, agree to have a fling. Within the framework of these ideas, adulterous affairs by married women were considered perfectly acceptable, and in many cases to be preferred to love within wedlock, since in an affair there would be no question but that the women's love was freely bestowed. These ideas were picked up with alacrity by an army of troubadours and troubaritz's (of whom Marie de France was one), and intertwined with the growing Arthur myth, made the basis of the new cult of Chivalry (see below). Eleanor heavily patronized the troubadours in both France, England, and Aquitaine. Not only that, during the middle years of her marriage to Henry, Eleanor set up shop on her own in Aquitaine, where she reportedly established "Courts of Love" in her palace at Poitiers. In these courts, panels of women sat as judges over men, setting penances for shortfalls in romantic behavior. This might be viewed as an aristocratic game of flirtation, which it was, since, except in cases where the women owned substantial property, all the real power was retained by the men, but it set up an arena of social interaction in which women had the advantage and raised their status accordingly. Throughout her life, Eleanor actively and substantially patronized the Order of Fontevrault, turning its establishments into a series of retreats, enjoyed especially by aristocratic ladies, but open to women of every class, even battered peasant wives and former prostitutes. In her final years, Eleanor herself retired to the Abbey of Fontevrault, and is buried there.

The most dramatic example of Eleanor's commitment to feminist ideas was her recruitment of a troop of Amazons to accompany her on Crusade. The significance of this was as follows: Medieval thought divided society into three functions; those who worked, those who prayed, and those who fought – and it was those who fought who ruled. Thus, to be a proper ruler in medieval society meant to be able to personally lead troops into combat. This concept continued as an operative fact of political life for several centuries after Eleanor's time (consider Henry V at Agincourt, or Henry Richmond and Richard III fighting it out at Bosworth field), and as an ideal accepted by many political leaders (Oliver Cromwell, Frederick the Great, George Washington, Napoleon Bonaparte) into the early Nineteenth Century. Put simply, in Eleanor's time, if you weren't prepared to appear on the battlefield, you couldn't rule. Eleanor wanted to rule. Not only that, her parents wanted her to be able to rule, and so Eleanor, like a considerable number of other aristocratic girls of her day, was taught how to ride and bear arms. Ordinarily, however, they would only do so when acting in the capacity of head of state, (as in the cases of Eleanor, Empress Matilda [Henry's mother], Stephania les Baux, Beatrice of Mauguio, and Ermengard of Narbonne, or delegated head, as in the case of Sybille of Flanders defending the country in her husband's absence.) But Eleanor had a point to prove.

Eleanor's Amazons did not ride in battle bare-breasted as the Amazons of Greek mythology did. That story is a Seventeenth Century invention, and is quite silly, as such antics would have been seen as not only pornographic, but suicidal. Rather, Eleanor and her Amazons wore crusader armor and tunics, made a bit more fashionable by the touch of red-leather riding boots. This was previously attested to by Byzantine historians who observed them, and now confirmed by Marie. It must be said, however, that Eleanor's Amazons did not do well militarily, and most who survived the Mount Cadmos pass massacre shipped back to France as soon as the Crusaders made it to Satalia. Until the publication of *Eleanor's Crusade's* we had no eyewitness accounts of Eleanor actually riding into battle during the

Crusade, but we did from later in her life. So there seems to be little call to doubt Marie's tale, as there is no reason to believe that a woman who was willing to charge an enemy on horseback in her seventies, would not do so in her twenties.

Medieval sketch of a troubaritz, or female troubadour. The new ideas of chivalry greatly enhanced the status of women, and were actively promoted by troubadours of both sexes. Marie de France is the best known troubaritz today, but there were many others.

Chivalry:

The Amazons were a failure, the Courts of Love did not much outlast Eleanor, and while the Abbey of Fontevrault persisted until the French Revolution, it was essentially a counter-cultural commune. The project of Eleanor's that was to have enormous lasting impact on western society at large was her promotion of the cult of Chivalry.

Early medieval knights were barbarian thugs. Their ethos defined a hero as someone with the strength to take whatever he wants, and to avenge whoever might offend him. The Church attempted to moderate the behavior of these knights through Christianity, but it didn't work. The knights simply would not accept an ethos that said that to be good was to be meek. They could, however, buy into the idea that a virtuous man was one who used his strength to defend the meek. This idea, which mixed Christian and barbarian heroic ideals, was combined by the troubadours with those of romantic love to create the ideology of chivalry. Thus, in contrast to the heroes of Greek mythology who seize the women who interest them without compunction, and gain bragging rights by doing so, the characteristic action of the ideal chivalric hero is to kill a dragon or villain to rescue a fair maiden, and thereby win her love. If dragons or villains are unavailable, the knight must find some other heroic deed to prove to the maiden that he is worthy of her. Promoted by the troubadours through the Arthur stories, these ideas became wildly popular, first among nobles, then propagating into the middle and lower classes, and they persist as a powerful theme underlying western notions of relations between men and women to this day. Contemporary feminists may sneer at Chivalry, but in fact these revolutionary ideas did much to civilize barbaric Europe, and greatly raised the status and dignity of women in the West from Eleanor's time down to our own. For a contrast, one has only to consider the Islamic world, which lacks such ideas and continues to regard women as chattels.

Rationalism:

Another key development within Twelfth Century France is the growth of rationalist philosophy, starting in the cathedral schools, and then gelling into the formation of the first universities. Abelard was the most famous figure involved, but there were plenty of others.

The key issue (as far as the future development of western society was to be concerned) is raised in the debate between Abelard and Father Stephen in Chapter 4. Blasting his opponent by pointing out that his position places him in agreement with Mohammed, Abelard says; "What madness is this, saying that it is God's inscrutable will that keeps the birds aloft? No, God made the birds, and God made the air, but it is the beating of the birds' wings against the air that keeps them aloft."

Abelard's argument quoted by Marie is remarkably similar that that found in an anonymous Christian gloss, written circa 1141, on a work entitled *Summary of the whole heresy of the diabolical sect of the Saracens.* It is clear that Abelard's position, while religious, allows for the possibility of rational investigation of the process by which birds fly, but Mohammed's cited view does not. In fact, during an earlier period, the Islamic world had included schools of philosophers who, setting aside Mohammed's denial of cause and effect, engaged in wide ranging rationalist inquiry themselves. However, by the Twelfth Century, Koranic fundamentalists had largely taken over the schools of the Islamic world, and shut down the work of the Islamic Aristotelians, or Mutazelites, with very destructive effects on Islam's intellectual life.

Abelard's position exemplifies a Christianized version of the ideas of Aristotle, who held that, after the initiating action of a Godlike "Prime Mover" to get things going, all other operations of the universe could be explained by natural laws of cause and effect. Furthermore, that the human mind, through rational inquiry, could discover such laws, and therefore ultimately understand how the universe works. These radical ideas, new to the Europeans of the Twelfth Century who had just had their first encounter with Aristotle's works through translations brought in from Moorish Spain, were quite controversial. But the decision by the Europeans of the Twelfth Century to embrace such thought put western civilization on a path that has led it to the Moon.

In later centuries, ossification of Christian establishment thought to mindless worship of Aristotle created problems, when new generations of thinkers developed scientific conclusions that contradicted particular findings of The Philosopher, but that conflict came much later. Nearly 500 years separate the banning of Abelard from that of Galileo. In the Twelfth Century, the Christian Aristotelians of Europe were rationalist revolutionaries.

The conflict between Christendom and Islam could thus be viewed as a war between pro and anti-rationalist societies, - between a society with a great future and one with a great past - but this is apparent only in hindsight. The average crusader was fully as barbaric as the average Turk, and   only

314

the most advanced intellectuals in Europe, such as Abelard, could have framed the issue in the terms described above.

However there is an aspect of the Christian-rationalist vs. Islamic-anti-rationalist dispute that would have been understood by many educated Christians, such as Eleanor, and that is the issue of the conscience. Medieval Catholicism was very clear in its belief that there is an intrinsic facility of the human soul, its conscience, that allows it to distinguish between right and wrong. This idea persists in the west, and is even taken for granted (for example, Jiminy Cricket's advice to Pinocchio that he should always let his conscience be his guide is not considered controversial). In fact, however, the doctrine of conscience is a radical individualist western notion, and it was not (and is not) shared by fundamentalist Islam, which insists that right cannot be determined by the individual mind, and that therefore right behavior can only be achieved through submission to the will of Allah as laid down in the Koran and derivative writings. Nor is it shared by other, more modern, forms of totalitarianism. In her speech to the troops before the battle of Damascus, Eleanor clearly attempted to draw this distinction.

It remains an idea worth fighting for.

Who's Who in Marie's Account

Eleanor of Aquitaine:
The beautiful, urbane, fun-loving heir to the sophisticated Duchy of Aquitaine, Eleanor was forced by politics to marry Louis VII, the monkish King of semi-barbaric France.

King Louis VII:
Louis was trained for the monastery, but was forced to become King when his older brother died after falling off his horse. Dull, cowardly, stupid, boorish, over-pious and sexually frigid, Louis abhorred contact with women. His marriage to Eleanor was like a snail married to a skylark.

Marie of France:
A troubaritz, Marie of France was the first western European woman to write a book. This work, a set of chivalric romances based on Breton tales, was published in England (in French) in the 1160s or 1170s, when Eleanor was Queen of England. The tales were quite popular, and were subsequently translated into English, German, and Norse. Until the discovery of *Eleanor's Crusades*, not much else was known of the historical Marie. She was residing in England when her work was published, and says she came from France and had lived for a while in Brittany. From the content of her work, which furthered the ideas of chivalry and romantic love, and the outline of her life story, many scholars have long believed that Marie was an associate of Eleanor. That hypothesis has now been confirmed

Henry of Anjou:
The future King Henry II of England, Henry of Anjou was an educated, brave, manly, and chivalrous youth, and while the two had plenty of rough moments, he was certainly a much better match for Eleanor than Louis.

Thomas à Becket:
Becket was a scholar in Paris at the start of Eleanor's reign as Queen. Later on he became a key retainer of the house of Anjou.

Peter Abelard:
A rock-star famous proto-rationalist rebel scholar in Paris during Eleanor's time, Abelard also had a notorious love affair with his student

Heloise. He was banned by the Catholic Church, with St. Bernard of Clairvaux doing the dirty work.

Gilbert of Poiree
A major rationalist scholar of Abelard's school, and a supporter of Eleanor. Eventually, he became Bishop of Poitiers, and successfully evaded attempts of more orthodox churchmen to purge him.

John of Salisbury
An important semi-rationalist scholar, John of Salisbury's more conservative views allowed him to pursue a successful career within the Church hierarchy.

Paul of La Rochelle
Born Jewish as Joseph of Valencia, Paul was educated in Moorish Spain, but went north after Muslim fundamentalist reactionaries ended the golden age of Al Andalus. Traveling to Aquitaine, Paul converted to Christianity and became a part of the Renaissance instigated by Eleanor's grandfather, Duke William of Aquitaine. Later he became a tutor to Eleanor and Raymond. In *Eleanor's Crusades*, we find the first extensive account of this important 12th century thinker.

The Cid
The great hero of Spain, the Cid led the defense of Valencia against the fanatical Almoravids when Paul (then Joseph) lived there as a young man.

Kate
Kate was a Cathar who served as Paul's housekeeper.

St. Bernard of Clairvaux:
Abbot Bernard was the head of the Cistercian Order, the white-robed new order of ardent monks. In contrast to the black-robed Benedictines and Cluniacs, who by then had gone decadent through their acquisition of worldly possessions, the Cistercians were still in their ascetic phase in the 1140s, a fact which gave them, and Bernard, great prestige. While intolerant towards rationalists like Abelard, Bernard was a vocal opponent of anti-Semitic violence.

Abbot Suger:

A member of the fine-art and good-food loving Benedictine Order, Suger was France's first great nationalist Prime Minister, and was the genius whose "God is Light" theology led him to design the first Gothic cathedral at St. Denis. (Technically St. Denis wasn't a cathedral, since no Bishop resided there, but everyone calls it a cathedral.) Suger had been born a peasant and had risen in the Church through his brains. He opposed the Second Crusade because he anticipated it would be a disaster, but this led him to form an unprincipled alliance with Peter the Venerable.

Peter the Venerable:

The head of the decadent Cluniac Order, Peter the Venerable was a major sponsor of important translation work that brought Moorish and classical knowledge into Europe. However he also was a raving anti-Semite and anti-Cathar, and strove to divert the Second Crusade into a war against the Jews and Cathars of southern France. He was defeated in debate on this issue by Bernard, Louis, and Eleanor, who for different reasons wanted to send the Crusade east. However Peter's dark vision was finally realized some 70 years later, when the notorious Albigensian Crusade was launched.

Lady Alicia of Bordeaux:

Lady Alicia was a close friend and confidant of Eleanor.

Alan of Cherbourg

Alan was a man destined for knighthood, who like Peter Abelard, opted for scholarship instead.

Prince Raymond of Antioch:

Formerly Count of Toulouse, Prince Raymond was Eleanor's uncle, and her closest living male relative. While ruthless towards his enemies, Prince Raymond's rule in Antioch was quite enlightened, and under him, Antioch was a magnificent cosmopolitan city where all religions were tolerated. The Byzantines hated him, and Eleanor adored him. Raymond wanted the Crusaders to join him in retaking Edessa, which was the militarily correct course of action, but which also smacked of self-interest, since being nearby, he would be able to add Edessa to his own Kingdom.

Princess Constance of Antioch

Raymond's young wife, and a very remarkable person in her own right.

Emperor Manuel of Constantinople:

A crafty double-dealing usurper, Manuel murdered many relatives to seize the throne, and treacherously made to deal with the Turk Nuradin to betray the Second Crusade. He also tried to kidnap Eleanor at sea during her return from the Holy Land.

Princess Anna Comnena:

The daughter of the Emperor Alexius, who ruled Constantinople at the time of the First Crusade (1097-1099), Anna was Manuel's aunt. He stole the throne from her, and she hated him for it. Anna had been a teenager at the time of the First Crusade, and met all the leading Crusaders of that generation. She wrote a book, called the *Alexiad*, about the reign of her father, and it includes the best description of the First Crusade. It also tells a lot about Anna's mind, and how she regarded western Christians. Terming them variously Latins, Franks, or Kelts, her attitude combines snobbish distain of barbarians with the fascination of a teenage girl for their raw animal power. Until the discovery of *Eleanor's Crusades* it was only suspected that Anna met Eleanor, but since she was still alive when Eleanor and the Second Crusade came through in 1147, and hated Manuel, it was suspected that she was the one to tip the Crusaders off to his plot. Now we know that she did.

Emperor Conrad (The German, or Holy Roman Emperor):

Despite his great reputation as a warrior, Conrad did even worse than Louis on the Second Crusade, and nearly his whole army was massacred by the Turks shortly after arriving in Asia Minor. Conrad and Manuel were married to sisters (Germans), which made him think that Manuel was his ally. Little did he know how the Byzantine mind worked.

Erika of Jutland:

Only a few of Eleanor's Amazon volunteers who were really prepared to engage in combat. Erika was one of them.

Queen Melisende of Jerusalem:

Regent for the boy King Baldwin, Melisende wanted to divert the Crusade from its true military objective of retaking Edessa from Nuradin to attacking Damascus, so she could add it to her Kingdom. This was a very bad idea, because the Emir of Damascus was an enemy of Nuradin, and by attacking him, the Crusaders united the two against the Christians.

Melisende was the cousin of Sybille of Flanders, and this gave her a lot of leverage in council.

Count of Flanders:
A mighty warrior, the most notable among the Crusaders of the Second Crusade. Flemings were at that time considered very fierce fighters, and frequently hired out by others as mercenaries. Flanders' men were therefore probably best soldiers among the Crusaders, excepting only the Templars.

Sybille of Flanders:
The tough wife of the Count of Flanders, Sybille joined the Amazons and fought by Eleanor's side all the way to Jerusalem. However, because she was related to Melisende, Sybille allied with her in promoting the Damascus campaign, which caused a falling out with Eleanor. Sybille did not go on to Damascus, however, as she had to return to Flanders to lead its defense against invaders while her husband continued the crusade.

Sir Robert:
A knight of Aquitaine, loyal to Eleanor.

Everard de Barres:
The Commander of the Knights Templar, who were the shock troops of overseas Christendom. The Templars were actually fighting monks; they had vows never to have relations with women, which vow they no doubt found easy to keep since they also had a vow to never wash. The Templars' headquarters were located above the ruins of the Temple of Solomon, in what is now the Al-Aqsa mosque. In their headquarters, the Templars kept what they claimed was the One True Cross, and on decisive occasions, carried this relic into battle with them.

The face of the young Eleanor? There is no definitively accepted representation of Eleanor in your youth. However these sculptures of a King and Queen from the Portal Royal of Chartres Cathedral date from the mid Twelfth Century. The King is Louis VII, which means that the Queen must either be Eleanor or Louis' second wife, Constance of Sicily. However, Eleanor is reported by medieval chroniclers to have been tall and strikingly beautiful, and the Queen's statue fits that description. Also, like Eleanor, she does not cover her hair. Furthermore, while her features are generally delicate, she shares the same strong nose and chin shown in representations of the older Eleanor (such as that on her tomb.) For these reasons, I believe that the above sculpture is a literal depiction of Eleanor of Aquitaine at the time of Marie's account.

Historical Chronology

The following are the actual dates of the events described in Marie's account.

Toledo taken from the Moors	1085
First Crusade	1097-1099
Battle of Valencia	1099
Almoravid Riots in Cordoba	1109
Raymond Born	1114
Phillipa founds Fontevrault	~1118
Eleanor Born	1122
Aragonese defeated by the Moors at Fraga	July, 1134
Eleanor marries Louis	July 25, 1137
St. Denis Construction Begins	1137
Communards Revolt in Poitiers	1138
Abelard Proscribed	1140
Abelard Dies	April 21, 1142
Battle of Vitry on Marne	1143
Consecration of St. Denis	June 10, 1144
Edessa Falls to Turks	Christmas, 1144
Daughter Marie (later Marie of Champagne) born to Eleanor	1145
Eleanor takes the Cross at the field of Vezelay	Easter, March 31, 1146
Second Crusade departs Paris	June 11, 1147
Eleanor reaches Constantinople	Oct. 4, 1147
Crusaders cross Bosphorus into Asia	Oct. 16, 1147
Total Eclipse of the Sun	Oct. 26, 1147
Battle of Meaender River	Dec. 25, 1147
Meaender Flood devastates Crusaders	Dec 26, 1147
Mountain pass massacre (near Mt. Cadmos)	Mid-January 1148
Crusaders reach Satalia	Late January 1148
Eleanor Reaches Antioch	March 19, 1148
Eleanor leaves Antioch	March 29, 1148
Crusaders reach Jerusalem	May 1148
Decision made in Council to attack Damascus	June 24, 1148
Crusaders reach Damascus	July 24, 1148
Crusaders retreat from Damascus	July 28, 1148
Retreating Crusaders reach Jerusalem	August 1148

322

Bretons, Normans, and English take Lisbon	1148
Eleanor and Louis sail from Acre	April 1149
Eleanor kidnapped and rescued in naval actions off Cape Malea	May 1149
Prince Raymond defeated and killed by Nuradin	June 1149
Eleanor has private audience with Pope Eugenius	Oct. 9, 1149
Eleanor arrives back in Paris	Nov. 1149
Baby Alicia born	Spring 1150
Eleanor's marriage with Louis annulled	March 21, 1152
Eleanor marries Henry of Anjou	May 18, 1152
Henry and Eleanor crowned King and Queen of England	Dec. 19, 1154
Marie of France publishes her book of stories	1160s-1170s
Henry dies	July 6, 1189
Eleanor dies	March 31, 1204
Fontevrault sacked by Jacobins	1789

Other Books About Eleanor

Fact

Eleanor of Aquitaine figures in numerous historical accounts, but many of these are slanderous, or derived from sources who are slanderous, as a result of Eleanor's adverse relationships with Louis, Henry, and the Church. The first modern historian to set the record straight was Wellesley professor Amy Kelly, in her indispensable *Eleanor of Aquitaine and the Four Kings*, published in 1951. A more recent book that approach's Kelly's in value is Douglas Boyd's, *Eleanor, April Queen of Aquitaine* (Sutton, 2004). Finally, worth mentioning if not on the level of the other two, is Marion Meade's *Eleanor of Aquitaine* (1977), whose focus on feminist inquiry, while limiting, also sheds some useful light in the present instance.

Fiction

Accounts of Eleanor in fiction are legion, but they tend to focus on her love affairs, real or imagined. Two recent novels that give a fair portrayal of her as a person of real character as described by Marie are Sharon Kay Penman's *When Christ and His Saints Slept*, and *Time and Chance*. The best depiction of Eleanor in film is the movie *The Lion in Winter*, where she was ably portrayed by Katharine Hepburn, a woman after her own mold. All three of these works deal with Eleanor in her middle years or later, and concern her activities as Queen of England. Eleanor thus enters Penman's saga at the point of her elopement with Henry. Marie's account, however, is the first we have of Eleanor in her youth, as the crusading Queen of France.

Books about Marie de France

Until the discovery of *Eleanor's Crusades*, we had virtually no information about the life of Marie de France. However her better known book, *The Lais of Marie de France* has been continuously in print since the end of the 12th Century. The introduction to the 1986 Penguin edition by Glyn Burgess and Keith Busby provided much speculation as to who she might have been, and effectively dismissed the theory that she was Eleanor. Burgess and Busby firmly placed first publication of the *Lais* in England (in French) in the 1160s or 1170s, with authorship by a person who emigrated from France and who had spent some time in Brittany. These facts, along with the romantic chivalric content of the *Lais* themselves were consistent with the theory that Marie was a companion of Eleanor. There can also be found in the *Lais* some tone of a bit of a chip on the author's shoulder, giving the feel that she was operating within a somewhat adverse social environment, as if she were surrounded by snobs who unjustly disparaged her work. While encounters with gender bias could explain this, some scholars have considered this to be evidence that she might have been of lower class origin than those around her. With the discovery of *Eleanor Crusades*, this hypothesis has now been confirmed, as Marie herself reports that she was a burgher by birth.

I find the contrast between these two most notable women of the Twelfth Century ironic. Eleanor's deeds are writ loudly across the pages of history, but we have barely any words from the famous Queen herself. Of Marie we knew until recently almost nothing, except that she had given us a book, and an international best-seller no less – the first written by a European woman. Many would follow in later centuries, from Mary Shelley and Harriet Beecher Stowe to Jane Austen and J.K. Rowling; indeed today over half of all published literature is written by women, collectively providing an enormous contribution to the intellectual life of our society. But Marie was the pioneer for them all- a genuine voice from the springtime of western civilization. She deserves to be remembered.

Now, with the discovery and publication of her long lost masterpiece of personal history, the memory of her remarkable life, times, and character is finally assured.

"The builders' trades include diverse crafts. There are the masons and stonecutters and glaziers, and many others, but the greatest of all are the enginators, those skilled in the secret and divine art of creating engines, or machines, as they are also known. For of what use would all the fine cut stone in the world be without the machines to lift them to their proper place? It is engines that allow weak men to move and lift all things, no matter how heavy, and by so doing transform mere rocks into mighty castles, noble palaces, and glorious cathedrals. The very word "engine" bespeaks a holy quality to this profession, as it shares its root with "genius" and "genesis," terms that name the quality necessary for, and the very act, of creation... So I am in no way ashamed to say that my father was an enginator."

—Marie de France

CPSIA information can be obtained
at www.ICGtesting.com
Printed in the USA
LVHW091333160120
643863LV00001B/20